Charles Henry Lee

The Judge Advocate's Vade Mecum

Charles Henry Lee

The Judge Advocate's Vade Mecum

ISBN/EAN: 9783744667036

Printed in Europe, USA, Canada, Australia, Japan

Cover: Foto ©Suzi / pixelio.de

More available books at **www.hansebooks.com**

JUDGE ADVOCATE'S
VADE MECUM:

EMBRACING A GENERAL VIEW OF

MILITARY LAW,

AND THE

PRACTICE BEFORE COURTS MARTIAL,

WITH AN EPITOME OF THE

LAW OF EVIDENCE,

AS APPLICABLE TO MILITARY TRIALS.

BY

C. H. LEE.

RICHMOND:
WEST AND JOHNSTON,
No. 145 Main Street.
1863.

Entered according to Act of Congress, in the year 1862, by
WEST & JOHNSTON,
In the Clerk's Office of the District Court of the Confederate States, for the Eastern District of Virginia.

PRINTED BY EVANS & COGSWELL, NO. 3 BROAD STREET, CHARLESTON, S. C.

PREFACE.

A practical Treatise on Courts Martial and the duties of Judge Advocate, seems to be called for at the present time. The works on these subjects by European writers can only be of partial application in this country; and besides being voluminous and expensive, are difficult to be obtained. The only book relating to them issued in America which is of much value is that published by Captain De Hart, in 1846. This appears to have obtained the approval of the military profession, and to be generally received as a standard authority.

The existing demand would, therefore, probably have been met to a great extent by a new edition of De Hart, could it have been fairly obtained; but, on further examination, it was believed that his work was susceptible of improvement, not only in its general plan and arrangement, but by the addition of the views of other authors upon most of the topics discussed by him, and particularly in respect to the office of Judge Advocate.

Instead, therefore, of issuing, as was suggested by some, a new edition of the Treatise of De Hart, it has been thought better to attempt a partial reproduction of his work, retaining only what appears of especial value, and incorporating with it such improvements as may be justified by the authorities to be collated and examined. In this way it is believed that nothing which is valuable in De Hart will be lost, while much that is important may be secured from other sources.

A laborious examination of the subjects discussed, and some experience in connection with them, will, it is hoped, justify the writer in the task he has assumed: at the same time, conscious of the many imperfections which will be found in its execution, he would here plead the difficulties which attend it, and invoke the indulgent forbearance of the critical reader.

It is proposed to consider the various subjects to be discussed in the order presented in the following table of contents.

Bedford county, Va., May, 1862.

CONTENTS.

I—Observations on Military Law in general.

II—The Origin of Military Courts; the sources of their jurisdiction, and the time within which such jurisdiction should be exercised.

III—The Judge Advocate; his qualifications; responsibilities; rights and duties.

IV—Courts of Inquiry; their objects, organization, and special duties.

V—Courts Martial; and herein,
1. Of their constitution and organization, as divided into General, Regimental, and Garrison Courts.
2. Their *particular* jurisdiction.
3. Their duties, general powers, and the punishments they may respectively impose.

VI—Military Trials; and herein,
1. Of the charges and other preliminaries to the trial.
2. The proceedings in the trial, and the incidents thereof.
3. The findings of the Court.
4. The sentence of the Court.

VII—Of the Final Proceedings; and herein,
1. The revision, and confirmation or disapproval of the proceedings and sentence.
2. The execution of the sentence.

VIII—Redress of Wrongs; and herein,
1. Of the new trial.
2. Of the particular modes of redress provided in the Articles of war.

IX—Lastly, the Law of Evidence, as applicable in military trials.

INDEX.

N. B. The figures in this Index refer to the *Sections* in the margin of the book.

A.

Absence without leave..344
Adams, John.. 12
Accomplice...315
    weight of his evidence..316
    when to be released..318
Adjournment of court—how ordered..............................141, 142, 149
        for what time..142
Alibi..347
Appeals...98, 286, 287, 289
Approval of proceedings..262
Arrest—of officers and soldiers....................................132, 184
    breach of..184, 185
    who to be..186
Articles of War—origin of..12, 17
        who bound by...17, 18
        violations of..137
        remarks on 34th and 35th articles....................282–285
        remarks on 83d article..................................348
Arraignment of accused...63, 69
Army, a legal body... 17
    followers of..21, 26

B.

Blackstone, Sir Wm..1, 3, 5, 189
Berrien, Mr..266
Bail...317
Breach of arrest..184, 185

C.

Camp followers...21, 26
Cadets, liable to military law...................................... 27
Cashiering..161, 162, 253
Capital punishment—See *Death*.
Cat-o'-nine-tails..270
Certainty in charge..175
    as to time and place..175
    person and facts..175
Chivalry, court of... 10

INDEX.

Citizen, right of..12
Civil action against court martial..............................37, 134, 168
Children, when may testify...308
Civil court no jurisdiction in military affairs................30, 31, 129
Cowardice..161
Contempts..114, 144, 145, 146, 152
Corporal punishment...158, 169, 270
Conspiracy..341
Constitution, the..12, 14
Civilians, authority of military court over.........................114, 144
Charges—duties of Judge Advocate as to.........................42, 43
        to be read in court..68
        not read to witness..226
        defective, not to proceed on.......................................68
        how altered..68, 173
        on reading, court cleared...147
        court to decide as to...147, 172
        not to accumulate..173, 291
        definition of...170
        rules in framing...175
        writings referred to in..176
        intention to be stated in...175
        technical terms in...177
        to use no figures in...177
        words of law in..178
        offences to the prejudice of good order, etc., in charge.......179
        duplicity in..180
        special matters in...181
        certainty in..175
        the whole to be exhausted..240
Challenge—Judge Advocate not to be..............................54, 193
        opportunity to...62, 67
        ground of to be stated...67
        court to decide...154, 194
        peremptory, not allowed..193
        rules as to..193, 194, 195, 201, 202
        grounds of.......................................195, 196, 197
        time for..199
        to be favorably viewed...200
        principal...195
        to the favor...195
        to the array...203
Character...311, 339, 340, 348
Circumstantial Evidence—grounds of..............................333
                importance of.............................334, 336
                cautions as to..................................335
                rules concerning................................337
                extenuating matters.............................338
Confinement—no place prescribed..................................184
Compulsion, legal..237
Conduct unbecoming an officer and gentleman......................348

INDEX.

Counsel—Judge Advocate not to have, except.................. 40
 "   "   allowed when 70, 110
 —   cannot address court 70
Counsel and Client..320
Court of Inquiry (see Title: *Inquiry*) 100
Court Martial—grounds of jurisdiction. 10, 15, 16, 17, 20, 32
            importance of 15
            legal liability of 37
            to aid civil courts 20
            power to appoint Judge Advocate for 49
            names of members registered by seniority 63, 120
            authority of 65, 142
            president of, powers..........................64, 65
            how and when cleared 143, 147, 65
            majority of votes in, when decisive 65, 142
            closing and opening of court recorded 66
            to decide propriety of questions to witness 77
            opinions how delivered 89
            question by court not to be objected to........... 77
            punishments voted................................. 90
            members vote on all questions..................... 91
            judgment how entered 92
            recommendation to mercy 93
            proceedings to be signed 94
              "   when remanded 95
              "   to be sent to War Department............. 96
              "   to commanding officer.................... 96
            final proceedings of 257
            time of sitting...................................113
              "   meeting......................... 120, 141, 189
            power to change time and place of meeting........141
            power to appoint court................. 119, 121, 122
            composition of...............................120, 123
            arrangement of members...........................120
            supernumeraries 122
            what officers not to be members of...............123
            number and rank of officers in, how decided..125, 126
            extent of jurisdiction.......................129-133
            civil responsibility of members..............37, 134
            powers confined to military persons 140
            general powers and duties 140, 141
            adjournment of court 141, 142
            proceedings not made known during the trial......146
            no control of prisoner out of court..............148
            to examine all charges 151, 240
            opinion of court may be given either party.......152
            mode of taking opinions..........................241
            powers before oath taken 153
            to judge law and facts, etc.................222, 293
            punishments they may order (see Titles: *Punishment—Finding—Sentence—Revision*) 154

IN...

...ing officer...
...dissolved...
... number...
...dissolve...
...ns of...
...ing decision...
...ound by...

D.

...for...
...an order...
...
...
...
...ate witness...
...Evidence)...
...for crime (see W...

E.

...thenticated...
...
...itted...
...be read...
...munications...
...court...
...vocate as to...
...urt of inquiry, when...
...
...
...what admissible...
...
...way...
...
...rs...
...issue...
...

INDEX. 11

  as to character 339
  substance of issue to be proved 344
  allegations to be proved..344
  names..344
  time and place.......................................345, 346, 347
  alibi..347
  affirmative of issue to be proved..............................349
  negative not generally proved..................................349
  best evidence produced...350
  primary and secondary..352
  secondary not received except..................................353
  exceptions to rule requiring best evidence.....................354
Evidence—See Titles: *Witness—Husband and Wife—Counsel and Client—Depositions—Circumstantial Evidence.*
Execution of sentence (see *Sentence*) 270

F.
Final proceedings...257
Fine..164
Figures, charge not to be in..176
Flogging...158, 165, 270
Followers of the army...21
Fraud (see *Embezzlement*)...161
Findings of Court—whole charge to be exhausted in....................240
    mode of giving opinion of court on................241
    votes to decide...................................242
    rule in stating decision..........................243
    special finding or verdict..................245, 246
    degree of guilt to be found by court..............247
    court may sentence prosecutor.....................248
    may find less guilt than charged..................249
    may consider extenuating circumstances............249
    minority bound by majority (see *Sentence*).......250

G.
Garrison Courts—See *Regimental Courts.*

H.
Habeas Corpus Act—care of England for 5, 6
    privilege secured in constitution................7, 8
    not to be suspended but by congress...........7, 8, 9
    opinions of Mr. Jefferson and others................9
Husband and wife..319
    who included as...................................320
Hanging..252, 271
Handwriting 352

I.
Inquiry, Court of—duty of Judge Advocate in.........................100
    proceedings in 100, 101, 104, 112, 118
    witnesses before..................................102
    authorized by law.................................104
    composition of...............................104, 106.

INDEX.

when proceedings, evidence................................105
oaths of...105
the president only to order................................105
special objects of.....................................107, 111
how far a judicial body....................................108
general objects of...108
accused to be present in 109
counsel allowed in...110
sits with closed doors.....................................111
expresses opinion when.....................................111
challenge in, for cause....................................112
time of sitting..113
copies of record of..113
when accused in arrest before..............................114
contempts before...114
opinions not divulged......................................115
revision of proceedings....................................116
statute of limitations in 117
how dissolved..118
members not to sit on court martial, when 108
accused not to criminate himself 109
governed by order convening it.............................111
Idiots and Lunatics, etc..235, 308
Interpreter, when allowed...106
Imprisonment 164, 165, 254, 273
Inferior officers—remedy for wrongs of....................................187
Incompetency of Witness—See *Witness.*
Interest—See *Witness.*
Intoxication of Witness—See *Witness.*
Issue—evidence to be confined to..337
    affirmative to be proved...349

J.

Jefferson, Thomas—opinion as to habeas corpus............................. 9
Jeopardy, twice in..15, 217
Jurisdiction of Military Courts—sources and grounds of 10, 15, 16, 17, 20, 345
                extent of.............................129, 140
                how limited.....................129, 140, 239
                how determined..................130, 131, 132
                where law is doubtful as to...............133
                where martial law exists..................136
Judicial Military Tribunals, who may appoint.............................122
Judgment of Court—how entered.. 92
         arrest of..234
         pleas in arrest of rarely employed...................................239
Judge Advocate—has no judicial power..................................... 58
         may remonstrate, when.......................................58, 59, 60
         may record his opinion..................................58, 59, 60, 85
         not to give opinion on sentence.................................... 60
         his duty on meeting of court....................................61, 62
         as to challenge.. 62

reads charges to court.................................. 63
not to proceed on defective charge...................... 63
may change form of charge............................... 63
opens the case.. 71
mode of address... 71
swears witnesses....................................72, 73
daily duties in court................................... 82
reply to defence....................................84, 232
sums up the case.....................................87, 88
cannot protest.......................................58, 88
takes opinions of court..........................89, 90, 241
to enter judgment himself............................... 92
form of entry of judgment............................... 92
duty on appeals... 93
to sign proceedings..................................... 94
qualifications of................................33, 34, 35
responsibilities of..........................36, 37, 38, 40
whether legally liable.......................37, 38, 39
not so regarded... 39
his general duties.......................41, 42, 43, 50, 51
authority to appoint.................................... 49
may assist prisoner..........................51, 52, 57, 58
not subject to challenge................................ 54
duty as to charges...................................42, 43
as to summoning witnesses...........................44, 46
prepares a brief.. 47
provides place of meeting............................... 47
duties in court, etc............................48, 50, 55
threefold character..................................50, 51
either party a right to his opinion.................53, 58
to conduct prosecution.................................. 55
independent of court as prosecutor...................... 55
duties as prosecutor............................50, 51, 55
should be impartial..................................... 56
legal adviser... 58
power of court over..................................... 99
duty in court of inquiry................................100

L.

Law—municipal... 1
military..2, 4
martial..3, 4, 136
Labor, hard.......................................138, 165
Language, construction of...............................177
Limitations, Statute of................................. 28
Liberty, personal, constitutional guards of..........7, 15

M.

Martial Law......................................3, 4, 136
Effects of... 5
Marine Corps..127
Majority—See *Votes.*
Marking with letter D...................................252

INDEX.

Messengers and Orderlies..191
Military Law 2, 4, 170
    Courts......................................10, 15, 16, 17, 20, 122
Messengers allowed...191
Misadventure..326
Militia, constitutional provision as to................................ 15
    officers on courts martial.......................................127
Military offences.. 22
Mutiny, English act of... 11
Mutiny, offence of.................................177, 252, 341, 342

N.

Navy Courts..13, 73
    Regulations.. 13
Names..175, 344
New Trials..276
    not after acquitted...277
    when granted..278, 279, 280
    application for, how made.......................................281
    proceedings on (see *Trial*)....................................289

O.

Oath—to court..61, 105, 204
    manner of... 62
    to witnesses...73, 105
    must be before a full court..................................... 73
Offences, military..22, 23
Office, incapacity to hold...162
Officer, punishments of..166
    not summoned, except...102
    may be suspended, etc..159
    reprimand of...160
    cashiering of..161, 162
    arrest of..182
    reviewing...264, 267
    succeeding...268
    conduct of...368
Opinions of court..89, 152
    not to be divulged...115
Order, to be read to court... 61
    copy provided... 68
    observed in court...143, 144
Orderly, etc..191
Oral testimony—See *Evidence* and *Witness*.

P.

Pardon...218, 278, 313
Parliament, English... 11
Place and time...170, 219, 345
Pleas, to be recorded.. 69
    of "not guilty"...69, 213
    of "former trial"..151, 216
    other pleas..209
    to jurisdiction..210

INDEX. 15

    in abatement 211
    of "guilty"...212
    special pleas...214
    of statute. of limitations.....................................214
    former acquittal..215
    pardon 218
    want of particularity 219
    general rules as to special pleas.............................220
    proceedings on pleas..222
    in arrest of judgment...234
    presumptions of law...360
Prisoner, all members must be present at trial of.............149, 150
    under guard without charges 182
    provision for keeping..182
    provision for release of 182
    brought in court 192
    allowed counsel..70, 207
    defence of 231
    guilt of—See *Finding.*
Punishments...89, 90, 154–169
    how voted for..89, 91, 251
    what forbidden 154
    what are cruel 154
    discretion of court as to 155
    limitations of....................................129, 165, 167
    checks to, etc...155
    capital...155, 156, 167
    when capital punishment may be inflicted 157
    of officers..166
    of soldiers..167
    by hard labor...165
    of spies..252
    corporal..252
    marking with letter 252
    of deserters..252
    of mutiny...252
President, the..264
    authority of..266
President of court martial...........................63, 120, 126
    to adjourn court 64
    general powers....................................65, 142, 143
    to sign proceedings..94
    to preserve order...143
    no casting vote...244
Prosecutor, Judge Advocate acts as 51, 55, 57
    when commanding officer is..................................119
Prisoner, list of witnesses given and received by.........44, 45, 188
    Judge Advocate to aid 51, 52, 57, 188
    arraignment of 63, 69, 208
    allowed a chair...64, 192
    to state ground of challenge.................................67

standing mute 69, 209
treated with respect 71
allowed time for defence..................................83, 231
several, to be separately tried.................................. 97
court no control of, out of court 148
Punishment, by incapacity to hold office..........................162
        by fine and imprisonment 164
        by cashiering..161
        by reprimand 160
        by reduction to the ranks 163, 167
        when particular directed by law............................167
        general rules as to 168
        observations upon 169
        different for same offence, not allowed (see *Sentence*) 167, 252

R.

Rank—in courts martial...120
Reduction to ranks..163, 167
Regulations of army..17, 18
        who they bind.....................................17, 18
Release 317
Record, revision of... 257
     to be written with care 62
     to be made up each day..................................... 62
     must be read to court daily................................... 82
     not read to witnesses....................................... 82
     to be sent to War Department................................ 96
     to be sent to commanding officer............................. 96
     cannot be contradicted......................................359
Retainer to camp.. 25
Reprimands 160
Recommendations to mercy.....................................93, 255
Revision, of proceedings..257
     proceedings may be returned to court, on.............258, 259, 261
     what court may amend......................................260
     approval after..262
     when court adheres to former decision........................263
     power to revise.......................................264, 267
     duty of revising officer.........................264, 265, 266, 278
     power of the President in reviewing.....................264, 266
     proceedings closed after 267
Regimental courts... 98
        proceedings on appeals from..............98, 286, 287, 289
        who to appoint.......................................121
        jurisdiction of 130, 131, 138, 139
        cannot inflict *death*................................. 158
        what crimes they punish...............................158
        proceedings in 288
        opinions of court on appeal (see *Appeal*) 290

S.

Safeguard, forcing..158
Sanity, presumed 171

Sentence of court (see *Finding*)..........251
    court may adjourn before..........251
    every member to vote..........251
    two punishments for same offence illegal..........252
    words of law to be followed in..........253
    term of imprisonment..........254
    solitary confinement..........254
    recommendation to mercy..........255
    court may change, etc..........256
    execution of..........270
    corporal punishment..........252, 270
    capital punishment..........271
    degradation..........272
    imprisonment..........272, 273
    to be strictly enforced..........275
    language of..........252
    marking with letter..........252
    against spies..........252
Spelling of name..........344
Special verdict..........245, 246
Spies..........252
Stoppage of pay..........163
Suspension of officers, etc..........159
Sutlers..........24, 26
Succeeding officer..........268
Supernumeraries..........193

T.

Technical terms..........176
Time and place..........170, 346
    for meeting of court..........190
Time of challenge..........199
    granted parties to trial..........231
Trials—general rules at..........191
    motion to postpone..........205, 206
    should be separate..........204
    former, how proved..........216
    what is a former trial..........217
    when former trial a bar..........217
    new (see *New Trial*)..........276

V.

Verdict—special..........245, 246
Variance—need not be pleaded..........221
Votes—majority decide, when..........65, 77, 150, 242
    equality, rule where..........244
    mode of taking..........89, 91, 150
    in capital cases..........150, 241
    president no casting..........244
    minority bound by majority..........250
    every member to vote..........251
    court vote till decision obtained..........250, 251

W.

War Department, proceedings of court to be sent to..........96

INDEX.

War, custom of 19
Wirt, Mr 266, 267
Witnesses—no one to be against himself........................... 15
    names of witnesses given...................................... 40
    retire from court, when...................................69, 95
    to be sworn before full court 73
    competency of, when objected to............................74, 76
    how examined 76, 77, 81, 83, 227, 228, 306, 324, 325, 326, 327
    examination not restricted to those summoned................. 44
    leading questions improper, etc.........................77, 325, 326
    questions to be in writing and all entered 77, 227
    court decides on question objected to......................... 77
    their testimony may be read to them when.................81, 229
    may correct testimony....................................81, 229
    may be recalled..86, 230
    how and when summoned............................46, 102, 225
    no form of summons... 45
    depositions of 45
    for prisoner..44, 45, 188
    who may be called as 189, 307
    separate examination a test...................................224
    sick witness...206, 225
    expenses of 305
    lunatics, when may be 308
    children, when 308
    intoxication of..308
    deaf and dumb...308
    want of religious belief in 307, 308, 309, 310
    infamy of character in 311
    treason in...311
    crimen falsi 311
    conviction of crime 312
    desertion..312
    incompetency of, how removed................................313
    interest in..314
    accomplice, when may be witness.............................315
    bail, when...317
    husband and wife, when 319, 320
    counsel, when 321
    credibility of...322
    how discredited 322, 324
    what questions they may decline to answer 329, 330
Wrongs—of inferiors......................................187, 276
    redress of (see *New Trial*) 187, 276
    under Articles of war..282
    of officers 282, 284
    duty of commanding general, under 34th Article of war....282, 283
    of inferior officers and soldiers........................284, 285
    appeals in cases of..186
    proceedings before regimental court in complaints of....288, 289
    redress only at request of party wronged 291

CHAPTER I.

MILITARY AND MARTIAL LAW.

Sir William Blackstone has defined Municipal Law to be "a rule of civil conduct prescribed by the supreme power of the state, commanding what is right and prohibiting what is wrong." But Mr. Chitty objects to the latter part of this definition as superfluous — the idea, as he contends, being completely expressed by the first clause. Admitting the correctness of this criticism, municipal law may be more accurately defined as "a rule of civil conduct prescribed by the supreme power of the state." _{Law. definition of.}

SEC. 2. The law thus established is of general application. It pervades all ranks of the body politic, and reaches every interest of society. As none are excluded from its benefits, so all are subject to its restraints. But military law, though not less powerful where it applies, is far less extensive in the circle of its operations. It is, as the term imports, designed for the military service, "or state, which includes the whole soldiery;" but is of no obligation in the affairs of civil life and conduct. Military law may, therefore, be defined as a "rule of" military "conduct prescribed by the supreme" authority; and must be understood as "that branch of the laws which respects military discipline and the government of persons employed in the military service." Though not exclusive of the common law, _{Military law.} _{Definition of Military law.}

it is, within its appropriate sphere, independent of that law—being administered under other forms and by different tribunals. Neither can properly infringe the jurisdiction or direct the duties of the other; nevertheless, it is made the duty of those who administer the former to be "aiding and assisting" the latter in arresting and bringing to justice offenders against the laws of the land.*

SEC. 3. There is yet a species of military law, of a different character and import from what should properly be understood by that term, but which is not unfrequently confounded with it—I mean what is now commonly called Martial law.

<small>Martial law.</small> Sir Wm. Blackstone himself seems occasionally to regard them as convertible terms. In discussing the military establishment of England, he says: "They, the militia, are to be exercised at stated times. Their discipline in general is liberal and easy; but when drawn out into actual service, they are subject to the rigors of *martial* law;" and again, "martial law, which is built on no settled principles, but is entirely arbitrary in its decisions is, as Sir Matthew Hale observes, in truth and reality no law, but something indulged rather than allowed as law. The necessity of order and discipline in an *army* is the only thing that can give it countenance, and, therefore, it ought not to be permitted in time of peace."†

SEC. 4. The censure of the military jurisprudence conveyed in these remarks is disclaimed by Mr. Chitty, as unmerited in his time. It is certainly so in our day and country; for excepting the very limited degree of discretion allowed in minor concerns, the Articles of war and the Regulations for the direction of the army, in conjunction with the custom or common law of the service, clearly define the duties and limit the authority of all connected with it; so that very little indeed is left to arbitrary discretion. The observations of Blackstone,

---

*See 33d Article of War. † Bl. Com., I, 413.

however, have been cited only to show that the proper distinction between the terms referred to has not always been duly observed. Yet they are clearly terms of different import when accurately considered, military law being, as has been already observed, a rule for the government of military persons only; while by martial law is understood that condition of things which results in the application of military rule to all persons indiscriminately.* The effect of martial law is not to apply to every one all the rules and minutiæ of the military code, but rather to bring them under the control of the military commander for the time being, whose action is regulated and restrained by the general principles of that code, and the necessities of the occasion—necessities, however, which, in former days, have subjected the citizen to imprisonment, to military trials, and summary executions. Such, in a few words, is *martial* law, as distinguished from military law. Martial law defined.

SEC. 5. Whether a system conferring power of such magnitude and importance may be lawfully introduced in these states by the decree of a military commander, or indeed by any authority, except that of the Congress, may well be questioned. Its effect, as has been already intimated, is to suspend for the time being all civil proceedings, and subject the liberty and even life of the citizen to a power which is independent of the forms and guarantees that distinguish a free government. Recent events have fully admonished us how difficult it is to resist temptations to the exercise of power, and how important to adhere to the safeguards of a written constitution. "Of great importance to the public," says Blackstone, "is the preservation of this personal liberty, for if once it were left in the power of any, the highest magistrate to imprison, arbitrarily, whomsoever he or

---

* De Hart, 2 Kent, 342—*note.*

his officers thought proper, * * * there would soon be an end of all other rights and immunities. Some have thought that unjust attacks even upon life and property at the arbitrary will of the magistrate are less dangerous to the commonwealth than such as are made upon the personal liberty of the subject. To bereave a man of life, or by violence to confiscate his estate, without accusation or trial, would be so gross and notorious an act of despotism as must at once convey the alarm of tyranny throughout the whole kingdom; but confinement of the person by secretly hurrying him to gaol, where his sufferings are unknown or forgotten, is a less public, a less striking, and, therefore, a more dangerous engine of arbitrary government. And yet, sometimes, when the state is in real danger, even this may be a necessary measure. But the happiness of our constitution is, that it is not left to the executive power to determine when the danger of the state is so great as to render this measure expedient; for it is the parliament only, or legislative power, that, whenever it sees proper, can authorize the crown, by suspending the *habeas corpus act* for a short and limited time, to imprison suspected persons."

Sec. 6. We have here an example of that watchful jealousy for individual rights which is so largely evinced in the history and jurisprudence of our English progenitors. Of such importance to the liberties of the people do they regard this writ that the parliament alone, in which is supposed to reside the wisdom and integrity of the nation, can suspend its operation, and then only *"for a short and limited time!"*

Sec. 7. Nor has the constitution of these states been silent upon this grave question. It has plainly declared when this privilege of such high dignity and value may be withdrawn: and as the writ itself, and the practice under it, were drawn from the courts of England, so, doubtless, was it designed to imitate the prudence of her legislation, which guarded them from arbitrary interference. The 1st Article of the Constitution, section 9, provides that the privilege of the writ of habeas corpus shall not be suspended, unless when in cases of rebellion or invasion the public safety may require it. And as this provision is found in the article enumerating the general powers of Congress, the inference is most natural, if not necessary, that to Congress only was it designed to refer the question as to when, and under what circumstances, the public safety may require the suspension of a privilege so highly prized by the citizen, and which can never be too scrupulously guarded from infringement.

Sec. 8. To Congress, moreover, is expressly reserved the exercise of all legislative power. The laws securing the privilege of the habeas corpus in cases where the civil courts have jurisdiction, are the result of the power so especially reserved. It will not be maintained that these laws can be directly repealed by any other authority. Yet the establishment of martial law is a virtual repeal for the time being of this act, and a suspension of all proceedings under it. And it would be difficult to assign any just reason for attempting indirectly what, if assumed in more open form, would be regarded by all as a gross usurpation of the legislative prerogative. The plea of necessity has indeed been offered as a reason for military interposition in special cases; but necessity, as has been aptly said, is always the plea of tyrants.

Sec. 9. This view will be fully justified by a reference to the opinions of such jurists as Judge Story, Chancellor Kent, and the present Chief Justice of the United States, Judge Taney, who all have denied the existence of any power, except Congress, to suspend this great writ. Mr. Jefferson himself declared that he was in favor of "the eternal and unremitting force of the habeas corpus laws." It is not likely, therefore, that he or his associates intended to bestow the right to interfere with them on any but the national legislature. It was once during his administration (in the time of Burr's rebellion) proposed to suspend the writ. The right was not claimed by Mr. Jefferson in any form, but a bill was introduced in Congress for the purpose, which passed the Senate, but failed in the lower House. Thus we have presented in striking harmony the theory and practice of earlier days on this important subject.*

---

*See 3 Story on Const., 208; 4 Cranch, 75; 2 Kent Com., 300, 323; Tucker's Blackstone, App., 292.

Chapter II.

OF THE ORIGIN OF MILITARY COURTS; THE SOURCES OF THEIR JURISDICTON, AND THE TIME WITHIN WHICH IT MUST BE EXERCISED.

Sec. 10. Before proceeding to consider the several subjects heretofore proposed,* it will be proper, in this place, to take a cursory view of the origin and general grounds of the jurisdiction of military courts.

The only military court of which we have any particular account in the history of English military laws, prior to the establishment of courts martial, is the Court of Chivalry, or Marshal's Court; so called because formerly held before the Lord High Constable and Earl Marshal of England jointly.† Of this court Blackstone says: "It hath, by statute, cognizance of contracts and other matters touching deeds of arms and war; and was in great reputation in the times of pure chivalry, * * * but is now grown almost entirely out of use, on account of the feebleness of its jurisdiction, and want of power to enforce its judgments, as it can neither fine nor imprison, not being a court of record." Court of Chivalry.

Sec. 11. The Court of Chivalry, in England, having gradually fallen into disuse, was succeeded by the law martial contained in the provisions of the Mutiny act, which is the first law authorizing the king to appoint a court martial. This Mutiny act is annually re-enacted by English Mutiny Act.

---

* See Preface.   † Bl. Com., III, 68.

Parliament, with such amendments as are found desirable, and may be traced back to the days of Henry the Sixth. "The sovereign power of the British nation is exercised by Parliament, and without its authority no military force can be levied or maintained." To the king alone belongs the executive power; yet, by the provisions of the Mutiny act, he is authorized to "ordain articles of war," and thus does he become, for his military subjects, possessed of both legislative and executive authority.

SEC. 12. The constitution has taken better care of the rights of our citizens, by securing to the Congress all legislative powers, which cannot be delegated, nor even administered, except under the restraints of a written law. In the exercise of this power Congress has itself ordained a military code, in the rules and articles of war, which each officer of the army is required to subscribe. The President, as commander-in-chief of the army and navy, is the executive, who is to administer this code. He can neither add to, nor take from it; and though he is authorized by the laws to make rules and regulations for both army and navy, they cannot be inconsistent with the fundamental law of the land, or with what may be called the groundwork of our military law, as expressed in the Articles of war; neither can he "ordain any penalty, or military crime not expressly declared by act of Congress."

<small>Articles of War.</small>

These Rules and Articles of war, having no limit as to their duration, must continue in force until repealed. They were first adopted in the United States service September 29, 1789, and afterward amended and readopted April 10, 1806. They were chiefly suggested by the elder Adams, who furnishes in his writings an interesting account of their origin, through the English, from the old Roman service. Thus have they come down to us, modified and improved, from a people who excelled in the art of war.

<small>Origin of.</small>

SEC. 13. It is in place here to note that regulations for the

government of the navy, were adopted by the United States Congress in 1775 and 1799; but these were sub- stituted by others provided in the Act of April 23, 1800. "The 35th article of that code provides for the convening of general courts martial as often as the President, the Secretary of the Navy, or commander-in-chief of a fleet, or commander of squadron, etc., shall deem necessary. These navy courts, like those in the army, are not to consist of more than thirteen nor less than five members. A marine corps is also organized and subjected to the laws governing the navy, except when in service with the army. See United States Navy Laws—titles, *Courts Martial* and *Marine Corps*.

<small>Navy regulations.</small>

SEC. 14. These provisions respecting the army and navy in the United States service are referred to because, until otherwise provided, they form a part of the organizations in these states, the Confederate Congress having, by act approved February 9, 1861, adopted all laws of the United States in force in the Confederate States November 1, 1861, not inconsistent with their constitution. So far, therefore, these establishments of the two governments rest upon the same general foundation.

SEC. 15. As courts martial are invested with judicial authority, which may be exerted in matters of grave and vital interest, extending to reputation, and even to life, it is important to determine the true character and extent of their jurisdiction.

<small>Importance of Courts Martial.</small>

The constitution provides for the right of personal liberty in the following terms: "No person shall be held to answer for a capital or otherwise infamous crime, unless on a presentment or indictment of a grand jury, except in cases arising in the land and naval forces, or in the militia when in actual service, in time of war or public danger; nor shall any person be subject, for the same offence, to be twice put in jeopardy of life or limb, nor shall be compelled in any criminal case to be a witness against himself, nor be deprived of life, liberty, or property, without due process of law." Const., sec. 7, par. 13; see also par. 14, same section.

Under the exception contained in this clause, says De Hart, "military courts take cognizance of such matters as fall within their competency, and proceed against defendants by due process of law, which terms, applied in reference to this subject, are convertible with those of 'by the law of the land.'"*

SEC. 16. In considering particularly the jurisdiction which may be exercised by courts martial, we will inquire:

<small>General grounds for the jurisdiction of military courts.</small>

1st. As to the subject matter out of which their authority may arise.

2d. As to the particular persons who are subject to that authority.

SEC. 17. So long as the army maintains a legal existence, in conformity to the laws by which it was originated and is preserved, it must be regarded as a "constitutional body." And as the means devised for its maintenance and government are derived from the same source as those which affect the masses at large, it becomes, and must continue, an object of legislative control.† The Articles of war, already referred to, are the result of the exercise of this power to control. They form, so to speak, the fundamental law of the army; and are designed to secure that order and discipline which are essential to its existence. To this end they define what are military offences, affixing, at the same time, either the appropriate penalty or the rule by which it may be ascertained; and herein they are "clear and explicit," and are sufficient for the observation of all military tribunals in the regulation of their proceedings. Whenever, therefore, these Rules or Articles are infringed, some military offence has been committed, and the jurisdiction of the court provided for its investigation at once attaches, and can be exercised lawfully by no other.

<small>The Articles of War the fundamental law of the army.</small>

---

* De Hart, 16. † Ibid., 19.

Sec. 18. Besides the Articles of war, the general regulations of the army furnish subjects for similar inquiry and examination whenever infringed by those to whom they are addressed. Although they do not, of course, possess the character and force of law, yet, as they proceed from the highest military authority, they are obligatory upon all to whom that authority extends. They are a "permanent body of rules for the better ordering and methodical arrangement of subjects of military concernment, and have a view to establish uniformity in the affairs of the army by determining, to a greater or less degree, the requisite minutiæ and detail. Their character, while mandatory, is also ministerial, and proceeding from the President, claims the utmost respect and obedience. They are not, it is true, in the nature of subordinate legislation to define and determine offences and affix penalties, for that belongs to Congress alone, * * but in the nature of orders pertaining to the executive and administrative branches of the service, and though they denounce no punishment in terms, yet the neglect, or breach of their requirements, are referrible to the established laws for the enforcement of discipline, to which they appeal for an appropriate sanction."* [General Regulations of the Army.]

Sec. 19. The third and last source of this jurisdiction, considered with respect to the *subject matter out of* which it arises, is the "custom of war"—more accurately defined as the "unwritten or common law of the army." [Custom of war a source of jurisdiction.]

"The common law of the land," says Chancellor Kent, "includes those principles, usages, and rules of action applicable to the government, * * * which do not rest for their authority upon any express or positive declaration of the will of the Legislature." Following this definition, we may say of the common law of the army, or custom of war, that it embodies the principles, usages, and rules of action applicable to the service, which do not rest [Definition of the term "Custom of War."]

---

* De Hart, 19, 20.

on any express or positive law or written regulation of the army. It must not, however, be opposed to any such law or regulation, and must always be well defined and certain in character. To be of any force, it must, moreover, relate wholly to the particular service in which it is applied, and not be of foreign growth. Hence, it would be inadmissible to refer for an interpretation or application of any custom of our service to the course or practice observed in another. And herein a difference may be observed between the custom or common law of military jurisprudence, and that which is so denominated in civil proceedings and courts. This "custom of war is sought rather as explanatory of some doubtful question, than as a source of authority by itself. It is an authority which should be well scrutinized before allowed to have a determining influence." And, finally, this "custom and usage of the army, when considered in contradistinction to the positive laws and regulations of the service, is generally well understood; and when adduced in illustration of the propriety of the forms adhered to, or the interpretation of acts, should have the certainty of an established fact."

SEC. 20. Having thus glanced at the jurisdiction of military courts as it results from particular sources, viz.: The Articles of war, the Regulations of the army, and the unwritten law or custom of the service, we come now to inquire as was proposed, in the second place, concerning the particular persons who are the subjects of that jurisdiction.

Persons conferring jurisdiction.

These persons are clearly described in the 96th Article of war, which declares "that all officers, conductors, gunners, matrosses, drivers, and other persons whomsoever, receiving pay or hire in the service of the artillery or corps of engineers, shall be governed by the Rules and Articles of war, and subject to be tried by courts martial in like manner with the officers and soldiers of other troops in the service." So, also, by the 97th Article, a similar provision is made as to the officers and soldiers of any troops, whether militia or others, who are mustered and in the pay of the government, when joined and acting with the regular forces of the Confederate States. These rules are, moreover, extended by act of Congress to all non-commissioned officers, musicians, artificers, and privates in the service. All such persons, therefore, as are described in these Articles, are subject to military control, and hence, to the jurisdiction of courts martial whenever the occasion arises for its exercise as to such persons.

SEC. 21. The followers of the army who accompany it and minister to its wants and comfort, are numerous and various, but have certain privileges allowed them — such as living in the camp boundaries, and protection to their persons and property. These privileges, of course, are granted on condition of fidelity to the state and subordination to the laws. The interests of the service, the discipline, and even safety of an army, render it necessary that such persons, though not belonging to the army, should, when accompanying it in the field, be subject, for actual crimes, to trial by courts martial. But this rule does not apply in time of peace and under ordinary circumstances, for where the civil jurisdiction exists and can be applied, camp followers are as much entitled to the usual mode of trial as others, and when charged with crime should be surrendered to the civil authority. *Followers of the army.*

SEC. 22. Where offences of a purely military character are committed by such persons, such as insolence to a commissioned officer, disobedience, or neglect of duty, though a court martial could not take cognizance of them, the offender may, nevertheless, be frequently sufficiently punished by dismissal from the camp and the prohibition of all intercourse with the troops. *Military offences by non-military parties, how punished.*

SEC. 23. The authority to punish individuals not strictly subject to military law, as above indicated, is the result of necessity; and as it owes its existence to no positive law, should always be exercised with prudence and caution.

SEC. 24. The 60th Article of war declares that "sutlers and retainers to the camp, and all persons whatsoever, *serving with the army* in the field, though not enlisted soldiers, are to be subject to orders, according to the rules and discipline of war."

<small>60th Article of war, sutlers, etc.</small>

These persons are designated by De Hart, substantially, as follows:

A *sutler* is a person who is permitted to reside in or follow the camp with food, liquors, and small articles of military equipment, or others, for general use or consumption. Every authorized trader within the bounds of a camp is a sutler. The mode of his appointment is designated in the Regulations of the army.

SEC. 25. *A retainer to the camp* is one connected with the military service, or business of the camp, by pay or fee. The term includes clerks, drivers, guides, and others who from time to time are employed in the public service and paid at the public expense.

<small>Retainers, etc.</small>

SEC. 26. *Persons serving with the armies.*—This includes all engaged in private service by wages from individuals who belong to the army, as well as those who serve by engagement for public hire.

<small>Persons serving with the army.</small>

"Mixed as they are in situation, business, and interests with the military body, it becomes necessary that they should be governed by the laws common to both. * * * *Sutlers and camp followers* entering into a new society having peculiar laws of its own, by their own voluntary act, must conform to those laws—as such is an understood condition of their admission. They are, therefore, liable to receive orders from their military superiors, and are to act in conformity thereto—though rather in a civil than a military capacity. These persons cannot be called on to perform military duty; but in all that relates to the maintenance of the peace and order of the camp, the observance of rights, public or private, the arrangement of their goods, horses, and carriages, and in matters pertaining to the police, safety, or convenience of the camp, they are as much liable to military command and punishment for nonobservance of the same as the enlisted soldier; though they are not compellable to perform the actual duties of a combatant."*

SEC. 27. Military cadets, under the opinion of Mr. Wirt, United States Attorney-General, are amenable to military law; and courts martial have, since that opinion, exercised jurisdiction over such cadets, though their authority was formerly doubted. The practice now is settled, in conformity to the opinion of Mr. Wirt.   *Cadets.*

SEC. 28. Having thus considered the several grounds of military jurisdiction, both in connection with the subject matter out of which it grows, and the various descriptions of persons amenable thereto, it will be proper, in concluding this part of the subject, to examine within what particular time this jurisdiction must be exercised.

In criminal proceedings before civil courts, no general statute of limitations† exists; and though military offences are to be regarded in the light of crimes, this general rule which allows them to be tried, for the most part, at any time, does not apply in cases before courts martial, inasmuch as the 88th Article of war provides that no person shall be tried by these courts for any offence committed more than two years before the issuing of the order for such trial, unless by reason of his having absented himself, or from other manifest impediment he shall not have been amenable to justice within that time.   *Statute of Limitations.*

The order directing proceedings against the party must, however, in all cases have been issued before the expiration of his term of service—for if once discharged from his enlistment, he cannot be afterward arrested for trial and punishment be-

---

* De Hart, 26.   † 4 Black. Com., 301, *note;* Wharton's Crim. Law, 212.

3

fore a court martial. But the expiration of his term of service even before sentence pronounced, would be no bar to the proceedings commenced before that time: the principle being that if the jurisdiction has once attached, it cannot afterward be ousted by mere lapse of time, but the court may, notwithstanding, proceed to sentence. Upon this subject our author remarks:

"It has been questioned whether a court martial can exercise jurisdiction over a person after the expiration of his term of service for an offence committed while acting in the capacity of a soldier or seaman prior to such period. The argument against such power is, principally, that unless there be some express provision giving the right, military authority of every description ceases necessarily with the period of enlistment; and that if such person be liable at all after the expiration of his term of service, he is liable at all times, at all places, and to all officers who have commanded him. * * * Every man who is not bound by military engagements, and the laws which govern those communities, is only subject to trial for any imputed offence by the common law courts of the land; and courts martial are divested of all jurisdiction over such persons — and, therefore, cannot enter into the question of guilt or innocence, and are not the proper tribunals to settle such fact.

Opinions as to Statute of Limitations.

"To which it is replied:

SEC. 29. "The general principle of law is that, whenever any act is prohibited under a penalty, and no limitation affixed to a prosecution, the offender is amenable at any time during his life; and were this principle not applicable to military persons, it is evident that offenders would frequently escape punishment, to the great detriment of the public service, because there are no other than courts martial which can take cognizance of particular crimes. It would also operate much to the prejudice of the public, were offenders in all cases to be brought to trial at particular periods within the statute of limitations, if any exist, and thus limit the authority to the mere time of the existence of a particular exigency when it might be unable to take cognizance of and decide upon a single offence.

"Authority is given (99th Article of war) to courts martial to take cognizance of the class of crimes indicated, and to punish, either by the arbitrary declaration of the law, or by the discretion vested in the court. If, then, the time is not limited by any statute when their jurisdiction of these offences ceases, it would seem to be putting at too great hazard the interest, the safety, and the reputation of the military and naval service to permit offenders to escape all punishment, and thus encourage insubordination and violence, asserting a privilege for the criminal because he had been prudent enough to restrain his temper or regulate his conduct until no judicial notice could be taken of his offences before the expiration of his term of service!

"If the object of these laws was intended to enforce obedience, and to promote discipline, and ensure order and safety, there can appear but little ground to doubt the jurisdiction of courts martial in cases like those now considered. Such object is apparent and admitted, and, therefore, the amenability of one, for the commission of military crime, to the authority of a special tribunal created for the trial and punishment of such offenders is not to be changed, because between the commission of the offence and the time of the assembling of the court he may have changed his official relations or professional character."

SEC. 30. It has been contended by some that the United States Supreme Court had appellate jurisdiction in certain military cases, and that a mandatory writ from that court would be obeyed by a court martial.* But this appears to be contrary to the opinions of the

<small>No jurisdiction of civil courts in military cases.</small>

---

* O'Brien's Mil. Law, 222.

best jurists, and to be supported by no precedent. No doubt both concurrent and appellate jurisdiction over military offences might have been conferred on the civil courts, but this does not appear to have been done, and in the absence of any provision to that effect, the jurisdiction of the military tribunals must be regarded as exclusive. Nor have the civil courts a right to take cognizance of a strictly military offence by the common law. On this point Chancellor Kent remarks: "Military and naval crimes committed while the party is attached to or under the immediate authority of the army or navy, and in actual service, are not cognizable under the common law jurisdiction of the civil courts.* It has, moreover, been decided by the New York courts that a party on trial before a naval court for alleged crimes committed on the high seas, was not amenable to the civil authority upon a similar charge.†

SEC. 31. The distinctions thus established by the United States Courts and jurists would, no doubt, be received as law in the absence of any special provision by Congress in the Confederate States.

SEC. 32. It remains to add that, as courts martial derive their authority from the same source as the civil courts, the decisions of the former within their proper sphere are equally entitled to consideration and respect. They are, however, in a general sense to be regarded as subordinate to the civil authority, inasmuch as their powers and duties are exercised only under a limited and special code, while the civil courts are charged with the administration of the general laws of the land. Hence, as already suggested, it has been made the duty of officers to aid in bringing offenders against those laws to trial before the civil authority, and to respect its orders and decisions in all cases arising under the Habeas Corpus acts.

Courts Martial subordinate to the civil courts, etc.

---

* 2 Kent's Com., 341. † Case of Captain McKenzie, 2 Kent, 342, 363.

Chapter III.

OF THE JUDGE ADVOCATE.

SEC. 33. We are now to consider the qualifications, responsibilities, rights, and duties appertaining to the office of Judge Advocate.

On these subjects we have no legislation beyond the very brief summary contained in the Articles of war. The rules and principles now existing for the guidance of this officer are the result of custom chiefly, and hence the difficulty so often experienced as to the authority of the court on the one side, and the rights and duties of the Judge Advocate on the other.* It is evident, therefore, that in the selection of a Judge Advocate regard should always be paid to his experience and previous knowledge, to enable him to discuss the questions which may arise, and to present and explain the rules and principles which ought to govern the court, and direct his own course in the conduct of the trial. *Judge Advocate.* *Selection of.*

SEC. 34. The Articles of war require that this office should be filled by some fit person; and it is important to ascertain, in the first place, the particular qualifications necessary to such fitness. *A fit person required.*

"It is generally conceded," says De Hart, "that for a proper discharge of this office there is needed qualifications and attainments of more than ordinary possession; *His qualifications.*

---

* De Hart, 301.

that as the duties are multifarious and highly important, and therefore responsible, there should be corresponding ability; a fitness, in a word, only to be derived from experience and knowledge of military life, its laws, customs, and modes of discipline, together with a competent acquaintance with the principles and maxims of criminal jurisprudence, and by which the proceedings in the ordinary law courts of the country are regulated. The particular rules for the government of military judicial proceedings cannot be found in the laws alone; they must be sought in the history of cases, or the treatises of military authors: for the experience of the most practiced individual is not large enough to embrace all the accidents and contingencies of circumstance, which give diversity to the subject."

Another author* remarks on this point: "In the investigation of criminal offences by military officers unacquainted with criminal law, unless the utmost precaution be used, there is too much probability that the sentences of courts martial will not unfrequently be altogether illegal, and that prisoners may, in consequence, be subjected to punishment — even to capital punishment — although such sentences were not sanctioned by law."

"It is to obviate the possibility of such occurrences," says Captain Hughes, "that Judge Advocates are appointed; that there may not in any case be a failure of justice, that irregularities and illegalities may be checked, and that the proper mode of procedure * * * may be brought to the notice of courts martial by a competent person."†

SEC. 35. Thus is it manifest that the proper administration *Importance of qualifications in Judge Advocate.* of justice in the army and navy depends in a large measure upon the ability and fitness of the Judge Advocate, in whom the qualifications and attainments of both the military and legal professions ought, to a reason-

---

*Kennedy, quoted in Hughes, 12, 187   † Hughes, 12.

able extent at least, to be united for this specific duty. Such a one would be a "fit person" for this important office; and hence it has been argued that the appointment of parties from civil life to officiate as Judge Advocates, while not opposed to any *law* of the service, is in many respects objectionable.*

SEC. 36. Having thus exhibited the *qualifications* necessary for the proper performance of the duties of Judge Advocate, let us next see what are his peculiar *responsibilities*.

The Judge Advocate is the law officer of the court. He is also required to prosecute for the government.† Upon his opinion and advice the members of the court rely to a great extent for direction in the discharge of their various duties.

<small>Responsibilities of Judge Advocate.</small>

SEC. 37. The question has hence arisen whether, in event of error in the court consequent on opinions given by the Judge Advocate, and to an extent resulting in damage to others, he is responsible therefor before the civil authorities.

<small>Question as to his legal liability.</small>

There seems no doubt that the members themselves are thus responsible; and it is claimed by some as a legitimate consequence that the party who is regarded as mainly concerned in assisting and advising the members, and to whose opinions they naturally, in a large measure, defer, should at least share in their responsibility.

<small>Members liable.</small>

There are no decisions of the courts on this point, and we are left in its discussion to the opinions of military men, and to deductions from general principles. An attorney it is said is bound to exercise care, skill, and integrity in his profession, but is not accountable for mere error or mistake.‡ If, however, he proves clearly deficient, or is guilty of

<small>No decisions on the point.</small>

---

* Hughes' Duties of Judge Advocate, 12.
† 69:h Article of War.   ‡ 3 Blackstone, 26—*note.*

gross neglect, he would be liable in damages to the injured party. Some English military writers have held the same principle to be applicable to a Judge Advocate, inasmuch as he is the legal representative of the government and its officers in the court; and Captain Hughes declares that, "if a Judge Advocate should mislead a court martial by counsel which is contrary to law, he is equally responsible to a court of justice as he is to his military superiors."* The same author remarks: "Let us suppose an action brought against a court martial for some illegal act * * clearly proved to have arisen from advice given by the Judge Advocate.  Is the person who thus misleads the court, who is expressly appointed to obviate a failure of justice, and for the more orderly proceedings of courts martial, whose peculiar duty it is to *prevent*, by pointing out such occurrences, an undue excess of authority, excess of jurisdiction, or illegality of proceedings, to escape the penalty of all other members of the court, collectively or individually? If the sole object of a Judge Advocate was merely to record the proceedings of the court, any clerk could perform this duty equally well; but the Judge Advocate is appointed for a different and more important purpose—it being his duty, in conducting and recording the proceedings, to obviate a failure of justice and the slightest deviation from either military law or custom, or the law of the land, to administer oaths, to advise on points of law, of custom, and of form—the very performance of which duties under military orders and instructions, renders him responsible to those who appoint him, and to the laws of the country, if he mislead the court, as whose minister he is appointed to guide and instruct."†

SEC. 38. These opinions are, perhaps, mainly founded on the phraseology of the English law, and cannot be relied on as of authority in our service. Nevertheless, there are strong rea-

Marginal note: Opinions on the question.

---

* Duties of Judge Advocate, 14. † Hughes, 192, 193.

some in favor of the doctrine they maintain, at least in cases of wilful or gross neglect, notwithstanding the opinion of De Hart, that to attempt to fix "responsibility on the Judge Advocate, even in such cases, would not only be unreasonable, but. approaching the ridiculous:" for it is a known general rule that negligence in the discharge of duty, which results in injury to another, subjects the offending party to damages. Where the fact of neglect is established, why should the rule not apply in military as well as in other transactions? It is true where the Judge Advocate is a commissioned officer he is responsible, as such, to the military authorities; but this appertains only to the discipline of the service, and affords no redress to the party suffering, who, in ordinary cases, might claim damages for the wrong received.

Sec. 39. And yet it must be admitted there is great difficulty in establishing a connection between the expressed opinions and advice of a Judge Advocate and the decision of the court with which he has been associated: for while one member may have been greatly influenced, perhaps guided, by such advice, by another it may have been wholly overlooked or disregarded. It ought also to be observed that the members of a court martial exercise, or at least ought to exercise, a full discretion in their decisions, and are under oath "well and truly to try and determine the matter" before the court, "without partiality, favor, or affection." But to whatever consideration the suggestions to the contrary may be entitled, the rule appears to be definitely settled in this country that a Judge Advocate is not responsible *civiliter* for his opinions; and this must be received as the law of the service, until otherwise determined by legislative enactment or judicial decision. Upon this point De Hart remarks: "The person officiating as Judge Advocate is frequently less fitted to advise the court than any individual making part of it; and of course, *in such cases*,

Judge Advocate not regarded liable in law.

De Hart's opinion on the question

his opinion, if ever asked, is received with very little deference."

"As courts martial," he continues, "must exercise a discretion of their own in the adoption of any opinion offered, or the acceptance of any rule for the government of their proceedings, and are not at all bound to follow the opinions of the Judge Advocate, it would seem that any decision of theirs should not involve in any liability to future censure or punishment that individual. It is true that his agency to determine their course may be very direct, but still he is without a judicative voice, and but expresses an opinion in the performance of a duty." If doubt exists, he adds: "the court may adjourn to make a reference of the question, and fortify their minds for future consideration" of the subject.

SEC. 40. But although the Judge Advocate is not liable before the civil courts, it must not be inferred that he is exempt from responsibility. The interests of the service, the court, and the accused, are frequently in a great measure entrusted to him, and demand his accountability to military law, for any neglect or inefficiency in the discharge of his duty. Hence it is an established rule, that no person can appear as Judge Advocate who is not subject to that law, so that, if one is appointed to that office from civil life, he becomes by accepting the position at once amenable to the same rules and conditions as a commissioned officer. In both cases the responsibility and obligation are the same. "Nothing," says Captain Hughes, "can be more conclusive than this, that although the duties of Judge Advocate are of a civil nature, yet he is responsible to the military authority who appoints him, and consequently is amenable to military law."* And this responsibility, small or great, must be borne alone. He cannot have the assistance of counsel before the court, *except as a mere legal adviser;* nor can counsel be allowed to aid in the prosecution at the

<small>Responsible to military authority.</small>

<small>Not entitled to counsel, except.</small>

---

*Hughes, 191—*note;* De Hart, 115.

instance and request of others. This would frequently result, as has been forcibly objected, in " mingling private animosities of personal resentments with the stream of public justice." In the case of Captain McKenzie, United States navy, who was tried in 1843, for murder on the high seas, the friends of Midshipman Spencer desired to employ two eminent lawyers to aid in the prosecution, by the examination of witnesses, etc., but the court after fully considering the subject decided that the request could not be granted. " In cases where it is necessary to have the assistance of the accuser or person who has suffered by the conduct of the accused, all that can be insisted upon on the part of the prosecution is, to ask of the court permission for such person to remain, after being examined as a witness, to whom reference may be made for information or particulars of the offence charged. And if a person bringing an accusation against any one in the army or navy is not himself an officer of either, he can only appear in court as an informer or witness."*

SEC. 41. Our next inquiry concerns the *duties*, and in connection with them, the *rights* of the Judge Advocate. It will be convenient to consider: First, such as devolve upon him prior to the meeting of the court; and, secondly, those in which he is engaged during the trial as an officer of the court. And first, as to his duties prior to the trial and meeting of the court. Duties of Judge Advocate.

SEC. 42. As soon as the Judge Advocate has received a copy of the order for the convening of the court, he should proceed to examine the charges on which they are to act. Sometimes a mere memorandum, or brief, is furnished him. In such cases, it devolves upon him to put them into proper shape. If they are sent him already prepared from head-quarters, and, nevertheless, prove upon examination to be defective, he ought immediately to return them for correction As to the charges.

---

* De Hart, 320.

—it being a doubtful question whether he can himself amend them under such circumstances. But in either case, it is his duty to see that the charges are properly framed, free from legal defect, and with the precision and distinctness which the law requires, before the prisoner is called on to *plead* to them. The particular nature of the charges, their form, substance, and the answers to them, will be considered in another place.

SEC. 43. Having ascertained that the charges are free from reasonable exception, the Judge Advocate is next to see that a copy of them is furnished the prisoner.

<small>Copy of charges to be sent prisoner.</small>

On this subject, Major Hough, quoted in the work of Capt. Hughes, remarks: "All writers on military law state that it is usual to furnish the prisoner with a copy of the charges on which he is to be tried;" and this "is not only proper, but advantageous." And Captain Hughes, quoting the Bombay Military Regulations, adds: "Although the prisoner cannot legally demand a copy of the charge on which he is to be tried, or object to any differences which may appear in it, he ought, nevertheless, to be furnished with one as early as possible, and also to be made acquainted with whatever alterations may be subsequently made."

De Hart states the rule in this connection in the following terms:

"It is considered the duty of the Judge Advocate to furnish the prisoner with a copy of the charges upon which he is to be tried at as early a period as possible, in order to avoid any delay in the progress of the trial. Where a prisoner has received a copy through another channel, as, for instance, the Adjutant-General, should any discrepancy exist between them and the charges submitted to the court, it cannot be pleaded in bar of the trial, but the court would under such circumstances, where the deviation was material, no doubt afford the prisoner time to prepare for the investigation by delaying the proceedings. This course is nothing more than common justice, inasmuch as an accused person should have a knowledge of the offences charged against him previous to trial, and sufficient time allowed to enable him to defend himself against them.

"To soldiers who cannot read, the charges are read by the Adjutant; or the Judge Advocate visits the place of confinement and instructs them as to the nature of their offences, and gathers their means of defence, list of witnesses, etc. The attention of the Judge Advocate to the consultation which the ignorance and peculiar situation of soldiers call for, is a happy means for the exercise of that portion of his functions which is, to some degree, expected of him as counsel for the prisoner, and to prevent the perpetration of injustice. With recruits especially, or very young men, apprehended at a distance from the station to which they are attached, and often without any previous investigation assigned to the guard-house, under charge of desertion, * * this intercourse is productive of the best results."

To soldiers who cannot read, etc.

SEC. 44. It next becomes necessary to summon the witnesses for the trial. The usual course is to append a list of those for the prosecution to the charges. This, however, cannot be demanded as a right; but, observes Captain Simmons, "unless there is some sufficient cause to justify its being withheld, it would not be in accordance with the existing practice to refuse the prisoner a list of witnesses for the prosecution. The almost universal custom is to give it as a matter of course."

List of witnesses furnished prisoner.

SEC. 45. The Judge Advocate also receives from the prisoner the names of such as he desires to be called on his part, and they are usually summoned. But here, too, a reasonable and sound discretion is to be exercised, subject to this limitation, that no witness, nor any commissioned officer, shall be called *at the expense of the government*, unless the ends of justice clearly require it. If sufficient cause appears why it should not be done, such as the great distance,

And received from him.

and important engagements of the witness, and heavy expense of his transportation, the Judge Advocate *may* decline to make the summons, and may submit the question for the decision of the court, who will direct what is proper. Where this course is adopted, the whole proceeding connected with it is entered on the record of the court. Nor is the examination restricted to such witnesses as are thus summoned; but either party may introduce such as are legally competent, so long as his case remains unclosed. Yet it is deemed desirable and "most expedient that the lists furnished the Judge Advocate should contain the names of every witness whom the parties intend to call."*

SEC. 45. No particular form is required in summoning a witness. In the English service, the Judge Advocate is invested with authority to enforce the attendance of civil witnesses. With us, no such authority exists; but under the provisions of the 74th Article of war their depositions may be taken — both parties being represented or notified of the time and place at which such testimony is to be given.

No form required in summons.

SEC. 46. In summoning military witnesses, it is only necessary for the Judge Advocate to advise the commanding officer, or the War department, of the names of the witnesses required. The proper instructions for their attendance is then issued, and, of course, obeyed. Lastly, it is important to observe that all witnesses should be summoned at the earliest practicable day. This is desirable not only to prevent vexatious delay, but to enable each party to be entirely prepared for the trial.

How summoned.

To be summoned early.

SEC. 47. Having progressed thus far, it is now desirable, though not incumbent, that the Judge Advocate should prepare a brief, or short analysis, for conducting the trial and for examination of the wit-

Best to prepare a brief for the trial.

---

*Kennedy.

nesses. This will greatly facilitate the operations of the court, and be of much assistance in the progress of the trial. In some cases the "task is delegated to him of arranging a prosecution on particular grounds designated by superior authority," and it is then his duty to ascertain the "facts in issue, and all the particulars relating thereto," and be prepared accordingly. He has lastly, under authority of the commanding officer of the post, or through the medium of an officer of the quartermaster's department, or in the absence of such, on his own responsibility, to provide a suitable apartment for the meeting of the court. This it is his duty to do. Provides place of meeting.

SEC. 48. We are now, secondly, to consider the *duties of a Judge Advocate in immediate connection with the trial, and as an officer of the court.* Duties as Officer of the Court.

The following summary of what may be denominated the cardinal principles, to be kept in view by the Judge Advocate, is given by Captain Hughes, and should be remembered by all who are called to discharge the duties of this responsible office: Main principles in view.

"That justice is the object for which a court martial is convened and the Judge Advocate appointed."

"That the great principle of a military court is honor; a conscientious adherence to substantial justice."

"That the business of a court martial is not to discuss points of law, but to get at the truth by all the means in their power."

"That a Judge Advocate is the mainspring of a court martial; that on him the court depends for information concerning the *legality* as well as the *regularity* of their proceedings, and if he errs all may go wrong."

SEC. 49. The authority to appoint a Judge Advocate whenever a general court martial is assembled is derived from the 69th Article of war. The observation of De Hart on this subject, is as appropriate here and now as Authority to appoint.

when he wrote. He says: "The broad interpretation given to all legislation, touching this authority, is, that he who has the power to appoint general courts martial has, incidentally as well as directly by statute, the power also of appointing some fit person to act as Judge Advocate."*

The 69th Article of war above mentioned, and to which the reader is referred, very briefly adverts to the special duties of this officer, and presents the leading idea of what they were designed to be.

<small>69th Article of War.</small>

SEC. 50. Besides this, there has been no special legislation by Congress on this subject. Nevertheless, the duties of the Judge Advocate are generally clearly defined by military writers. Says General Kennedy: "A Judge Advocate appears at a court martial in three distinct characters. 1st, as an officer of the court, for the purpose of recording its proceedings and administering the requisite oaths; 2d, as the adviser of the court in matters of form and law; 3d, as public prosecutor. In the first of these characters he is of course subject to the orders of the court, who may direct their proceedings to be conducted and recorded as they think proper; but in the other two characters the court can exercise no control whatever over the Judge Advocate, as in the performance of these duties he must be allowed to act according to his own judgment and discretion."

<small>No other special legislation.</small>

<small>Yet his duties generally defined.</small>

And Captain Simmons remarks: "The duties of a Judge Advocate are various and important. He records all the acts of the court, and all oral evidence—as near as may be the very words of the witness; he notes the hour of assembly and adjournment, and generally all incidental occurrences, particularly the clearing of the court, the cause thereof, and, where interlocutory judgments are given, the decision. He advises the court on points of *law, custom,* and form, and invites their attention to any deviation therefrom."

---

* Page 308.

Sec. 51. The Judge Advocate may, to a limited extent, assist the prisoner, notwithstanding he is required to *"prosecute"* for the government. Yet, in the discharge of the duties of his office, he does not always occupy precisely the position of prosecutor. This is evident from the three-fold character which, as already shown, he bears before the court, as *officer, adviser,* and *prosecutor.* Upon this point General Kennedy thus lays down the rule: "It is expected that the Judge Advocate, if consulted by either a private prosecutor or by the prisoner, should give him the best information and advice in his power; but an opinion which was long prevalent in the army, that it was the official duty of the Judge Advocate to assist the prisoner in the conduct of his defence, appears to be no longer maintained. To affording him, however, such assistance, if requested as a favor, I suppose no Judge Advocate would ever object; and if a prisoner, therefore, wishes to avail himself of it, he is merely to make the requisite application, which will, no doubt, be complied with. It is, however, to be observed, that the Judge Advocate ought not for a moment to forget his duty as prosecutor; and though he ought on the defence, as well as at all other times, to restrain the prisoner from advancing anything which might criminate himself or prejudice his case, he is still bound, by the cross-examination of the prisoner's witnesses, to give every effect to the prosecution. In court, therefore, it is not in the power of the Judge Advocate to afford the prisoner any effectual assistance, for there he could neither advise him nor frame questions for him, nor cross-examine the prosecutor's witnesses, which acts could alone be of any essential benefit to the prisoner; but out of court there can be no impropriety in the Judge Advocate pointing out to a prisoner the manner in which he might best conduct his defence for him. A defence, however, cannot be made without a knowledge of the circumstances of the case, and it would, therefore, seldom be prudent for the

How far he may aid the accused.

prisoner to acquaint the Judge Advocate with the real nature of the transaction alleged in the charge, or to disclose to him the grounds on which he intended to rest his exculpation. A prisoner, however, may give to the Judge Advocate a memorandum of the points on which he wishes his own witnesses to be examined, and the opposite party cross-examined, or a list of questions to the same effect, and request him to put only such interrogatories to the witnesses as he thinks necessary, and to frame the questions in his own words."

SEC. 52. So, likewise, DeHart referring to this subject observes :

"It is evident that the provisions of the 69th Article of war were intended for the benefit of enlisted soldiers, whose ignorance makes the counsel of the Judge Advocate much more necessary than in other cases, and to whom it most forcibly applies. It would, consequently, be incumbent on the Judge Advocate to see that no improper advantage be taken of the prisoner by the admission of illegal testimony, but that he direct him how to present the facts on which his defence may hinge in the most effective light to the court. The prisoner may give a memorandum of the points on which he wishes his own witnesses examined, and the opposite party cross-examined, to the Judge Advocate, and request him to put the questions in his own words. In general terms it may be remarked, that it is the duty of the Judge Advocate to shape questions in legal form; to solve all difficulties as to the relevancy of facts adduced by either party; to see that the prisoner shall not suffer from a want of knowledge of the law, or deficiency of experience, or ability to elicit from witnesses a full statement of the facts bearing on his case; and to this extent both the court and Judge Advocate are bound to give their advice to the prisoner. He should also give him reasonable aid in his defence either in point of law or justice, and where doubtful questions arise,

Judge Advocate to see no improper advantage taken of prisoner.

rather incline to the side of the prisoner; and, above all, never *omit* any circumstances of the proceedings having a tendency to palliate the charges against the accused. As to the propriety of speaking with the prisoner before trial, Major Hough says, "he conceives great good may often result, particularly in the case of a private soldier, as the Judge Advocate is more free from bias it may be supposed than any other person."

There is some difference, it will be noticed, between the opinions here quoted from Captain Simmons and Captain De Hart, as to the duty of the Judge Advocate to the accused *while in court*. But, under the language of the 67th Article of war, there would seem to be very little doubt that the views expressed by the latter writer are correct; and leaning as they do to the side of the accused, should be preferred, especially where he is without the aid of counsel.

SEC. 53. It is conceded, therefore, that either party has a right at least to the opinion of the Judge Advocate, whether in court or out of it, upon any questions that may arise in the course of the trial, or in connection with it.

SEC. 54. We are thus brought to consider the duties of the Judge Advocate in open court. And here it should be premised that this officer, being the representative of the government at general courts martial, is not subject to challenge on any ground. He may, moreover, be absent, though this is not desirable, during part of the time, and may afterward resume his duties without invalidating the proceedings. <small>Judge Advocate not subject to challenge.</small>

SEC. 55. We have already adverted to the two-fold duties of Judge Advocate, as public prosecutor and legal adviser of the court.

Let us consider them more particularly, and in their order. Under the authority of the 69th Article of war, it is settled that the Judge Advocate only, or person appointed to act as such, can appear as prosecutor before a court martial.* The

---

* De Hart, 317.

Judge Advocate to conduct the prosecution. conduct of the prosecution devolves upon him. In the discharge of this duty, he acts agreeably to his own judgment and discretion; and although, as an *officer* of the court, it may direct him as to the particular manner of recording and arranging the proceedings, yet it cannot control him in the exercise of his peculiar office as *prosecutor*—as by directing him to withdraw or alter a charge, to withhold evidence, denying his right to reply, or placing any obstacle in his way while engaged in the proper discharge of his duties—for he is appointed wholly to *conduct* the prosecution, "to search out the truth and obviate a failure of justice." He is therefore "bound to lay before the court the *full* particulars of the circumstances which are considered to have been an infringement of the ordinances of the army, or perhaps of the state; and in so doing must produce, without partiality or favor to either party, *all* evidence that tends to elicit the truth. However painful it may be to his feelings as an individual to sustain a prosecution, whether the evidence tends to conviction or acquittal, his duty to the state, the maintenance of discipline, and above all *justice*, demand a faithful discharge of the duty."*

SEC. 56. Impartiality is one of the first duties of this office, though from the natural desire which is felt to succeed in what is undertaken, this high obligation is too frequently overlooked. The Judge Advocate should, therefore, "be particularly careful not to let one part of his business prejudice him in the conducting of another, nor lead him to endeavor to bias the court by any ambiguous explanation of the law, or of other matters. Truth and equity ought to be conspicuous in courts martial, but chicanery never permitted to enter the door. A Judge Advocate should never omit anything in the record which may be of service to the prisoner; nor, on the other hand, is he to let the cause of pub-

Duty of impartiality in Judge Advocate.

---

* Hughes, 118.

lic justice suffer and a criminal escape unpunished through lenity, or any other motive whatever.*

SEC. 57. But while it is the duty of the Judge Advocate thus to prosecute, he is at the same time, in some sense, to regard himself as the friend and counsel of the prisoner. He must not himself put leading questions, and should object to their being put by others. He should also observe the same rule as to questions tending to criminate either the prisoner or a witness. Particularly is a Judge Advocate to prevent any improper advantage being taken of the prisoner, and to record fully and fairly all that appears in his favor, so that it may be brought to the view of the court and of the revising authority.† He should treat the prisoner liberally, and be careful that nothing is brought against him by surprise.‡ In short, his whole duty consists in so conducting the prosecution that the whole and nothing but the truth shall be revealed and put on record, and entire justice done to the state, the service, and the individual. *[side note: Judge Advocate the friend of the accused.]*

SEC. 58. Next, and intimately connected with the duty of the Judge Advocate as public prosecutor, is that of legal adviser of the court. This latter duty is very accurately defined in the following passages from Tytler: *[side note: Duty of Judge Advocate as legal adviser.]*

"Another important duty of the Judge Advocate during the trial is the instructing or counselling the court, not only in matters of essential and necessary form, with which he must be presumed to be, from practice, thoroughly acquainted, but in explaining to them such points of law as may occur in the course of their proceedings, for which purpose a Judge Advocate ought to instruct himself in the general principles and rules of law and in the practice of criminal courts.

"In the performance of this duty he will always be guided

---

* Captain Adye, in O'Brien's Military Law, 282.
† O'Brien, 284.   ‡ O'Brien, 285.

by a just sense of his official character and situation;
as he has no judicial power, nor any determinative
voice either in the sentence or interlocutory opinions
of the court, so he is not entitled to regulate or dictate those sentences or opinions, or in any shape to interfere in the proceedings of the court, further than by giving counsel or advice, and (unless the court demand it) his own discretion must be his sole director in suggesting when that may be seasonable, proper, or necessary."

<small>Judge Advocate has no determining voice or judicial power.</small>

"On every occasion when the court demands his opinion, he is bound to give it with freedom and amplitude, and even when not requested to deliver his sentiments, his duty requires that he should put the court upon their guard against any deviation either from any essential or necessary forms in their proceedings, or a violation of material justice in their final sentence and judgment.

<small>Must give his opinion when required.</small>

"A remonstrance of this nature urged with due temperance and respect will seldom, it is presumed, fail to meet with its proper regard from the court; but should it happen that an illegal measure or an unjust opinion is, nevertheless, persevered in, the Judge Advocate, though not warranted to enter a dissent in the form of a protest upon the record of the proceedings (for that implies a judicative voice), ought to insert therein the opinion delivered by him upon the controverted point, in order not only that he may stand absolved from all imputations of failure in his duty of giving counsel, but that the error or wrong may be fairly brought under the consideration of the power with whom it lies, either to approve and order into effect, or to remit the operation of the sentence."

<small>May remonstrate.</small>

SEC. 59. It is both the right and duty of the Judge Advocate where a difference of opinion arises between himself and the court, to insert the opinion he has given in the proceedings or annex it to them. Indeed, Gen-

<small>Right to record his opinion.</small>

eral Kennedy observes, his attendance on the court would be of no use whatever, if he were not permitted to insert in the record any opinions of importance he may give during the trial, whether adopted by the court or not. "But," he adds, "a Judge Advocate ought certainly to refrain interposing his opinion except on occasions where he apprehends the probable occurrence of some irregularity or illegality, or where questions of importance arise to the proper decision of which he may think that the expression of his sentiments might contribute. It is, however, his most particular duty to object to the admission of improper evidence, and to point out to the court the irrelevancy of all such matter as may be adduced which does not tend to prove either directly or consequentially the charge under investigation." And "should he observe the court inclined to find a verdict contrary to the evidence, it is undoubtedly his duty to endeavor, by the expression of his opinion, to prevent it from deciding so erroneously."

Captain Hughes* refers to a case mentioned, he says, by Major Hough, wherein a court, having acted contrary to the advice of the Judge Advocate, was thus rebuked by the reviewing authority:

"*Disapproved:* Because the court, having taken upon itself the decision of a question of law, instead of having permitted the exposition of law given by the district Judge Advocate-General to guide it, has permitted the error of finding the prisoner guilty of manslaughter, with the exception of the words 'feloniously and wilfully'—the first of those words being indispensable to define the crime of manslaughter; thus the court has affirmed the crime, after having abstracted the essence which constituted it: if the act was not feloniously done the crime charged was not committed."

SEC. 60. When the court is considering the sentence, the

* Page 124.

Judge Advocate should express no opinion. He is
Judge Advocate to give no opinion as to sentence. not responsible for the punishment adjudged, to whatever extent he may be answerable for the correctness of the finding. But after the sentence has been passed, there is no objection to the Judge Advocate pointing out any error or illegality in the nature or degree of the
Or in closed Court. punishment awarded by the court.* He should not assume the office of prosecutor or adviser in a closed court, nor give any opinion at such time unless required by the
Except when? court. This is the general rule; exceptional cases may, however, occur, in which the Judge Advocate must exercise a sound and proper discretion. If the court is manifestly proceeding in the sentence, or any of its deliberations, in opposition to established law or the custom of the service, it would then be his duty to interpose with his opinion and a statement of the law on the subject. But the general rule is as already stated. In no case where the question is within the discretion and competency of the court should the Judge Advocate attempt to interfere, so long as the limits of legal authority are duly observed and respected.† It
Not to seek points for discussion. is never desirable to seek after *points* for discussion, or to intrude advice upon immaterial questions; much less should a Judge Advocate insist on placing on record his opinions upon subjects of no importance. Such a course naturally tends to irritate the court and unnecessarily to consume its time.‡

SEC. 61. The court having now met, the first duty of the
Judge Advocate to see Court is legally constituted. Judge Advocate, after reading aloud the order convening it, is to see that it is legally constituted. To this end it is essential that the number of officers required for a quorum is present, and are so by competent authority. He should also, before proceeding to trial,

---

* Kennedy. † De Hart, 328. ‡ Same, 328, 329.

be careful to administer the oath required by the 69th Article of war; and be himself sworn by the President, as directed by the same Article. The mode of administering these oaths is thus described by De Hart: "The members of the court and the Judge Advocate stand; the persons to be sworn lift the right hand ungloved, when the Judge Advocate recites, in an audible voice: 'You, Colonel A B, Major C D, Captain E F (thus naming, with his rank, each member of the court), do swear that you will well and truly try and determine,' etc., following the form of the oath prescribed in Article 69. The presiding officer then administers the oath to the Judge Advocate, observing the form prescribed for that officer in the same Article; during all which time the members of the court remain standing, and observe the most decorous silence and attention." *Oath.* *Mode of administering.*

In military as well as civil courts oaths may be administered by kissing the book or, as above described, by affirmation. In the case of Jews, they should be sworn on the Five Books of Moses, with the head covered—the Jew not regarding any other oath as valid.*

SEC. 62. The Judge Advocate must, moreover, see that the proper opportunity is offered the accused or prisoner to object, by challenge, to any member of the court; and if the public interests require it, he should himself exercise this right of challenge where it is demanded. These requirements must not only be observed, but it must appear on the record, in each case, that they have been complied with. This record must be written out each day, as free from erasures and interlineations as possible, always stating by what authority the court has been convened. *For the form of this heading, see Appendix.* *Opportunity to challenge allowed.*

SEC. 63. The names of the members are registered on the

---

* 1 Starkie, 82.

Names of members registered, etc. proceedings according to seniority, the rank and regiment of each being properly set forth. As no president is appointed as such, the first named officer in the order directing the court is the president thereof, and is the senior. *No Presid't detailed as such.* The name of the Judge Advocate is inserted last on the list. This, though forming part of the record of the court, had better be prepared beforehand.

As a matter of convenience, and to afford a better idea of the arrangement and relative position of the officers composing a court martial, the annexed plate is copied from the work of Captain Hughes, with his explanation. "The Judge Advocate," he says, "sits opposite to the president, the interpreter a little to the right, and the witness on the left of the Judge Advocate; the prosecutor and prisoner, a short distance behind the Judge Advocate, should each have a small table to enable them, or their counsel or friends, to write upon; but none of the parties should sit with their backs to the court; the public, military and civilians, take their seats around the room at a short distance from the court."

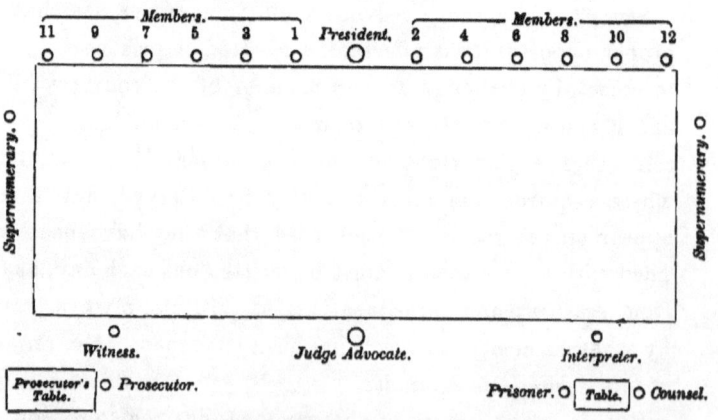

SEC. 64. The court being thus formed, the prisoner or accused is brought before it, and this is noted by the Judge Advocate as follows:

At a general court martial convened at —— on the —— day of ——, by virtue of General Orders, No. — (here describe the order), was arraigned and tried Captain ——, of the Regiment of ——, upon the following charges and specifications—which should then be separately and distinctly set out. *(Form of arraignment and order.)*

It is usual to allow an officer a seat upon his own application. This application is, however, in the cases of non-commissioned officers and soldiers, made by the Judge Advocate. But in all cases the accused or prisoner should stand while the charges are read, or whenever he proposes a question or addresses the court. These rules apply equally to witnesses. *(Prisoner allowed a seat.)*

SEC. 65. When the court is once assembled, none but the authority by which it has been called together can in any manner interfere in its proceedings. The president of the court only has the power to assemble and adjourn it, and to preserve order during its sittings. But he has no further power except as a member, as all questions of whatever nature which arise during the deliberations of the court must be decided by a majority of the votes.* *(Powers of President.)*

The deliberations of the court are with closed doors. At other times it is open to the public. Upon all questions respecting the admission or rejection of evidence, and upon points of law or custom, a majority of the votes decide.† *(Closed doors, when. Votes.)*

SEC. 66. The facts of closing and opening of the court must always be noted on the proceedings. The result of deliberation of the court upon any question must also be stated. *(Closing and opening to be noted on record.)*

SEC. 67. It has been already suggested that the prisoner has the right of challenge, and that before proceeding to trial he should always have the opportunity to exercise it. If no ob-

---

* Kennedy. † Simmons.

<small>Prisoner to state ground of challenge.</small> jection is made, the trial proceeds. But if the prisoner object, he is required to state the grounds of the objection, with any evidence he may have to sustain it. All this should be recorded regularly and at length in the proceedings. Who are liable to be challenged, and the manner and ground thereof, will be considered hereafter. It is only necessary here to remark, in this connection, that the distinction taken in the English books between the mode and effect of the challenge in the case of the president of the court and that of an ordinary member does not exist with us. In the English service the appointment of the president is by special warrant, and the objection to him is decided by the appointing power, to whom the question is formally referred; but here the members of the court are all appointed by the same authority, and if the challenge to the president should be sustained, the officer next named in the order would succeed to his position.

This right of challenge belongs as well to the Judge Advocate as to the accused, and should be exercised when occasion requires.

SEC. 68. All questions of this nature having been disposed of, the court properly organized, and the record up to this point completed, the court is next directed to be cleared.

<small>Court cleared, when.</small>

The Judge Advocate having provided several copies of the order by which the court is convened, for its use (the court being cleared), the charges are distinctly read in the hearing of the prisoner. This, says Sir C. J. Napier, is essential to ascertain "if they are specific, for unless the court clearly understand what they are to inquire into, and the prisoner what to defend himself against, the court should refuse to receive the charges;" and it is the duty of the Judge Advocate, notwithstanding he has examined them previously, to remonstrate against proceeding upon any charge which is ascertained to

<small>Judge Advocate reads charges in court.</small>

<small>Defective charge not to be proceeded upon.</small>

be defective. But whatever doubts arise or objections are urged, ought to be recorded in the proceedings. It should be remembered, however, that when a charge has been approved by proper authority, and ordered to be investigated, neither the Judge Advocate nor any other person can alter it, without the consent of such superior authority having been first obtained.* But as charges are chiefly confined in their preparation to form and phraseology, the Judge Advocate may generally modify or change them, either as legal necessity or particular rules require, subject to the limitation just stated. No charge to be altered, except.

Sec. 69. The charges being thus read in the hearing of the prisoner, who has been previously regularly called, the Judge Advocate now inquires:

———: You have heard the charges against you just read; how say you, are you guilty or not guilty? Arraignment of prisoner.

Sometimes the prisoner stands mute, sometimes he confesses by the plea of guilty. But the usual plea is "not guilty." In either case, says Captain Hughes, the trial proceeds, for it is essential to know the facts and particulars, and to report them to those who are to pass upon the sentence pronounced by the court. Pleas.

Besides these, pleas in bar are not unfrequently employed. But whatever the nature of the plea, it must be recorded. Where a written statement, or defence, is made, it must be appended to the proceedings, with the decision of the court thereon. Plea to be recorded.

We shall have occasion hereafter to treat more at large of the defence of the prisoner, and the various pleas employed for that purpose.

When the plea is thus presented, the question is ready for trial; and the Judge Advocate directs all witnesses to retire until called. Witnesses to retire.

---

* Tytler.

SEC. 70. Application may at this stage of the proceedings be made to the court by either party,* for permission to introduce counsel. It is conceded by all that the prisoner is entitled to such assistance. Counsel can in no case, however, *address* the court, and should be so advised by the Judge Advocate. The prosecutor, also, may be allowed the aid of counsel, but such assistance is always "restricted to giving advice, framing questions, and offering in writing legal objections that may appear necessary.† "It is certain," says De Hart, "that under the language of the law no other than the Judge Advocate can appear as the prosecutor before a court martial." He admits, however, that some writers entertain a different opinion—but the Judge Advocate may, as just stated, have the advice and assistance of counsel in intricate cases where it is desired.

<small>Parties now apply for counsel.</small>

The restriction of the law referred to by De Hart does not exist in the naval service, and, therefore, it is said, a different rule as to the admission of counsel prevails in that service.

SEC. 71. The parties being thus prepared, the Judge Advocate proceeds to open the case by a brief statement of the matter to be tried and the evidence to be submitted. The only restrictions imposed upon him are that he must introduce nothing disrespectful to the court or reproachful to the prisoner, and must confine himself to the subject matter of the trial, avoiding as much as possible all that is foreign to the charges and the proofs in support of them. This is a leading rule in all trials, and nowhere is it more important to be observed than before a court martial. This opening of the Judge Advocate may be spoken or written. In either case it ought to be recorded.

<small>Judge Advocate opens the case.</small>

Although there are obvious advantages in this manner of proceeding in the opening of the case, the practice in trials in

---

*See *ante*, section 40.   † Kennedy.

the United States service has been different. "The address," says De Hart, "is deferred until the evidence has been rendered and recorded, and the defence made." The Judge Advocate's speech or address is then made as a "*reply*, and embodies the whole subject."*

SEC. 72. All writings laid before the court and *received by it* must be dated, and duly authenticated on the part of the party presenting any such; and it is the duty of the Judge Advocate to see that this is done.† Writings must be authenticated.

SEC. 73. The swearing of witnesses is next in order. The oath is prescribed in the 73d Article of war, and is that ordinarily administered to witnesses. This duty Oath of witnesses. is performed by the Judge Advocate according to the custom of courts martial, though not prescribed by any law. In naval courts the oath is administered by the president. It is important to observe that this oath must always be administered to the witness before a full court — that is, all who sit on the trial; it is otherwise nugatory and of no value — "for no act performed by part of a court can be legal."

SEC. 74. Objections to the competency of witnesses should be made invariably before they are sworn; and the objecting party ought to state his reasons fully and at the same time, in order to avoid delay. These objections should always be entered by the Judge Advocate on the proceedings of the court, of which they sometimes form an important part in the eye of the reviewing authority. Objections to their competency made before swearing.

SEC. 75. It has already been observed that when the charges are read, the court is usually cleared and the witnesses directed to retire. It is not desirable that they should hear the charges read; as that, it is said, "has a tendency to put them upon a narrative," and to furnish them with dates and facts. So important is this precau- When and why witness retires.

---

* De Hart, 149.   † Hughes, 54.

tion, that the regulations in the Bengal service, and for the Bombay army, expressly prohibit the reading of charges to any witness.*

Testimony of each witness recorded separately. SEC. 76. The testimony of each witness should be recorded separately, and General Kennedy suggests the appropriate manner as follows:

"Lieutenant A B, of —— regiment, called into court and duly sworn." The evidence being given in and concluded, an entry to that effect is made by the Judge Advocate.

"It is," says the same writer, "most usual to take down the evidence by way of question and answer; and on recording each interrogatory, the party putting it should be distinctly noted, thus: *Question by Prosecutor. Question by Judge Advocate. Question by Prisoner. Question by the Court.* Sometimes, however, a witness gives his testimony in the way of narrative; in which manner it must be taken down in writing, and the Judge Advocate is bound to adhere to the precise words of the witness." The Judge Advocate should, also, insert at the commencement of each examination by what party it is made, as for example: Examined by Prosecutor, Court, or Judge Advocate, as the case may be; cross-examined by Court, Prosecutor, or Judge Advocate; or re-examined by the Court, Prosecutor, or Judge Advocate," etc.†

How recorded.

Regular order of examination to be preserved. It is essential to the proper conducting of the trial that the regular order of examination should be maintained, and that neither party should question the witness until he is surrendered by the other. The Judge Advocate may question a witness who has been examined by the prosecutor, and should follow the interrogatories of the latter, making one and the same examination.‡ But he is not permitted to examine *in chief* any witness who has been cross-examined by the accused; although he may *re-examine*

---

*Quoted in Hughes, 59, 60.   †60 Kennedy.   ‡Same.

as to new matter which has been elicited by the cross-examination.*

Sec. 77. The mode of examining witnesses, of taking their depositions, and the various questions relating to evidence in this connection, will be more properly discussed in the chapters relating to trials and to evidence; but it will be useful here to remark that leading questions are improper, and should not be employed. All questions must also be reduced to writing by the party offering them, and then read aloud by the Judge Advocate. If objection is made to any question the court is cleared, and a majority of voices determines whether it shall be asked the witness or rejected. It must always be entered; but if afterward refused, should generally be expunged from the record, unless otherwise agreed between the parties. If the question is such as to render its reading before the witness objectionable, the Judge Advocate should request to have the court cleared before it is announced, and then state his objection, otherwise the witness might be improperly led in his testimony.†

<small>Leading questions improper.</small>
<small>Questions to be reduced to writing and entered.</small>

No question by the court can be objected to by either party. The examination of witnesses must be before the whole court; and whenever a member leaves it, the Judge Advocate should suspend his record of the proceedings.

<small>Questions by court.</small>

Sec. 78. Documentary or written evidence is of two sorts—original and secondary—the latter being such as is embraced in *copies* only. The general rule is to require the original to be produced, where it can be obtained. Where the court is satisfied that the original cannot be had, a copy is admitted. For this reason copies of official records or other official papers are usually admitted, as it is generally impossible to produce the original in

<small>Documentary evidence. rules as to.</small>
<small>Copies, when admitted.</small>

---

* Kennedy.   † De Hart, 156.

such cases; but these copies must always be properly authenticated. Where a document, whether original or copied, is introduced, the whole must be read, and not a part.

SEC. 79. These subjects will be recurred to again in the chapter on evidence, and it is unnecessary to enlarge upon them here. The Judge Advocate should, however, be careful that all written evidence introduced at the trial be recorded just where it is appropriate—that is, evidence bearing on one charge should not be mixed with that referring to another, but only in connection with the particular charge it is designed to sustain.

Judge Advocate to see that documentary evidence is recorded.

It is usual when written proofs are introduced to note the fact in the following manner, or to this effect: "The prosecutor, witness, or prisoner, as the case may be, here hands to the court [describe the letter or document] which is read, admitted by the court, and marked No. 1, 2, 3; or A, B, C, and attached hereto."

Manner of recording.

SEC. 80. There are certain privileged and confidential communications which the Judge Advocate should remember cannot be demanded or used in evidence; thus, a witness in employment of the government cannot be required to make known the character of his instructions, or any secret communication, nor can the correspondence between the government and its agents be required as evidence. This, with the military instructions and orders of a commander-in-chief, are regarded as confidential, and privileged from disclosure.

Confidential communications.

SEC. 81. When the evidence of a witness is reduced to writing, it is the duty of the Judge Advocate to read it over in open court, or before the witness leaves the court, if he so requests, and thus afford an opportunity for the correction of errors. Such corrections are always to be entered in the proceedings. "But it would be obviously improper to read over the record to a witness, or per-

Judge Advocate to read evidence of witness in open court.

mit him to refer to it, when under, or previous to a cross-examination." The object of reading the evidence to the witness being only to avoid mistakes, it should only be done when his testimony is closed; and "no erasure or obliteration" should ever be allowed.*

General Kennedy remarks that a "witness may even correct his testimony the day after it has been recorded." The explanations or corrections must, however, in all cases be recorded separately, and not interlined, or written over erasures. Witness may correct his testimony.

No further questions remaining to be asked, the witness is directed to withdraw. This must be noticed on the record, that it may appear that no two witnesses were examined together. Two witnesses not to be examined together.

SEC. 82. The Judge Advocate should likewise note on the record the hour of meeting and adjournment of the court each day; and at the close of each day's proceedings he should make a fair copy of the whole, and so continue through the trial. At the meeting of the court on each day, he should call the name of each officer composing the court, noting those who are present and the cause of absence as to those who do not appear. This done, if a quorum is present, the Judge Advocate reads aloud the proceedings of the previous day, and having recorded this fact also, the trial proceeds. If any errors occur in the record of the previous sitting, they should always be corrected when the proceedings are read. This custom of reading the record is said by Major Hough not to be obligatory upon the court, and ought never to be allowed in the presence of the witnesses. It is much better, however, that the record should be carefully read over each day *to the court*, as errors and omissions are thus more certainly excluded. Proceedings from day to day. Record not to be read to witnesses.

---

* Simmons, in Captain Hughes.

Sec. 83. When the prosecution has been brought to a close, the Judge Advocate makes a minute of the fact, and no further testimony on the part of the prosecution can afterward be admitted.

Prosecution closed.

The defence is then opened. But the court will always allow time, at the prisoner's request, to enable him to prepare further for his defence, if this be at all necessary.

Defence opened.

The same course of examination, as to witnesses, is here observed as in the case of the prosecution—that is to say, the examination in chief, cross-examination by the prosecution, and re-examination by the prisoner. When his evidence is closed, he may address the court, and present whatever considerations he can to defeat the prosecution. If, however, he should introduce new matter into his defence, the Judge Advocate may rebut it by additional evidence.

Examination of witnesses.

When the defence is closed the Judge Advocate notes the fact on the proceedings, and no evidence of any kind can afterward be admitted on the part of the prisoner.

Defence closed.

Sec. 84. The Judge Advocate may now, if he desire, reply; and, if necessary, time is allowed him for preparation. He cannot introduce new evidence, unless, as already intimated, for the purpose of rebutting such new matter as may have been brought out by the defence. But he may, says Tytler, "recapitulate and methodize the import of his evidence, and strengthen it by argument; or show the weakness and insufficiency of the reasoning and proof on which the prisoner has rested his exculpation."

Judge Advocate replies.

Captain Simmons is of opinion that the Judge Advocate is not entitled to reply in cases where the prisoner has only drawn inferences from the evidence of the prosecution, or elicited something from the prosecutor's witnesses on cross-examination, even though the tendency of such observations be to reflect on the prosecutor. And Captain De Hart considers that addresses to the court are seldom called for, and are quite unusual; though cases may occur in which the parties deem it advantageous to claim and exercise the right.

SEC. 85. "It has been said it is not the duty of the Judge Advocate to weigh opposing evidence, and discuss the same for the purpose of influencing the decision of the court; yet it is undoubtedly his duty, should he observe the court inclined to find a verdict contrary to evidence, to point out the same, and prevent, if possible, a wrong decision, and to enter his advice, thus given, on the record. Duty of Judge Advocate in examining the evidence.

"The value of the opinions of the Judge Advocate entered upon the record may, at some future period, be well demonstrated for the protection of the members of the court, by presenting with more particularity to the attention of the approving authority the merits of the controverted points, and thereby preventing, at times, the execution of their judgment, which, if illegal, would render them liable to damages in a civil action."

SEC. 86. The court may, at any time before the finding of the sentence, recall the witnesses and re-examine evidence of any sort. All the parties, however, should be present when this is done, and the particulars attending it must invariably form part of the record. Court may recall witnesses.

When the evidence on each side has been adduced, and the addresses completed, the trial is at an end, and these facts ought to be distinctly recorded. Trial closed.

The court is now closed, and the Judge Advocate reads aloud from a fair copy of the proceedings the whole, or such portion of them as may be deemed important.

SEC. 87. It is here that the Judge Advocate is sometimes called on, in special cases, to discharge the important duty of "summing up," as it is called, the whole cause. Summing up of case.

Upon this point, Tytler remarks: "In complicated cases, in circumstantial proofs, in cases where the evidence is contradictory, or where a number of prisoners are jointly arraigned, it is expedient that the Judge Advocate should arrange and methodize the evidence, applying it distinctly to the facts of the charge, and bringing home to each prisoner the result of the proof against him, balanced by the evidence of exculpation or alleviation. In ordinary cases, a charge of this kind is not so necessary."

"The summing up," says Major Hough, "should not assume facts to be proved. That should be left to the court to decide upon. There is a duty to be performed to show the relative bearing of the whole evidence, but no opinion should be given by the Judge Advocate." And again: "besides applying the evidence fairly to each side of the question, the Judge Advocate should inform the Court of the legal bearing of the evidence; for it may be that the evidence may morally satisfy the court, and yet be deficient legally; or something may have been admitted which ought to have been rejected;" and it is the duty of the Judge Advocate to see that on these points, also, the court is correctly informed.

SEC. 88. Another delicate and important duty devolves upon the Judge Advocate when the court has been closed, in the discharge of which he must exercise a sound discretion, and this is to "guard the court against deviation from essential forms, or the violation of justice in their final judgment." In doing this, he should keep in view his duty to the prisoner no less than the government, and never attempt to urge or procure a verdict of condemnation by presenting an argument. It would be proper for him to point out, says De Hart, the relevancy of testimony, or its legal value, but not to attempt to weigh it and decide on its preponderance to the one side or the other—for that is the peculiar and exclusive duty of the court. He should distinguish between the mere ministerial

Duty to the prisoner.

and the judicial character. Of the first it belongs to him to speak, but with the latter he cannot in any manner interfere. He cannot even *protest* against the wrong doing of the court, as that, it is said, implies a judicative voice; but he may enter his opinion given to the court on the record, for the consideration of the reviewing authority. His office here, in short, is only to counsel and advise, and never to order or direct. And such counsel and advice he is to give fully, and to the best of his ability, when required by the court; and always, even when not requested, to call their attention to such facts and circumstances as may tend to avoid error and injustice.* Peculiar duties of Judge Advocate. Cannot protest.

From such considerations, De Hart deduces the rule "that when the court is deliberating upon the findings or the sentence, the Judge Advocate should interpose an opinion only when there is danger of an irregular or illegal decision being made; and that in all questions within the discretion or competency of the court to determine, he should take no part. To the members themselves attaches a responsibility for every act; and while they honestly observe the limits of legal authority defined for their guidance, they are independent of all other control." General rule as to opinion of Judge Advocate.

SEC. 89. The court having closed their deliberations, are next to pronounce their several opinions. General Kennedy thus states the practice in the military courts of Great Britain: "The Judge Advocate now proceeds to take the opinions of the members, by putting to each the following questions, beginning with the *youngest:* 'From the evidence given for and against the prisoner, and from what he has said in his defence, are you of opinion that he is guilty or not guilty of the charge preferred against him?' And as they declare their opinions, he writes them down severally." But Opinions of the court.

---

* De Hart, 323, 324, 325.

How taken.

as it is not desirable that the opinion of the court should generally be thus openly expressed, a different plan may be adopted, and the members, therefore, frequently write on a slip of paper the opinion "guilty" or "not guilty," or with such qualifications as may be required, which being handed to the Judge Advocate, he ascertains and announces the *result:* when the opinion of each member is read. This latter course is perhaps the most approved, and is usually followed in this country. But whichever plan is adopted, in arriving at the vote, the Judge Advocate should 'remember that the court is "bound to exhaust the whole of the charges which come before them, by expressly acquitting or convicting the prisoner of each allegation that is contained in them."* If a charge consists of several specifications, the vote should be taken on each, and the result stated in the record. "As the vote for each member is given," says De Hart, "the Judge Advocate makes a minute of the same, which should be carefully retained and kept by him, to meet the possible contingency of proceedings in the common law courts touching the legality of the acts of the court martial. * * * He is the proper depository of such secrets, and the written notes made at the time the only sure defence against uncertainty and error."

SEC. 90. The court having decided upon the guilt or innocence of the prisoner, are next to determine, in event of conviction, the punishment to be inflicted. And even though a member may have voted for acquittal in the *findings*, he must, in the sentence, vote *some* punishment. The Judge Advocate, therefore, proceeds to take the vote of each member upon the punishment to be awarded, in doing which he observes the same forms as in the findings of the court.

Punishments voted for.

SEC. 91. Each member should vote on all questions pre-

---

* Kennedy.

sented; and it is important that this fact should at least be capable of proof by the record, inasmuch as it may be necessary to know what the particular vote may have been—whether a majority, as in ordinary cases, or two-thirds, as is required when the extreme penalty of the law is inflicted. *[Members vote on all questions.]*

Where the judgment of members differs as to the nature of the punishment, it is usual, says Captain Simmons, to separate the questions: first to ascertain the *nature*— the majority deciding; then the *quantum*. This, however, need of course only be done in those cases in which the punishment is not already fixed by law. *[Questions may be divided.]*

SEC. 92. The findings and sentence of the Court being thus ascertained, as the judgment of the court, must be entered on the record; and this, observes Kennedy, must always be done in the Judge Advocate's own handwriting. *[Judgment to be carefully entered.]*

Great particularity is requisite in drawing the sentence of the court, upon which Captain Simmons remarks that, "with respect to the wording of the sentence in cases discretionary with the courts, no special form is necessary. It should obviously be expressed in clear and unambiguous language. In cases not discretionary, the court would do well to adhere as literally as possible to the terms of the statute or Article of war by virtue of which the punishment is awarded."

The findings and sentence of the court may be drawn up as follows:

FINDINGS AND SENTENCE.

The court having maturely weighed and considered the evidence adduced in the case, do find the prisoner, Captain A. B., Regiment of ———, as follows: *[Form of entry.]*

Of the 1st Specification of — Charge: "Guilty."
Of the 2d Specification of — Charge: "Not Guilty."
Of the 3d Specification of — Charge: except the words ——— ———, "Guilty."

Of the 4th Specification of — Charge: "Guilty, but attach no criminality thereto," and "Guilty of the Charge."

And (having proved the prisoner guilty, as above specified) the court do sentence the said Captain A. B., — Regiment, ——— ———, "to be dismissed the service."

Dated at ———

J. F. L., Colonel, etc.,
President of the Court.

S. W., Captain, etc.,
Judge Advocate.

Or, should the prisoner be acquitted, (following the form in the heading above):

Of the 1st Specification of — Charge: "Not Guilty."

Of the 2d Specification of — Charge: "Not Guilty, and Not Guilty of the Charge."

The court do, therefore, fully acquit the said ——— of every part of the aforesaid charge.

[Signed as above.]

SEC. 93. If mitigating circumstances appear on the trial, such of the court as desire on that account to recom-
Recommendations to mercy. mend the prisoner to mercy, may do so, in a *separate* paper, which should be signed by the concurring members only. This the Judge Advocate should attach to the record, or it may be written at the end of the proceedings, but never incorporated with the findings and sentence of the court.

SEC. 94. The Judge Advocate should sign the proceedings
Proceedings to be signed. after the president has done so; and they are not complete until the signatures of both are duly affixed to them.

SEC. 95. It sometimes becomes necessary to remand the proceedings to the court for revision of the findings
Sometimes remanded. and sentence. In such cases, the Judge Advocate should note the fact to the following effect:

The court reassembled at ——, by order of —— president [such members as appear, which, of course, must be the same as before].

The Judge Advocate having then read the order reassembling the court, and stated the alleged defects in the findings and sentence, the court proceeds to reconsider them. The proceedings are all recorded by the Judge Advocate, as before, and the conclusion of the court is stated as the "revised findings and sentence," which should be signed by the president and Judge Advocate, as already indicated.

SEC. 96. The 90th Article of war provides that the Judge Advocate of every general court martial shall transmit, with as much expedition as circumstances admit, the original proceedings and sentence to the Secretary of War, to be there preserved, to the end that the persons entitled to copies may obtain them. To be sent to Secretary of war.

Provision is also made in the army regulations on this subject. They require the proceedings to be sent, without delay, to the officer having authority to review them by confirming or disapproving the sentence, who is to state his decision and orders at the foot of each case. The whole proceedings are then, in cases of general courts martial, and which shall require the decision of the president, under the 65th and 89th Articles of war, forwarded to the War department, through the Adjutant-General, accompanied by copies of all orders confirming or disapproving the sentence. And to commanding officer.

SEC. 97. The regulations also require that where the same court tries more prisoners than one, arraigned on separate and distinct charges, the court is to be sworn at the commencement of each trial; and the proceedings of each case must be made up separately. A copy of the order appointing the court is, in all cases, to be entered on the record. Prisoners to be separately arraigned.

Sec. 98. The 35th Article of war authorizes any inferior officer or soldier, thinking himself wronged by his superior, to complain to the commanding officer of the regiment, who is to summon a regimental court martial, from the decision of which either party may *appeal*.

Appeals from Regimental Courts, etc.

The duties of the Judge Advocate are thus stated in this connection by Captain Hughes: The court having assembled, the appellant and respondent are called before it, and the orders for assembling the court, etc., are read. The Judge Advocate then informs the court that the case is an appeal from a regimental to a general court martial. Both parties have the right of challenging, and the Judge Advocate should put the usual question on this point, to the appellant first, and then to the respondent, minuting such question, and the answer thereto, on the proceedings. The members and Judge Advocate are duly sworn. The statement of the appellant's wrongs is now read and recorded, who first addresses the court and lays his grievances before it, and then adduces evidence in proof thereof. The appellant should not, in any case, be sworn. The examination of witnesses, who must all give their evidence on oath, is taken in precisely the same manner as on other courts martial. When the appellant's case is fully before the court the respondent then replies to it, adducing such evidence as he thinks necessary. Neither is he sworn, unless appellant requires it, or the court considers it necessary that *he may depose to facts*. The trial being finished, the opinion of the court is now given, and may be thus recorded:

Duties of Judge Advocate on appeals.

Proceedings on appeals.

1. The court, having maturely weighed and considered the evidence adduced in this case, is of opinion that Private ———, ——— regiment of ———, has failed to substantiate the grievances complained of (or, as the case may be, has substantiated, etc.), viz:

2. The court are further of opinion (should such be the case)

that the appeal made by —— ——, private of —— regiment, is vexatious and groundless.

3. The sentence of the court is then recorded.

SEC. 99. In concluding his remarks on the duties of a Judge Advocate as an officer of a general court martial, Captain Hughes appropriately observes: "It may be well to remind the Judge Advocate that, as *officer* of the court, in recording and conducting the proceedings of general courts martial, the court may direct him to perform these duties in *any* manner it may deem proper. In obeying, however, and carrying the orders of the court into effect, the Judge Advocate must bear in mind that *he* has also a most responsible duty to discharge, and that it is *incumbent* on him to submissively and respectfully point out to the court the slightest deviation which may occur in their orders from established forms and rules, whether it be at variance with the custom of war or the laws of the land." He is responsible that the laws "relating to trials by courts martial are fully acted up to; and in the absence of official rules, that the customs of the army are adhered to; and above all, that those who are appointed jurors and judges discharge their duties without exceeding the power vested in them, so that under all circumstances 'there may not be, in any case, a failure of justice.'"

Power of court over the Judge Advocate. what.

SEC. 100. The duties of a Judge Advocate before a court of inquiry are, in many particulars, similar to those he is required to discharge before a court martial, though much more limited. They are, moreover, often varied by the instructions he receives from the authority appointing the court, and the particular subjects to be examined.

Duties of Judge Advocate in courts of inquiry.

Having prepared the case for investigation, the next duty of the Judge Advocate is to summon the witnesses required, and give proper notice of the time and place of meeting. He does not act as prosecutor, but he is both to administer the required oaths, as set out in the 93d Article of war, and to examine all witnesses brought before the court. It is his duty to assist the court in a full and honest inquiry into all subjects ordered to be investigated, so that a just conclusion as to the necessity of further proceedings may be arrived at. To this end he should arrange and methodize the evidence, copy all original documents into the proceedings, and record the entire transactions of the court, so that the whole case be clearly and explicitly presented for consideration to the proper authority. Although, as just stated, not the prosecutor here, he is still, as before a court martial, the legal adviser of a court of inquiry, and as such, bound to instruct the members in matters both of form and law, and to object to the admission of all improper evidence.

SEC. 101. The Judge Advocate or Recorder of a court of inquiry is not sworn to secrecy as before a court martial, but simply to record impartially and accurately the proceedings of the court, and the evidence adduced before it.* In conducting the proceedings, the same rules as to form and order are generally to be observed *mutatis mutandis* as before a court martial. Opportunity for objecting to the members, by the usual inquiries, to be put by the Judge Advocate, must always be afforded the accused. He should also make out, from day to day, a fair copy of the proceedings, to be read to the court every morning. A full copy of the order convening the court should be inserted in the record; and the Judge Advocate should be careful to state that the court was regularly organized as the law requires, that the necessary oaths were duly administered both to the court and the Judge Advocate, and that the accused was asked if he had objections to any member of the court. When so required, but not otherwise, the opinion of the court should be given on the merits of the case. When special instructions are given in any case,

How sworn.

---

* 96th Article of War.

they should be read to the court by the Judge Advocate, and entered on the record. This record, when completed, should be duly authenticated by the signatures of the president and the Judge Advocate, and by the latter transmitted to the authority convening the court.

SEC. 102. In summoning witnesses, the Judge Advocate should remember that, without an order from the court, no witness is to be called at the expense of the government, nor any officer summoned, unless it is clear that the testimony is necessary to the ends of justice.* Witnesses before.

SEC. 103. We have thus completed an examination respecting the important office of Judge Advocate. It has no doubt been observed, that topics have been introduced in the present chapter which appear to have an immediate connection with other parts of the subject; but it has also been seen that they are, at the same time, nearly related to the duties of the Judge Advocate; and it was thought better, in order to present a connected and coherent view of those duties, not to separate them in the discussion.

---

* See Army Regulations.

CHAPTER IV.

COURTS OF INQUIRY.

The composition, objects, and duties of courts of inquiry are next to be considered in the order proposed.

SEC. 104. In European armies, the authority for such courts is an incident to prerogative which does not exist in this country. They are, therefore, expressly provided for by law. The 91st Article of war directs that they shall consist of one or more officers, not exceeding three, and a Judge Advocate, or Recorder, to reduce their proceedings and evidence to writing; all of whom, it directs, shall be sworn to the faithful performance of their duty. It also confers on the court power to summon witnesses and to examine them on oath. They are directed not to give their opinion on the merits of the case unless specially required to do so. The accused is to be permitted to interrogate and cross-examine all witnesses adduced, so as to investigate fully the circumstances in question.

Court of Inquiry provided for by law.
Composition of.

SEC. 105. The 92d Article of war requires the proceedings of courts of inquiry to be authenticated by the signatures of the Judge Advocate and president, and then delivered to the commanding officer. These proceedings may then be used in evidence before a court martial in cases not capital, and not extending to the dismission of an officer, provided oral testimony cannot be obtained. No court of inquiry can be ordered unless, by direction of the president, or at the request of the party accused. The oaths to be

Ordered by the Presid't.

administered to the court and the Judge Advocate or Recorder are prescribed in the 93d. Article of war. The witnesses are to take the same oath as witnesses sworn before a court martial.

SEC. 106. It thus appears that the composition of a court of inquiry is exceedingly simple. It is to consist of not more than three members, and a Judge Advocate or Recorder. When indispensable, an interpreter is allowed.

We have just seen that the President only can direct a court of inquiry, unless one is demanded by the accused. In the latter case, the court may be convened by the commander-in-chief of an army, or an officer commanding a military department. *Who else may order.*

SEC. 107. Having shown how the court of inquiry may be properly convened, we are next to consider its *special objects and duties*. As the term imports, this court is chiefly designed as a means of investigation and inquiry. It is, therefore, preliminary to something beyond, as upon the result here depends the question of further proceedings before a court martial. *Special objects.*

SEC. 108. This court is so far a judicial body, as it is authorized to summon witnesses, and to examine them upon oath. But it pronounces no sentence, nor should it even express an opinion on the merits of the case, unless expressly so required. No opinion of this body should be made public, and the members are precluded from sitting on any general court martial growing out of their proceedings as a court of inquiry. *How far a judicial body. General objects.*

SEC. 109. While the accused has an obvious right to be present at an examination of his case by the court, and cannot, on the other hand, disobey a summons to appear, he is at the same time at liberty to decline taking any part in the proceedings. But it is considered better that he should not forego the advantage of an opportunity thus *Accused ought to be present at.*

afforded him to explain, if necessary, any doubtful circumstances in his case, and by cross-examining the witnesses, elicit whatever might otherwise, through inadvertence or neglect, be omitted in their testimony. He cannot, however, be required to make any statement that would criminate him; and hence is not obliged to respond to questions of such a tendency.

SEC. 110. Both the accused and accuser are entitled to counsel before a court of inquiry. Nor can there be any reasonable objection to this, for the reason that such assistance may aid materially in the chief object of the examination, which is to determine whether there is just ground for a trial.
<small>Counsel.</small>

SEC. 111. It is usual for courts of inquiry to sit with closed doors. But this, unless otherwise decided by the authority convening the court, is a matter of discretion with them, in which they should be governed by the circumstances of each case. Where the subject of inquiry is of such a nature as to render its publicity improper or inexpedient, the court should, of course, be closed. Their special duty in either case, as defined by the Article of war already cited, is "to examine into the nature of any transaction, accusation, or imputation against any officer or soldier." The objects for which the court is convened should be set forth in the order, with particular instructions requiring a report of facts ascertained, or an opinion upon the merits, as may be deemed best. By such order and instructions the court is always to direct and limit its proceedings, and in no case are they competent to depart from them.
<small>Sit with closed doors.</small>
<small>Duties.</small>

SEC. 112. The *mode* of proceeding is to be determined by the court. When this is done, the complainant and accused are called in, and the subject to be examined is then stated by the Judge Advocate.
<small>Mode of proceedings determined by court.</small>

The right of challenge is allowed, *for cause*, to either party, and this for the reason that the investigation, whether accompanied by an opinion of the court or not, may
<small>Challenge for cause.</small>

in some way affect the reputation of the party accused, or the public interest; and as the right is to be exercised subject to the discretion of the court, there is little danger of its abuse.

SEC. 113. Trials before courts martial are limited by the 75th Article of war as to time, between the hours of eight in the morning and three in the afternoon; but there is no such restriction upon the proceedings of courts of inquiry. *Time for sitting.*

There is no provision made for furnishing copies of the proceedings, or any documents connected with them, to the accused, as in courts martial; nor can they be rightfully demanded, inasmuch as the inquiry is preliminary only, and designed exclusively for the information of the authority by which it was instituted. *Copies of record.*

SEC. 114. An officer accused before a court of inquiry is not under arrest, except there exists a necessity therefor. But contempts *from military persons* before a court of inquiry may be punished as if committed before a court martial. For such an offence the court may direct the *arrest* of an officer, and confinement of a soldier. The provisions of the 76th Article of war, guarding the dignity of courts martial, do not appear to have been extended to courts of inquiry in terms, and the power thus conferred could not, perhaps, be exercised by the latter. Hence it seems that, conceding the right of courts martial under that Article to punish contempts committed by citizens or persons not subject to military law, no such authority could be claimed by a court of inquiry, whose only remedy in such cases would be an appeal to the civil tribunals, and, in the meantime, the expulsion of the offending party from the presence of the court. *When accused is in arrest. Contempts before.*

SEC. 115. As already observed, a court of inquiry is not sworn to secrecy; but it would be regarded as a gross breach of military decorum should any member divulge the opinion of the court prior to its being officially announced. *Opinions not to be divulged.*

Sec. 116. This court may be reassembled whenever necessary, the witnesses recalled, and new questions put to them with a view of eliciting every fact connected with the subject of inquiry. Their proceedings may, moreover, be revised as often as requisite, in which respect the practice, if not the law of the service, has established a difference between them and courts martial.

May be reassembled.

Revision of their proceedings.

Sec. 117. The 88th Article of war is the military statute of limitations. It prohibits trial by a general court martial for any offence committed more than two years before the issuing of the order directing its trial, except in certain specified cases. This prohibition rests on the same broad principle which underlies all similar restrictions—that of preventing vexatious accusations and stale demands, which, from lapse of time and loss of evidence, it might prove impossible either to refute or defend. And thus the spirit of this law as certainly applies to investigations before courts of inquiry as to any other; and though they are not named in the article referred to, yet, when it is remembered that the object of all investigations before courts of inquiry, especially when not instituted at the request of the accused, is to ascertain if there exists a necessity for the trial of the offender, there can be little doubt as to the propriety of extending this prohibition to them. This may now be considered the better opinion, although some military writers* appear to think differently.

Statute of limitations applies.

By Act of Congress, approved April 21, 1862, it is provided, that any commissioned officer convicted of drunkenness before a *Court of Inquiry* shall be cashiered, or suspended, or publicly reprimanded.

Act to punish drunkenness.

Under this act the court are only to collect the evidence, and report the facts, with their "*findings*," to the Secretary of

---

* McComb and O'Brien.

War, and are not to pronounce any sentence in the case. This belongs to higher authority.

SEC. 118. It is not necessary to publish the proceedings of a court of inquiry, although justice to the accused, and the public interest may sometimes require this to be done. The court is dissolved by the same authority which convened it.

<small>Proceedings not published.</small>

Chapter V.

OF COURTS MARTIAL.

We come at length, in the course of our inquiries, to the subject of *courts martial*, and are to examine as was proposed:

1. Their particular organization, as divided into *general, regimental*, and *garrison courts*.
2. Their particular jurisdiction.
3. Their general powers and duties, and the punishments they may respectively impose.

SEC. 119. The power to appoint courts martial is derived directly from the act of Congress, approved March 6, 1861, establishing a code, or "Rules and Articles for the government of the Confederate States." In this law the peculiar composition of these courts, and the persons by whom the power of appointment is to be exercised, are definitely prescribed and limited. By the 65th Article of that code, any general officer commanding an army, or colonel commanding a separate department, may, when necessary, appoint a general court martial.

Power to appoint courts martial.

An act of the United States Congress, the provisions of which are operative here, passed in 1830, provides that if such commanding officer or colonel shall be the accuser or prosecutor of any officer of the army commanded by him, the court for his trial shall be appointed by the President. But independently of any such provision, the President, as the commander-in-chief of the army, is *ex officio* competent to order courts martial whenever they prove necessary.*

SEC. 120. Under the terms of the 64th Article of war, general courts martial are to consist of any number of commissioned officers, from five to thirteen inclusively; but cannot consist of less than thirteen, when that number can be convened without manifest injury to the service. Where the maximum number cannot be obtained without such injury, the order assembling the court should state that fact. The time and place for the meeting of the court should also be designated in the order. Composition of.

The members detailed take place in the court according to their rank, and no decision by the proper authority on a question of rank can be overruled by the court. No president is formally appointed; but the officer having the highest rank in the court is president.†

SEC. 121. The same law authorizes every officer commanding a regiment, or corps, to appoint courts martial therefor, to consist of three commissioned officers, for the trial and punishment of offences not capital. For the same purpose, officers commanding garrisons, forts, barracks, or other places where troops consist of different corps, may assemble courts martial of three commissioned officers, and decide upon their sentences.‡ The authority thus conferred cannot be delegated, but is to be exercised only by parties designated in the law. Hence the order directing the convening of any court should issue immediately from the officer upon whom such power has been bestowed.§ A consequence of this law is that when an army is assembled in a body none but the commanding officer, who is to be also a general officer, can order a general court martial; and in military departments this privilege Regimental courts.

---

* De Hart. ‡ Army Regulations.
† 64th Article of War, act of March 6, 1861. § De Hart, 6.

is limited to the commanding officer, having at least the rank of colonel.

SEC. 122. *What military courts allowed.* It thus appears that the only judicial tribunals in the military system are the *general, regimental,* and *garrison courts martial,* before referred to. Of these, the general court martial is the highest, and, as already observed, can only be appointed by the President, or general officer commanding an army, or a colonel commanding a military department; while regimental courts may be ordered by the commanding officer of a regiment, and garrison courts by the commanding officer of a barrack, fort, etc.—the two last having only a limited and inferior jurisdiction.

SEC. 123. *Minimum and maximum numbers.* A court martial of full jurisdiction cannot consist of less than five members. But sometimes more than the maximum number, thirteen, are detailed, the excess being counted as *supernumeraries,* who sit with the court, but take no part in its proceedings, except by discussion, as they have no voice in any sentence pronounced, and no vote as to any question to be decided.* *Supernumeraries, object of.* Such supernumeraries are, indeed, detailed only in important cases, to prevent delay from vacancies which might occur through sickness, death, or other cause.

SEC. 124. *What officers not to sit as members of court.* There is a class of officers who, although regularly commissioned (such as surgeons, quartermasters, etc.), are not considered as having military rank, and who, while they may be employed in the capacity of *Judge Advocate* to a court, cannot be detailed as members. The same has been determined as to chaplains, who, as such, indeed, have no military rank.† *Cadet may be detailed as such.* It is held, however, that a cadet brevetted to a lieutenancy is a commissioned officer, having the lowest rank, and may, therefore, on necessary and suitable occasions, be detailed as a member of a court.‡

---

* O'Brien's Mil. Law. † O'Brien, 227. ‡ De Hart, 41, 42.

Sec. 125. The direction in the Articles of war that a court martial shall not consist of less than *thirteen* members, when that number can be convened without injury to the service, is addressed to the officer convening the court, and his decision of the question whether that number can be convened without such injury is conclusive. This point was so determined by the United States Supreme court,* and is now settled by the army regulations to the same effect.

Sec. 126. The Articles of war provide that general courts martial are to be composed of commissioned officers, without prescribing the particular rank in any case. Rank of officers. This question is, therefore, left to the discretion of the appointing power, in determining which he can only be guided by the rank of the party accused, and the importance of the subjects to be decided by the court.† As already observed, no president is formally appointed, the senior member present being entitled to that position, so long as the court does not fall below the minimum number of five. And while the court can be kept up to this number it is competent to transact the business before it.

Sec. 127. By the 68th Article of war, it is provided that, when necessary or convenient, officers of the marine corps may be associated with those of the land forces Marine corps. in courts martial for trying offenders belonging to either; and in such cases the orders of the senior officer of either corps present and duly authorized shall be obeyed. Such is not the case, however, with the militia; for although the 97th Article of war subjects the militia, when mustered into the service of the general government, to the Rules and Militia. Articles of war, and renders them liable to be tried by courts martial, it at the same time requires such courts to be composed entirely of militia officers.

---

*112 Wheaton, 35. † De Hart, 46, 47.

Referring to this provision, De Hart remarks: "It would appear but just that this rule should be reciprocal; for if the militia are not to be subjected to the judgment of officers of the regular service, it is very inconsistent to measure the opinions and acts of the latter by the judgment of the former. The reason of the law would, undoubtedly, exclude militia officers from a court convened for the trial of persons belonging to the regular service."*

SEC. 128. The court having been assembled, the names of the members and Judge Advocate duly registered according to rank, seniority, etc., the challenge, or opportunity therefor presented, and the members and Judge Advocate all sworn according to the prescribed forms, their organization is complete.

<small>Organization of court when complete.</small>

SEC. 129. II.—We are now to examine the particular jurisdiction of courts martial, and herein,

1. Of General Courts Martial:

We have heretofore adverted to some of the principal rules which appertain to military jurisprudence generally, but it will be necessary to refer to them more particularly in the course of the present chapter.

Until Congress shall see fit to confer either appellate or concurrent jurisdiction upon the civil courts in military matters, the better opinion is that the jurisdiction of the military tribunals is exclusive, and can in no way be interfered with by the civil authority.*

The 65th Article of war, which authorizes the appointment of general courts martial, applies no limit to their jurisdiction. It is, therefore, claimed, and generally admitted, that as they are courts of the highest authority, they may take cognizance of any military offence whatever. But, although they have conferred upon them this jurisdiction, they

<small>Extent of jurisdiction.</small>

---

* De Hart, 45.   † 1 Kent, 341, *note.*

are yet, in all cases which are cognizable by the inferior courts, restricted by necessary implication to the punishments prescribed to the latter; were it otherwise, "the security proposed for offenders against the higher degrees of military punishments, by confiding their cases to the cognizance of an inferior court," would be wholly defeated. It is true the 37th and 47th Articles of war refer to punishments to be inflicted at the "discretion of a regimental court;" and hence a doubt has been expressed whether in such cases authority can be exercised by other courts. But, as the terms of the law respecting general courts martial are very broad, and do in no way confine their jurisdiction, the limitation of the 37th and 47th Articles may be construed with reference to the particular punishments referred to, and not to the tribunal by which they are to be pronounced—that is, as already suggested, the general, or court of larger jurisdiction, can inflict no greater degree of punishment than the court of inferior jurisdiction. Moreover, there are "violations of duty which a soldier might be guilty of which do not amount to capital crimes, and yet, considering the circumstances under which the act is perpetrated, and the consequences flowing from it, demand more serious consideration or severer chastisement than a minor court could give. It is true, a knowledge of the circumstances attending the offence ought, in most instances, to determine the tribunal to which the case should be referred for trial. But as such may not be known to the appointing authority, or not succinctly enough set forth in the charges, such a rule cannot always apply, and therefore it becomes necessary that a more definite course should be determined. An offence, for instance, like that specified in the 45th Article of war, illustrates what is here intended—of so heinous and dangerous a nature is it, that a commissioned officer convicted of the same is *ipso facto* cashiered; and yet the same act in a non-commissioned officer or soldier is left to the discretion of the court how to punish.

If, then, the crime should be submitted for investigation to a regimental, or garrison court martial, how disproportionate, when compared to the penalty declared against an officer, would the sanction be. For such cases, and when the power to punish in the court is a discretionary one, as the above quoted Article of war exemplifies, it would appear necessary that a general court martial should have proper cognizance thereof."*

SEC. 130. It is usual, however, and better, that offences of an inferior nature should be disposed of by the minor tribunals, when it can be conveniently done. And in determining what particular jurisdiction should attach in given cases, it will be convenient to recur to three distinct particulars: 1st, the punishment to be pronounced; 2d, the person by whom; and 3d, the offence for which such punishment is inflicted. Now, by the Article of war, neither a regimental nor garrison court can take cognizance of capital cases, or of any matter appertaining to a commissioned officer. Here reference to the *punishment* and the *person* decides the fact that in such cases a general court martial has exclusive jurisdiction. The Articles of war also provide that the minor courts shall not inflict fines exceeding one month's pay, nor imprison nor put to hard labor any non-commissioned officer or soldier for a longer period than one month; so that, where their offence is such as to require a greater degree of punishment than is here specified, the trial must be before a general court martial; but where less, or only equal, the inferior court may take cognizance of the case.

How to determine.

Instances in which the particular *offence* alone is to be regarded in determining the jurisdiction, may be found in the 20th and 45th Articles of war; the first denouncing against the crimes specified the punishment of death; and the second

---

* DeHart, 50, 51.

that of cashiering, or such other punishment as the court may select. Here we see that, if the offence requires the punishment of death, or cashiering, as the inferior courts are excluded in such cases, the general court martial only can act; but if, on the other hand, the offence is trivial, and merits but a low degree of punishment, the regimental, or garrison court is authorized to try the case.

SEC. 131. De Hart deduces the following as the several classes of crimes exclusively within the jurisdiction of general courts martial:

1. Those which are expressly committed to their jurisdiction.

2. Those against which particular penalties are denounced, exceeding the authority of the minor courts to inflict.

Classes of crimes subject to jurisdiction of general courts martial.

3. Those which, from the nature of the crime committed, demand severe punishment beyond the power of the inferior courts to order.

4. Those which offend against the principles of good order and military discipline, and though subject to trial before the minor courts, may yet require, for speedy punishment and conviction, to be investigated by a general court martial.

He then presents a summary of the various offences, designating them by name, which are by law made cognizable by a general court martial only, as follows, viz:

"Beginning, exciting, causing, or joining in any mutiny. Article 7.

"Knowing of, and not informing of any intended mutiny, and not endeavoring to suppress it. Article 8.

"Striking, or drawing, or lifting any weapon, or offering violence against a superior officer in the discharge of his duty. Article 9.

"Desertion. Article 21.

"Persuading to desert. Article 23.

"Enlisting in any other regiment, etc., before being regularly discharged. Article 22.

"Disobedience, or drawing a sword upon any inferior officer in quarrels or frays. Article 27.

"Selling, losing, or spoiling, through neglect, horses, arms, or accoutrements. Article 38.

"Sentinel sleeping on post. Article 46.

"Violence to persons bringing provisions or necessaries to camp, etc. Article 51.

"Misbehaving before the enemy, abandoning post, throwing away arms, quitting colors to plunder. Article 52.

"Making known watchword, or giving a different watchword from that received. Article 53.

"Forcing a safeguard, etc. Article 55.

"Relieving, harboring, and protecting the enemy. Article 56.

"Holding correspondence with, or giving intelligence to the enemy. Article 57.

"Compelling a commander to surrender. Article 59.

"Spies, etc. Article 59, section 2. And all other cases in which a commissioned officer is to be tried."

"All such cases," he adds, "as have been referred to, coming under the 38th and 45th Articles of war, and any others of similar description, should, for uniformity of rule and substantial justice, be made subject to trial by a general court martial."

SEC. 132. Referring to the fact that general courts martial may exercise jurisdiction over every species of offence which is named in Articles of war, the same author observes:* "It becomes necessary that such courts should discrimi-
Courts to discriminate between crimes. nate between crimes confined exclusively to their jurisdiction, and such others as might be tried by an inferior court, so far as their own discretion to award punishment may be affected." In those cases in which, by the Arti-

---

* Page 64.

cles,* "a jurisdiction is saved to the regimental court, it would appear as a just interpretation of the law that the punishment for such was intended to be limited according to the competency of a regimental court to award it, and therefore a general court martial, when considering such cases, should not vary in kind, nor exceed in degree, the punishment which the inferior court could decree. This rule is not only just in the abstract, but, considering the trial as a criminal proceeding for the infliction of punishment, it is of legal obligation,"† and should therefore be obeyed. The evidence adduced enables the members to determine whether the subject could have been disposed of by an inferior court, and to shape its sentence accordingly.

SEC. 138. The language of some of the Articles of war is very indefinite, and leaves it doubtful as to the particular courts to which the jurisdiction of certain cases is intended to be confided. Where such doubtful terms are employed, the only safe rule is to consider the several Articles bearing in any manner upon the same subject, so as to gather, as far as practicable, their true meaning and intent. If two meanings apparently attach to a particular Article, and yet one of them is opposed to the manifest construction of another Article, it is obvious that the inconsistency should be avoided by adopting that meaning in the doubtful Article which tends to harmonize the whole. Thus, for example, the 38th Article provides for the punishment, by *a court martial*, of certain offences committed by non-commissioned officers, and soldiers, by weekly stoppages of their pay, not exceeding half pay, as such court martial shall judge sufficient for repairing the loss or damage; and by confinement, etc., *as the crime may deserve.* But what court is here intended? A regimental court may try the parties specified, and may likewise inflict punishments of

Rule where doubtful language in law.

---

* 37th and 47th Articles.   † Pages 64, 65.

the nature designated: and yet a "*loss or damage*" is to be repaired which it may be difficult, perhaps impossible, for any inferior court to have done by "weekly stoppages" of the offender's "half pay," inasmuch as the 67th Article of war declares that no regimental or garrison court shall inflict a fine exceeding one month's pay. Here it appears that the construction to which the 38th Article is liable, whereby regimental and garrison, as well as general courts, might claim jurisdiction in some cases, is controlled by the 67th Article, which expressly limits the action of the inferior courts to those cases only which do not require a fine exceeding one month's pay, and remits such cases as require a greater degree of punishment to the cognizance of a general court martial.

SEC. 134. But apart from the express directions of the law, and those obvious considerations of a public and professional nature which should limit and control every court in the discharge of its duty, there are others of a private character not to be overlooked, inasmuch as each member "is responsible in the civil courts, not only for any abuse of power, but for any illegal proceedings of the court, if he has voted for or participated" in them. And a case is reported in England of a marine who recovered one thousand pounds damages against the president of a court martial which had convicted him on illegal evidence, and the judge informed him that he was at liberty to bring an action against any other members of the court.* Perhaps this latter part of the decision would not now be sustained; but should a court martial in any case exceed its jurisdiction, or pronounce sentence where it had no jurisdiction, a claim for damages might arise, to be settled by the civil authorities.

Civil responsibility of court.

SEC. 135. It should be remembered, in this connection, that the 88th Article of war prohibits trial by general courts martial for any offence committed two years

Statute of limitations.

---

* O'Brien, 222, 223.

beyond the date of the order for such trial; excepting, however, those cases in which certain impediments, recognized in the Article, are shown to have existed to the trial.

SEC. 136. When the authority of courts martial is extended by the Executive, by proclamation or otherwise, to certain departments or districts of country, by the establishment of martial law, the court should be satisfied, before taking cognizance of any case, that it is embraced in the purview of the order and of their jurisdiction, otherwise their proceedings might prove to be illegal and void.* Caution as to jurisdiction where martial law exists.

SEC. 137. In concluding this head, it may be observed that all violations of the Articles of war should be tried and punished *as such*, no matter before what court the charges are brought; nor can the objection that they are not so charged be obviated by changing the form of the charge, and "classing the offence under the denomination of disorders and neglects, to the prejudice of good order and military discipline."† Violations of Articles of war tried as such.

SEC. 138. 2. Of the Jurisdiction of Garrison and Regimental Courts:

These inferior courts are designed for the trial and punishment of minor offences. They are essential to the success and discipline of the service, as without them many wrongs and delinquencies would go unredressed, where from circumstances the requisite number of officers for the regular court martial could not be procured, which is frequently the case on marches, on detached service, or at distant posts. Design of.

Their jurisdiction,‡ as before noticed, is very circumscribed, and cannot extend to capital cases, nor to commissioned officers. This is expressly prohibited by the 67th Article of war, which also forbids their inflicting a fine Jurisdiction limited.

---

* O'Brien, 226. † De Hart, 61. ‡ See secs. 130, 131.

exceeding one month's pay, or the imprisonment or putting to hard labor any non-commissioned officer or soldier for a longer period than one month. The offences named in the 37th and 47th Articles of war may be tried more properly by a regimental court, as it is expressly named; but it has been shown that its jurisdiction is concurrent with that of the general court martial, and not exclusive. The same remark is applicable to the 35th Article of war, which confers on a regimental court the power to examine complaints of soldiers against their officers. It is usual and most proper that this examination should be made by the regimental court; but there appears no good reason why the higher court should not act even in such a case, if circumstances render it necessary.

SEC. 139. The general rule as to regimental and garrison courts may be stated in a few words. They possess jurisdiction over all offences by non-commissioned officers and soldiers "which infract the ordinary proprieties of military service, as irregularities and disorders which are not of a grave and serious description, beside such specific offences as are named in the Articles of war as subject to their authority."*

<small>General rule as to.</small>

It remains here to add, that no court martial can take cognizance of offences not conceded to its jurisdiction by the law or the custom of the service, either "as crimes against the military state, or as disorders and neglects tending to the prejudice of good order and military discipline."

<small>General limitation of jurisdiction.</small>

SEC. 140. III.—Of the General Powers and Duties of Courts Martial, and the punishments they may respectively impose:

1. The authority of courts martial is strictly limited to military persons and subjects. Although subordinate to the civil authority, yet, as they derive their being from the same source—the written laws of the land—

<small>Limited to military persons.</small>

---

* See sec. 133, *ante*.

they are entitled within their legitimate bounds to "the same respect to their character and acts which every citizen is required to observe toward the ordinary courts of civil judicature."* The persons who are subject to the control and jurisdiction of military courts and law, have already been pointed out.† As to all such, those courts, and the laws they administer, are of the same binding obligation as is the common law of the land upon the community in general.

Sec. 141. When a court is once regularly assembled and organized, it is a legal body, possessed of definite and independent powers. No authority, therefore, not even that by which it was convened, can interfere with its proceedings. The court may, indeed, in doubtful cases, ask instructions from a superior source, but even these when received are not binding, to whatever respect they may be regarded as entitled. The legal existence of the court continues till it is dissolved by competent authority. If the prisoner has been arraigned, the court must proceed to judgment, unless by sickness or death its members have been reduced below the requisite standard, or where the illness of the prisoner renders the prosecution of the case impracticable. Where a member is prevented by sickness or other cause from attending, the court adjourns from day to day for a reasonable time before proceeding to business; and if a member's seat is permanently vacated, they may nevertheless organize, unless their number is below the required minimum; but no judicial act can be performed, except by a court legally organized. The day and place of the meeting can only be changed by the authority convening the courts; and if such change becomes necessary it should be reported to the proper authority, and its sanction first obtained before any order for it is made by the court.

General duties and powers of courts martial.

---

* De Hart, 9. † Page —.

Sec. 142. The president of a court martial is charged with the duty of seeing that the proper forms of procedure are duly observed. He directs the ordinary adjournments from day to day, but in those cases where a longer adjournment is requisite, as from Saturday to Monday, the vote of the court is necessary. The president is not entitled to any special authority *ex officio* beyond what is needful for the preservation of order and decorum. In voting, and in the ordinary discharge of his duties, he is not distinguished from his comembers. Upon questions of order, and such as relate to individual members, and in "the daily routine of business, he decides of his own motion."*

<small>President of court martial, duties and powers.</small>

But if an adjournment is announced by the president, it may be excepted to for good reason by any member, who is generally to be allowed to state his objection for the decision of the court. The adjournment is usually from day to day, between the hours prescribed by law, though, if necessary, it may be for a longer time; but upon an adjournment *sine die*, the court can only be reassembled by the authority which originally convened it.

Sec. 143. The court is cleared by order of the president, for deliberation, or other purposes, as occasion demands, and generally at the request of a member or the Judge Advocate. Its deliberations are always with closed doors. On other occasions it is open to the public. The utmost decorum and order should be observed in the court, and no improper behaviour or indecorous words should be tolerated. The authority of the president, where a sense of duty is insufficient to restrain members, will generally enable him to suppress all such exhibitions; otherwise, it is his duty to report the facts for the action of the officer ordering the court.

<small>Court cleared, how and when.</small>

<small>When with open doors.</small>

---

*De Hart, 93.

Sec. 144. The 79th Article of war provides that no person shall use "menacing words, signs, or gestures in presence of a court martial, or cause any disorder or riot, or disturb their proceedings, on the penalty of being punished, at the discretion of the said court martial." *Contempt of court punished.* The authority thus conferred for the punishment of contempts extends to all persons, civil as well as military. This is the practice in the military courts of Europe, and is clearly conferred by the Article of war just quoted, which makes no exception in favor of civilians. He who voluntarily presents himself at the bar of a court martial (and no civilian can be there by compulsion) subjects himself for the time being to the rules which govern them; and if he suffers from a violation of those rules, has only his own imprudence or folly to censure. Nor does this right to protect itself depend on the rank of the members. It is a power vested in them as a legal tribunal by the law of the land, supported and strengthened by the general principle that, as such a tribunal, it is entitled both to a proper degree of respect and the means of securing it; and hence, as has been justly observed, "the prosecution, prisoner, and witnesses, although they happen to be of superior rank in the army to those who form any such court martial, are equally bound to observe the lawful injunctions of the court as if the same had been altogether composed of officers of a more elevated rank."*

Sec. 145. Where a contempt is committed before a general court martial, it may at once pass judgment on the offender without regard to his rank. But if he be a commissioned officer, and the offence is before a regimental or garrison court, as they cannot in such cases award any punishment, the only remedy is to impose an arrest on the offender, and report the facts to the proper authority.

---

* Samuel on Mil. Law, 535, 536.

The contempts, says De Hart,* which may be thus summarily punished by a court martial, are those committed before the court, of a public and self-evident kind. But the party should have an opportunity to make such explanations to the court as he may desire.

The court before whom a contempt has been committed is the proper tribunal to judge of the fact, and, with the exceptions just indicated, to pronounce the penalty.

SEC. 146. "In order to promote the ends of justice, to guard against the prejudicing the public mind in regard to any trial, as well as to secure an honest and sincere declaration by the witnesses, courts martial may forbid the publication of their proceedings before the termination of the trial. A violation of such an order would be a contempt of court, liable to be noticed and punished as any other species of contempt may be."†

Proceedings of court not made known.

SEC. 147. With regard to the duty of the court relative to the charges submitted for trial, Captain Simmons advises that the court should "invariably be cleared on the reading of the charges before the arraignment of the prisoner, to consider their relevancy." Referring to this remark, De Hart observes‡ "that it is the duty of courts martial, upon being duly organized, and when the charges are read, to judge of their propriety;" and it would be well, "previous to the arraignment of the prisoner, to clear the court, and then consider the character of the charge submitted." This mode of procedure, he adds, "could never militate against the interests of the accused, and might save much useless trouble and individual responsibility."

Court to be cleared on reading the charges.

To decide on their propriety.

SEC. 148. A court martial has no control over a prisoner except in court. It cannot, therefore, bestow upon him any indulgence or favor by enlarging his freedom, or otherwise, when not in court. His custody

No control of prisoner out of court.

---

* Page 103.   † De Hart, 108.   ‡ Page 111.

concerns his commanding officer, and is subject to his discretion; and all that can be required of him is, that reasonable and proper assistance which may be necessary to advance the business of the court and ensure justice.

SEC. 149. All the members necessary to constitute the court should be present at its opening, and so continue, and if the court is reduced by any cause below the minimum number, the better course, by far, is to dissolve it, and convene a new court—although it is held by some military writers that new members may be detailed, even without consent of parties, and certainly, it is said, with such consent, inasmuch as the record enables them to become familiar with the preceding portions of the trial. But this practice is so objectionable that it has few advocates, and is very rarely admitted. In this connection, De Hart remarks: "should a court be reduced below the minimum number an adjournment *sine die* follows, or for a different period, according to circumstances, and the facts are reported to the proper authority, which may declare the court dissolved, and issue a new warrant for the trial. The members who composed the first, may make part of the second court; but are liable to challenge with the new members, and the proceedings *ab initio* must be *de novo.*" {.sidenote: All the members of court must be present. New members not desirable.}

SEC. 150. As already observed, the names of members are called according to seniority, and they take their places in the same manner on each side of the president. An absent member, who has been so during any part of the trial, cannot resume his place without violating the whole proceedings. Neither can any member, after the court has been called to order, leave his place without permission from the president. The vote is taken on each question until a majority, or such number as is required for the decision, is obtained; and this decision, when announced by the court, binds the minority. The majority vote {.sidenote: Absent member not to return, when. Votes, how taken.}

decides all questions except the findings and sentence in particular cases, where, as in capital offences, the law requires a two-thirds vote.*

SEC. 151. A court martial is bound to examine all charges presented by competent authority for their consideration, and will not be justified in ignoring any complaint so presented, by reason of a former arrest or trial of the accused. Such facts must be brought to the notice of the court by *plea*, and except when this is done, the court is not bound to notice them.

<small>Court to examine all the charges.</small>

SEC. 152. Upon questions of law, the practice of the service and the custom of war, either party is entitled to the opinion of the court, and may request it at any time.

<small>Parties may have opinion of court.</small>

SEC. 153. The Articles of war require the members of all courts martial general, regimental and garrison, to take a prescribed oath; but every court martial is to be regarded as a legal body, for certain purposes, even before it has been sworn, and may, therefore, punish contempts, decide questions relating to the challenge of its members, and dispose of all matters which are merely preliminary in their character.

<small>A legal body for some purposes, before oath.</small>

SEC. 154. 2. Of the Punishments which courts martial may inflict:

The constitution declares that excessive fines shall not be imposed, nor cruel and unusual punishments inflicted. These terms are explicit, and hardly require comment. It is obvious that all punishments are *cruel* which violate the dictates of humanity, and are not necessary to vindicate the claims of justice. Every punishment, moreover, is to be esteemed *unusual* which is unknown to the law and the custom of the service, and is purely arbitrary in its origin.

<small>Cruel punishments, what.</small>

---

* See 87th Article of War, and sections 89, 91, *ante*.

Sec. 155. In awarding punishments, a large discretion is necessarily allowed to military courts. But as authority is generally liable to abuse, where it is unrestrained by law, great watchfulness is required lest the proper bounds of a reasonable and just discretion should, under any circumstances, be exceeded. There are, however, two important and valuable checks upon this power of the court, which are to be found: 1st, in the reviewing authority, whose duty it is to correct every such abuse of power by returning the case to the court for reconsideration, or by disapproving the proceedings altogether; and, 2dly, in the individual responsibility of the members, as already explained. Where the law is express in its directions as to the *kind* or *quantum* of punishment, it must, of course, be obeyed; where it is silent, or of too doubtful import to be applied, the punishment, as just observed, must be determined by the court, and hence the general rule in awarding punishments may be stated to be a just and reasonable discretion, to be exercised always in strict subordination to the law and custom of the service, and according to the merits of the case. *[Discretion in punishing. Rule in awarding.]*

Sec. 156. We have already shown that the general court martial is the highest military tribunal. It may, therefore, impose whatever punishment the law and facts of the case demand—from that of death to the lowest degree of fine and imprisonment. Capital punishment, however, it must always be remembered, cannot be inflicted at the arbitrary discretion of the court, but only in such cases and for such offences as are specifically named in the law. *[Capital punishment.]*

Sec. 157. The offences for which the punishment of death is thus denounced, and may, therefore, be inflicted at the discretion of the court, are as follows:

The beginning, exciting, causing, or joining in any mutiny or sedition, by any officer or soldier.

The failure by any officer, non-commissioned officer, or soldier, present at such mutiny or sedition, to endeavor to suppress the same.*

Desertion in time of war.†
Persuading another to desert.‡
Sleeping of sentinel on post.§
Occasioning false alarms in camp, etc.‖
Doing violence to any person bringing provisions or other necessaries to the camp or quarters of the army in cases specified in the Article of war.¶
Misbehavior or bad conduct before the enemy, shamefully abandoning any fort, post, etc., or inducing others to do so, casting away arms, ammunition, etc., or quitting his post to plunder, etc., by any officer or soldier.**
Making known the watchword; giving a different watchword or parole from that received.††
Forcing a safeguard in foreign parts; relieving or protecting the enemy; corresponding with, or giving intelligence to the enemy.‡‡
Compelling the surrender of any commander of a post, garrison, or fortress.§§

SEC. 158. And here it must again be observed that, in the various cases above cited, with only a single exception, the punishment of death is not commanded, but only permitted at the discretion of the court, who may inflict "such *other punishment,*" as circumstances justify. The exception referred to is the offence of forcing a safeguard in foreign parts, for which the penalty of death is peremptorily denounced in the 55th Article of war. But it is expressly declared in the 87th Article that no person shall suffer death *but by the concurrence of two-thirds of the members of a general court martial;* nor except in the cases

<small>Capital punishment permitted, not commanded.</small>

<small>Two-thirds vote required in sentence of death.</small>

---

*See Articles of War, 7, 8.
† Art of War 20; Act U. S. Congress, May 29, 1830; Confederate Congress, 1861.
‡ Article of War 23.   ‖ Article 49.   ** Article 52.   ‡‡ Articles 55, 56, 57
§ Article 46.   ¶ Article 51.   †† Article 53.   §§ Article 59.

expressly mentioned in the Articles themselves. By the 67th Article of war, the trial of capital cases is prohibited to any garrison or regimental court, and is thus limited to general courts martial only. And the 99th Article provides that all crimes not capital, and all disorders and negligences to the prejudice of good order and military discipline, though not mentioned in the Articles of war, may be taken cognizance of and punished by a general or regimental court, according to the nature and degree of the offence, *at their discretion*. Punishment by stripes can only be awarded by a general court martial, and is limited to the crime of desertion, nor can more than fifty lashes be inflicted for any one such offence. Inferior courts-not to inflict. What to punish.

SEC. 159. *Suspension of Commissioned Officers* from pay and command may, under the provisions of the 84th Article of war, be directed by a general court martial according to the nature of the offence. This punishment is in the discretion of the court—which may direct the suspension of the officer only from his command, or may in addition suspend his pay and emoluments at the same time. In this connection it has been well observed: "In the determination of such mode of punishment, courts martial in the cases of commissioned officers should take a liberal view of the subject before pronouncing judgment, and refer not only to the merits or demerits of the individual, but to his appropriate place in society as a gentleman, and the possible influence which his acts, habits, and associations, which are all more or less dependent on his means of support, may exercise, through public opinion, on the military service. * * * If the power given in the Article is considered merely as a means of punishment * * it is certain that it is deficient in a very essential feature of distributive justice, to wit: equality and uniformity of operation when applied to different persons. What in one case would be a severe deprivation, and a source of anxiety and pain, would in another be regarded with total indifference; and this from the mere accidental circumstances of the parties."

SEC. 160. *Reprimands and admonitions,* either public or private, are a mode of punishment frequently awarded against commissioned officers, and are authorized by long continued custom rather than by express provision of law.

Reprimands.

SEC. 161. *Cashiering or dismission* is a severe but sometimes necessary punishment. The various offences to which it may be applied are indicated in the Articles of war, though it is not expressly restricted to the offences thus specified. The 14th and 45th Articles, however, render it obligatory on the court to cashier every officer who shall be convicted of the crimes indicated therein, while as to the delinquencies mentioned in the 32d Article, the court is authorized to cashier *or otherwise punish* the offender. The 85th Article further directs that where a commissioned officer is cashiered for *cowardice* or *fraud,* it shall be added to the sentence that the crime, name, etc., of the offender shall be published, etc.

Cashiering.

SEC. 162. To the sentence of cashiering or dismissal may be added the incapacity to hold office under the government. But this addition, says De Hart, can only be made in cases specially named in the law.

This incapacity to hold office was perhaps formerly implied in the sentence of every officer who was *cashiered,* and it was supposed that the latter term itself imported a greater degree of infamy than mere dismission. Both terms are employed in the Articles of war, and applied to different offences; as for example, in the 83d Article, which directs *dismission* on the conviction of conduct unbecoming an officer and gentleman; and the 85th Article, just referred to, directing that when an officer is *cashiered* for cowardice or fraud, he shall be published, etc. Whence it appears that the supposed graver term of cashiering is appropriated to mere breaches of discipline, while for more serious offences the punishment of dismission is deemed sufficient! This inconsistency can only be explained by assuming that no distinction was designed to be observed in the terms referred to; nor does any seem now to be admitted in the practice and understanding of the service. The danger of misapprehension on this point may generally be avoided by adhering, in the sentence, to the terms of the law directing particular offenders to be cashiered or dismissed, as the case may be; and by clearly expressing the intention, wherever entertained, to debar the convicted party from the honors and emoluments of office.

Sec. 163. There are two offences specified in the 39th and 48th Articles of war respectively, viz: embezzlement or misapplication of money, and the "conniving at the hiring of another" to perform duty, etc., by any non-commissioned officer, which may be punished by reduction to the ranks; and in the case of embezzlement by the addition of the necessary "stoppages until the money is made good." These cases may be tried by a general, regimental, or garrison court, as circumstances justify or require. The same tribunals, under authority derived from the custom of the service, exercise the right for various other offences, of reducing non-commissioned officers to the ranks. In some cases this right is confirmed by the regulations of the army, and seems to be necessary in many instances where further punishment is requisite, inasmuch as a non-commissioned officer can neither suffer imprisonment nor corporal punishment before he has been reduced to the ranks.*

Sec. 164. *Fine and imprisonment* is a common mode of punishment with military courts. And that of *hard labor* is sometimes added, according to the exigencies of the

Embezzlement.

Stoppages.

Reduction to ranks.

Fine and imprisonment.

---

* De Hart.

case. The authority for these punishments is found in the 67th Article of wár, which provides that no garrison or regimental court shall inflict a fine exceding one month's pay, nor imprison nor put to hard labor any non-commissioned officer or soldier for a longer time than one month.

Hard labor.

SEC. 165. The punishment of imprisonment *and* flogging cannot be imposed, *for the same offence,* in the discretion of the court. There must be express authority for it.

Flogging.

It should, moreover, be observed that the restriction in the 67th Article extends only to the inferior courts. Offences, however, may be committed, and sometimes are, of which the general court martial would have either concurrent or exclusive jurisdiction, but for which no specific punishment is provided, or where the limited degree of punishment allowed to the other courts would prove inadequate. Where this is the case, these modes of punishment, by fine and imprisonment, and hard labor, may be resorted to by the general court martial. This is authorized not only by the custom of the service, but by the practice of the civil courts, in which fine and imprisonment is usually imposed for those offences to which the law has affixed no other mode of punishment. Where the jurisdiction, however, is assumed to be concurrent, and is exercised by a general court martial, care should be taken never to inflict a greater degree of punishment than that which might lawfully be imposed had the case been tried by a garrison or regimental court.*

Hard labor.

SEC. 166. The punishments inflicted on commissioned officers are thus shown to be admonitions or reprimands; suspension from rank, and forfeiture of pay; cashiering, or dismissal from the service.

Enumeration of punishments for commissioned officers.

Those usually awarded against enlisted soldiers are confinement, solitary or otherwise; flogging; forfeiture of

---

*See sec. 129.

pay and allowances; marking by letter on the hip; reprimands, and drumming out of service. <small>For soldiers.</small>

SEC. 167. Non-commissioned officers are frequently sentenced to loss of rank, and this must always be done before they can be punished by stripes. In other respects, they are, as to punishments, to be regarded on the same level with ordinary soldiers. <small>Reduction to ranks.</small>

The punishment of death may be awarded against an officer, non-commissioned officer, or soldier, under the restrictions of the 87th Article of war. If a particular penalty is annexed by law to any offence, no other can be imposed by the court; nor can two essentially different punishments be inflicted for the same cause, unless by express direction of the law. <small>Death.</small>

Should it happen, remarks De Hart, "that an offence, falling within the jurisdiction of a court martial, be not provided for by a special penalty, but left to be determined by the discretion of the court, such sentence must be in accordance with the common law of the land, or the custom of war in like cases; a departure from this would make the sentence unusual, and as such, unlawful."

SEC. 168. We have thus endeavored to point out briefly the law and general principles which should govern courts martial, in determining both the kind and degree of punishment to be awarded against offenders. The directions of the law, and the discretion of the court, controlled by the customs of the service and a just humanity, are generally a sufficient safeguard for the conduct of military courts in this respect. The violation of these rules might subject the members of the court to a civil action from the person whose rights have been disregarded and infringed by their judgment; and must tend to the prejudice of that wholesome influence and authority which should be exercised in the military community.* <small>General rule as to punishment.</small>

---

* De Hart, 69.

SEC. 169. Those who are called to discharge the important duties devolving on military tribunals, cannot study too carefully the rules and principles which should direct their course. Not only are the interests and dignity of the law to a large extent confided to them, but the reputation and personal rights of individuals are frequently at their disposal. Even trivial errors are often productive of pernicious consequences, which, however regretted, cannot always or easily be corrected. "The power of discrimination," says De Hart, "by which members of courts martial are enabled to distinguish the path before them, is not intuitively derived. A habit of reflection and study of the laws can alone place it within their reach, and thus save them from the expression of inconsistent opinions or the commission of illegal acts which react upon the individual and the profession." He only is a wise and just magistrate who diligently seeks to discharge his whole duty, so as while, in the words of Blackstone, he avoids "oppression on the one hand, on the other are stifled all hopes of impunity or mitigation, with which an offender might flatter himself, if his punishment depended on the humor or discretion of the court."

Importance of the subject.

Chapter VI.

OF MILITARY TRIALS AND THEIR INCIDENTS.

Sec. 170. We are thus brought to the subject of military trials, and shall consider, as was proposed:
  I. The charges, and other preliminaries to the trial.
  II. Particular trials and their incidents.
  III. The findings of the court.
  IV. The sentence of the court.

I. Of the charges, and other preliminaries to the trial.
1. As to the charges:
A charge is the formal, written accusation on which is based the trial before a court martial of any person accused of crime or other delinquency, and should contain a brief and accurate statement of those circumstances which are necessary to ascertain. the existence of all facts essential to sustain the accusation. It will lie against all military persons who are guilty of a violation of the military laws and regulations of the service, the customs of war, and the orders of any competent military authority. <small>Definition of charge.</small>

Sec. 171. It is only here proposed to bring to view the principal rules which seem necessary to a comprehension of the particular form and manner in which charges are preferred before military courts. Before stating these rules, however, a few general remarks will be in place.

Says Blackstone: "It is a general rule that no person shall be excused from punishment for disobedience to the laws of his country, unless he be expressly defined and exempted by the laws themselves.

"All parties are considered responsible to the law of the land, with a few marked exceptions, the character and extent of which are expressly limited and defined.*

"Every person at the age of discretion is, unless the contrary be proved, presumed by the law to be sane, and accountable for his actions. †

The object of military trials is, by the proper punishment of offences and delinquencies, to preserve the dignity, order, and discipline of the military service. All *charges* should, therefore, be "founded in public utility," and never made the occasion of "gratifying private or personal resentments."

Object of military trials.

SEC. 172. When the charges are read to the court, which, as stated in a previous chapter, it is the duty of the Judge Advocate to do, the court, after being properly organized, should examine and decide as to their character and fitness respecting the statement and definition of the crime charged, and the precision of the language employed. If sufficient objections appear on such examination, as, for example, that the offence is cognizable only in the civil courts, or the accused is not amenable to military law, proceedings should be suspended, and the question submitted to the authority which convened the court. And if the charge is manifestly erroneous or illegal, it is said the court ought at once to reject it.‡ So, also, if the charge is prepared in a loose and indefinite manner, may the prisoner demand a precise statement of the facts on which he is to be tried. The Judge Advocate may also remonstrate against proceeding to trial upon any charge which is deficient in precision and accuracy of statement.

Court to examine charges.

---

* Wharton's C. L., 81. † Archibald's C. Pl. ‡ De Hart, 100, 101.

Sec. 173. Previous to arraignment, it is competent for the party ordering the trial, and also for the Judge Advocate, if so authorized, to alter or amend any charge. But this would be irregular *after plea*, except on a plea of abatement, as for a misnomer or a wrong addition.* And after arraignment and swearing of the court, no additional charge can be entertained. Additional charges can only be reached by reswearing the court after the previous charges are disposed of, and then proceeding as in a new trial.

Charge may be amended when.

It is never proper to allow the causes of any accusation or charge to accumulate, for the purpose of forming a crime of such magnitude as will then justify prosecution. This course, says De Hart, is prohibited by the regulations of the army, so that if "the facts as they arise are not of a kind to be made matter of charge *at the time*, they should not at a future period be revived."

Not to be allowed to accumulate.

Whether the charges should be read to the witnesses, is matter of serious doubt. They certainly should not be where the language is such as to be suggestive of answers.

Sec. 174. While that technical strictness which is observed in the ordinary courts of law on the subject of pleading does not obtain in military tribunals, there are, nevertheless, certain requirements not to be lost sight of in framing the charges, and the answers or pleas thereto. It is as essential in the one court as the other that accuracy and conciseness of statement should be observed and diligently practised.

Sec. 175. We have already shown what the term *charge* implies.† In framing it, as just noticed, technical nicety is not requisite, yet it should always contain such a "description of the offence that the defendant may know what crime he is called on to answer, and the court may be warranted in their conclusions" respecting it.

Charge— what it should contain.

---

* Ibid, 101, 102.   † Section 170.

What, then, are the principal rules to be observed to this end?

1. *A charge should be stated in definite, accurate, and direct terms:*

<small>General rules in framing.</small> To secure this, all circumlocution and argument should be avoided, and only plain, brief, and positive language employed. All surplusage should be rejected, and no variant or inconsistent statements should be allowed.

2. *Certainty* is at all times necessary to a properly framed charge. This is requisite both as to the *party accused* <small>Certainty.</small> and to *time and place*. The "defendant must be described," says De Hart, "by his title or rank, christian name, and surname, and the addition of the company, regiment, or corps to which he belongs." Care must be taken to set forth his name with accuracy, and a mistake in any part of the name will be fatal; though it seems that if the sound of the name is not affected by the misspelling the error is not material.* Such difficulties, common in civil courts, are not likely to occur in military trials, where the name of the defendant is so easily ascertained and generally known.

Certainty as to time and place.—In law, time and place must <small>Time and place.</small> be attached to every material fact averred in an indictment.† And it is said that the same minuteness is required before military courts in specifying time and place as in the statement and description of the offence. It is, however, admissible, when doubt exists as to the precise time, to state the fact as having occurred "on or about" a particular day, which must always be within a reasonable time. But if either a precise time or place forms a necessary ingredient in the offence, it must be accurately and truly set forth.‡ Time, says De Hart, is a "necessary ingredient in the offence, when the circumstances or conduct would on one occa-

---

* Wharton's Crim. Law, 154.
† Chitty on Pleading.   ‡ De Hart.

sion constitute a particular crime, though at another it would be different in its character. Thus, where an officer is charged with being drunk on duty, under the 45th Article of war, it would be necessary to set forth the nature of the duty and the precise day, or nearly so, that the time may not be confounded in the testimony, and thus lead the court to adjudge him guilty of a crime the penalty of which is arbitrarily fixed by law."

Still, it is admitted that a much greater latitude is allowed in military than in the civil courts, in respect to allegations of time; but this privilege, according to Tytler, is always accompanied with the proviso that the "charge is in other respects sufficiently precise." This indulgence, he adds, "is granted only from necessity, and in no case where it is possible for the prosecutor to mark the time with certainty and precision ought he to be allowed such latitude, as it deprives the prisoner of all opportunity of proving an *alibi*." And under any circumstances, care should be taken that wherever *time* forms a necessary ingredient in the offence charged, it should be so stated as to avoid all difficulty in ascertaining from the evidence the true time involved. And although, adds De Hart in this connection, "there is no military crime to insure conviction of which it is essential that the precise day should be set forth and proved, yet it is essential for a conviction in some cases that the time should be so nearly declared that, if found, it may not appear to be a different day from the one in which the offence could have been committed. That is, the allegation of time should be so well ascertained as that the alternate words (usually employed) 'on or about the said time,' should leave no doubt of their truth."

<small>Time.</small>

The same rules generally apply to allegations as to *place*. In the latter case it would seem, indeed, that less indulgence should be allowed, as precision in this respect is generally much more easily obtained. But it will be found

<small>Place.</small>

a safe rule that both time and place should be plainly and consistently alleged in every material fact.

Certainty as to the person.
3. *A charge should be certain as to the person against whom the offence is alleged:*

Name, etc.
Offences are sometimes committed against the person and property of individuals, or there may be breaches of discipline with respect to particular persons. In such and similar instances, where the offence is made the subject of a charge, the name of the injured party, if known, must be accurately set forth. If at the trial a *variance* in this particular is proved, it will prove fatal.* But if the name proved be *idem sonans* with that in the charge or indictment, and different in spelling only, the variance will be immaterial;† as, for example: "*Keen*" for Keene, "*Segrave*" for Seagrave, etc. The name given must be that by which the party is generally known. And where third persons cannot be described by name, it is sufficient to charge or describe them as "a certain person or persons unknown."‡ These cases, however, are exceptions to the general rule, for wherever the name of the injured party is known, or can be ascertained, it must be fully and correctly stated.

4. *The charge must be certain as to the facts involved, and the intention of the accused:*

Certainty as to facts.
It is not sufficient to state in general terms that a particular offence has been committed, or any incumbent duty neglected, "but the facts and circumstances must be specifically set forth, and the offence must appear on the face of the charge as a distinct, substantial offence. A man cannot be charged with being an habitual violator of orders, or a common thief; but the charge must set forth every fact and circumstance which is necessary to make up the offence. In the ordinary courts of law there are exceptions to this principle, growing

---

* Wharton's Crim. Law, 277. † Ibid, 287. ‡ Ibid, 158.

out of necessity. As, for instance, a man may be indicted for being a common barrator, without detailing the particulars of the barratry; or a woman may be indicted as a common scold, without detailing the particulars of her conduct. But this cannot be done in military courts, because there particular acts or conduct constitute particular crimes. Under this rule, therefore, an officer cannot be charged with being a common liar. There is no military law which recognizes the specific offence of lying; but conduct of that character, according to the attendant circumstances, would necessarily be laid under the eighty-third (83) or the ninety-ninth (99) Article of war, as conduct "unbecoming an officer and a gentleman," or "prejudicial to good order and military discipline." The particular acts or circumstances, then, by which the violation or disregard of truth was evinced by the defendant must be cited in the charge, and thus be shown in evidence.*

Although *intention* is incapable of actual proof, and a man is presumed to intend the necessary consequence of his acts, so that when a wrong act is committed its guilty intent may commonly be inferred—it is, nevertheless, proper to state the intention of the party in the charge as an ingredient of his offence. Knowledge and intent are usually necessary to constitute crime, and, when material, ought to be averred in the charge.

Sec. 176. 5. *Written instruments:*

Where written instruments constitute the gist of the offence, they should be set out in words and figures. It is not necessary, however, in such cases to insert the vignettes, letters, or figures in the margin, as they are no part of the instrument. When it becomes necessary to set forth any writing, it is usually preceded by the words "to the tenor following," or "in these words," or "in the

Written instruments, how set out.

---

* De Hart.

words and figures following." The words "in manner and form following" do not profess to give more than the substance. *Tenor* means an exact copy. *Purport* implies the substance of the instrument as read on its face.*

Not to be in figures.
No part of a charge, it is said, should be in figures, except where it becomes necessary to set out some writing or instrument containing them. And where particular words are material to the substance of the charge, they should be particularly set forth; or when this is inexpedient or impracticable, the words employed should be averred to be of the like meaning and import with those on which the charge is based.†

SEC. 177. 6. *Technical terms, and other words:*

Technical terms.
Language is to be fairly construed, according to its ordinary acceptation in the country. If technical terms are employed, they should be regarded in their technical sense; and if terms of a doubtful meaning occur, they should be so construed as to be consistent with the general scope and intent of the subject. Thus, says De Hart, sometimes "the law has adopted certain expressions to show the intention with which an offence is committed; and in such cases the intention must be expressed by the technical word prescribed, and no other—thus, for instance, the fifteenth (15) Article of war says; "Every officer who shall knowingly make a false muster of man or horse; and every officer or commissary of musters who shall willingly sign, direct, or allow the signing, etc., etc., shall etc., be cashiered." Thus, a charge exhibited against an officer for making a false muster must be laid to have been done "*knowingly;*" and for signing a false muster roll, to have been done "*willingly.*" The words "*mutiny*" and "*sedition*" are technical terms, purely, when applied to military offences, and can only be used and understood according

---

* Wharton's Criminal Law. † De Hart.

to the fixed acceptation of them, determined by legal precedents, and the customs of war."

SEC. 178. When a larger punishment is by law annexed to the commission of any offence than might otherwise be awarded, in order to make the offending party liable it must be expressly charged that such offence was committed under the circumstances contemplated by law. Thus, offences against an "officer *in the execution of his office*," specified in the 9th Article of war, must be charged as having been so committed. So, drunkenness, if charged under the 45th Article, must be laid in the charge as drunkenness *on duty*, which here is the gist of the offence, and the particular duty should also be set forth.* The same rule is to be observed as to offences created by statute. The charge in all such cases must represent the offence or delinquency to have occurred under the particular circumstances designated in the law, as in the 52d Article of war: the "misbehavior" must be "*before the enemy*," and the *quitting* of post or colors" must be with a view to "*plunder*," etc. Hence, in framing the charge, the intention of the delinquent must be set out in the words of the law.

<small>Offence to be charged in words of the law.</small>

SEC. 179. The 99th Article of war provides that "all crimes not capital, and all disorders and neglects which officers and soldiers may be guilty of, to the prejudice of good order and military discipline, though not mentioned in the Articles, are to be taken cognizance of by a general court martial, according to the nature and degree of the offence, and punished at their discretion." In this connection it has been remarked, that "it is not desirable to specify the offence as committed in breach of a particular Article of war. In cases where the offence comes within a particular enactment, it should be set forth in the terms used

<small>Offences to the prejudice of good order and military discipline.</small>

---

* De Hart, 297.

therein; but where the alleged offence is a disorder or neglect not specifically provided for, it must be charged "as conduct to the prejudice of good order and military discipline."

SEC. 180. 7. *Lastly: Duplicity, or double statements, should be avoided:*

Any count which contains charges of two distinct offences is defective.* Thus, it would be improper to embrace in any one specification a charge of a capital offence and of drunkenness, or any other crime. The statement of the crime may be varied in terms in different specifications of the same charge, so as better to meet the evidence; but they should be consistent, and never embrace in any single specification more than one distinct offence.

SEC. 181. In concluding this branch of the subject, we may observe that it is a general rule that the special matter of the charge should be set forth with such certainty that the offence may judicially appear before the court.† "*Certainty and verity*," said Lord Coke, should appear in every accusation. And a distinguished judge‡ of the present age, remarks: "The law secures to every man who is brought to trial on a charge of crime that the acts which constitute his alleged guilt shall be set forth with reasonable certainty in the indictment which he is called upon to plead to. This is his personal right, indispensable to enable him to traverse the facts, if he believes them to be untruly charged;' to deny their asserted legal bearing, if in his judgment they do not establish the crime imputed to him; or to admit at once the facts and the conclusion from them, if he be conscious of guilt. It is important for his protection, also, in case he should be a second time charged for the same offence, that there should be no uncertainty as to that for which he was tried before. And beside all this, which may be supposed to regard the accused

Special matters, how to be charged.

---

* Wharton's C. L., 192.　　† Wharton's C. L.　　‡ Judge Kane.

alone, it is necessary for the proper action and justification of the court that it should clearly appear, from facts patent on the record, that a specific, legally defined crime has been committed, for which sentence is to be awarded according to the laws that apply to it."

Sec. 182. II. We are now to consider certain subjects which may be regarded as *preliminary* to the regular trial by a court martial. " Whenever any officer shall be charged with crime, he shall be arrested, and confined to his barracks, quarters, or tent, and deprived of his sword by the commanding officer." *See 77th Article of War.*

The 78th Article of war directs that "non-commissioned officers and soldiers, charged with crimes, shall be confined until tried by a court martial, or released by proper authority." But, as if to guard against any abuse or arbitrary exertion of power, the 79th Article immediately adds: "No officer or soldier who shall be put in arrest shall continue in confinement more than eight days, or until such time as a court martial can be assembled." In the same spirit, the 80th Article declares that "no officer commanding a guard, or provost marshal, shall refuse to receive or keep any prisoner committed to his charge by an officer belonging to the forces of the Confederate States, *provided* the officer committing shall, at the same time, deliver an account in writing, signed by himself, of the crime of which the said prisoner is charged." At the same time, the 81st Article declares that no. "officer commanding a guard, or provost marshal, shall presume to release any person committed to his charge without proper authority for so doing."

<small>Arrest of officers and soldiers.</small>

The general regulations of the army with reference to this subject have provided that prisoners under guard *without written charges* shall be released by the officer of the day at guard mounting, unless otherwise ordered by the commanding officer, who in his discretion may

<small>Prisoners under guard without charges.</small>

enlarge the limits of any officer in arrest, on his own application.

Thus it will be observed that while on the one hand the law has amply provided for the arrest and safe keeping of military offenders, it has on the other taken care that no undue rigor or oppression shall be exercised against them. For, beside the special restrictions of the Articles of war, a discretion is conferred on the commanding officer who may even, in a proper case, release the prisoner before the expiration of "eight days."

SEC. 183. It has been made a question whether, if a prisoner is committed to the officer of the guard *without written charges* or statements as to the cause of the arrest, the officer is bound to receive such prisoner. It is said the English rule is in favor of the obligation to receive the prisoner under any circumstances. Perhaps the strict reading of the 80th Article of war would not require this to be done unless the cause of arrest is given in—but as there might exist reasons why this could not be done at the time, and injury to the service might result in a refusal to receive the prisoner, and more especially as the officer of the day is required to release all prisoners confined without written charges, the better opinion is that all such objections ought to be waived by the officer commanding the guard. "So far," says De Hart, "as any personal responsibility may attach to his act, he may exercise a becoming prudence, and satisfy himself of the character of him who commits and of him committed; that is, whether the one is authorized so to act, and the other amenable to such, or military authority. It is a safe rule, then, which ought to be observed, that whenever a prisoner thus offered is amenable to military law, and the officer confining him is known, and responsible, the officer commanding a guard, or provost marshal should invariably receive and keep in custody the prisoner so presented."

Question on the subject.

Sec. 184. When an officer is placed in arrest, it is regarded as a breach of discipline to pass beyond the limits assigned him. If the crime alleged against him is of so serious a nature as to induce any attempt to escape, he should be placed in confinement, or at least in charge of a guard. It is moreover directed by the Articles of war that the commanding officer shall deprive the party arrested of his sword. This is not done formally, but the announcement of the proper agent of such commanding officer to the subordinate that he is placed in arrest deprives him of the right to wear arms, or to exercise any official function, for the time being.* Breach of arrest.

The Articles of war do not prescribe any particular mode or place of confinement for non-commissioned officers or soldiers; but the regulations of the army direct as to the first, that they shall be kept "in quarters or other limits," except where escape is anticipated; and as to the latter, it is usual to confine them in the guard-house or prison-room. No officer can be relieved from arrest except in the regular and legally appointed manner, that is, by the authority imposing such arrest, or by a superior officer. Confinement, usual place of.

Sec. 185. What constitutes a breach of arrest has been sometimes matter of argument and doubt. The offence is of a very grave character, and subjects the guilty party to serious consequences; it is therefore important that it should be well understood and defined. And there ought to be, indeed, no difficulty in this, for however certain acts or conduct of an officer under arrest, appearing to exercise the privileges of his commission, such as passing an order, wearing his sword, or visiting his superior, are to be treated, whether as mere improprieties, liable to reprimand and censure, or as violations of some special regulation, and, as What a breach of arrest.

---

* De Hart.

such, to be duly punished, they do not, of themselves, constitute the specific offence here spoken of. That only should be regarded as a breach of arrest, which comes within the terms of the law. The consequences of this crime are too serious to justify any strained or enlarged application of its meaning. The 77th Article, which directs the arrest of an officer charged with crime, as already pointed out, clearly distinguishes the breach of that arrest to be the *leaving his confinement before he is set at liberty by his commanding officer, or by a superior officer.* There can be no reason or authority for changing or enlarging this definition so as to embrace other and different offences. On the contrary, the law being penal, is to be strictly construed.

SEC. 186. "The 27th Article of war confers extraordinary powers on officers of every grade and degree for the suppression of quarrels, frays, and disorders, and in cases contemplated by the Article, a senior is liable to arrest by his junior, and the law requires on the part of all persons subjecting themselves to the exercise of such authority of the junior, or other, to give the most implicit obedience to the same. This is a wholesome check to the exasperation of feeling, and tumult of passion, which might, in some circumstances, be exhibited by men whose rank, years, and services would operate as a very hurtful example to others, youthful and inexperienced, and, therefore, a strong motive to suppress such violence was necessary to be offered, which should at the same time appeal to their professional interests and personal pride."*

<small>Arrest, who may be.</small>

SEC. 187. The law has wisely provided a means for the redress of grievances on the part of inferiors who may consider themselves wronged by those who are placed in command over them. Thus, the 34th Article of

<small>Inferior officers, redress for wrongs of.</small>

---

*De Hart.

war provides "that if any officer shall think himself wronged by his colonel or the commanding officer of his regiment, and shall, upon due application being made to him, be refused redress, he may complain to the general commanding the state or territory where such regiment shall be stationed, in order to obtain justice, who is hereby required to examine into said complaint, and take proper measures for redressing the wrong complained of, and transmit, as soon as possible, to the Department of War a true state of such complaint, with the proceedings had thereon."

This Article is in its nature *remedial*, and is, therefore, to receive a liberal interpretation. Its benefits are to be extended to every officer of the army, whether under a regimental organization or not. It "presents. to each inferior officer a means for the redress of wrongs committed by his superiors," and is not to be confined in its literal meaning, as might be inferred, to "wrongs committed by "a colonel or commanding officer of a regiment;" for in a just and liberal construction of the law, "the particular grade of the person who inflicts the injury, be he a regimental or a general officer, cannot affect the means or the right of the sufferer to seek redress."* The particular mode of this redress is also pointed out in the Article of war. The "proper measures" are required to be adopted by the commanding general, where redress has been refused by the colonel or regimental officer, and proceedings reported to the War Department. No form of proceeding is prescribed, and it would appear that the duty of the general officer is merely to examine and report the facts as directed in the Article of war.

In addition to the remedies provided in the Article just quoted, the 35th Article of war provides the means of redress for "any inferior officer or soldier who shall think him-

<small>Construction of 34th Article of war.</small>

---

* De Hart.

self wronged by his captain, or other officer." Unlike the remedy proposed in the preceding Article, the commanding officer is required to summon a regimental court martial to do justice to the complainant — from which either party may appeal to a general court martial.*

SEC. 188. We have in previous chapters discussed the duties of the Judge Advocate in connection with the charges presented, the propriety of reading them to ignorant persons when accused, summoning witnesses, and rendering them such other assistance as may be consistent with their position, previous to the trial. We have also stated the general practice of furnishing with the charges a list of the witnesses called for their support, though this is not conceded as a right so much as a favor to the prisoner. It is, however, proper that he on his part should furnish the Judge Advocate the names of all witnesses he requires; and should that officer decline to summon them, as for satisfactory reasons he may do, it is yet the right of the prisoner to have submitted to the court through the Judge Advocate an application to direct the summoning of the witnesses thus refused. This application may be supported by any reasons the prisoner has assigned, and should be communicated by the Judge Advocate to the court.

Prisoner— rights of referred to.

His witnesses.

SEC. 189. Whether a court martial can call any witness not produced by the prosecution or defence, De Hart says, has been made a question. The utmost, he remarks, "which according to military writers has as yet been conceded on this point, is to allow a court to examine an individual who has been alluded to in the course of the trial, and whose testimony may elucidate some point referred to." He then declares his own opinion that to permit such a practice would be a "violation of the principle upon which

Who court may examine as witness.

---

* See title, Redress of wrongs.

depends the impartial administration of justice." It is difficult to conjecture how such a question could well be raised. The court are sworn to decide, according to the evidence, the matter before them; they are jurors only, and not parties to the trial. To allow them to "originate evidence," or of their own motion to introduce witnesses, would be contrary to all precedents in other courts, and a manifest infringement of the rules of equity. No officer can of right *demand* a court martial, either for himself or another. If in possession of facts likely to render a trial necessary in any case, he can only report them, or present them in the shape of charges to the commanding general or other officer capable of ordering a court martial, who is to judge of its expediency or necessity.

SEC. 190. The regular hours for the transaction of business by a court martial are fixed, as has been before stated, between eight in the morning and three in the afternoon; and no proceedings can be legally had at other hours, except when in cases requiring "immediate example" it is otherwise ordered by the authority convening the court.

SEC. 191. II. *Of the proceedings in the trial, and its incidents:*

In treating this subject, some degree of repetition must be expected in regard to certain general principles and rules which are of common use and application, and to which recurrence cannot therefore be avoided. As in other judicial bodies, so in military courts there are certain formalities and rules, which, though not written out, are yet well understood and carefully observed.

Thus, order and decorum must at all times be maintained; the court invariably deliberates with closed doors; and the party addressing the court should always respectfully rise from his seat. The prisoner, if a commissioned officer, should be addressed by his name and title, and is attended by a guard or an officer, as his rank and

General rules on the trial.

other circumstances require. A guard is also posted at the door of the court, and the necessary number of orderlies are detailed as messengers to aid the Judge Advocate in summoning witnesses, conveying notices, and for other purposes.

The members of the court take their places, as before explained, according to their rank; and when the requisite preliminaries are arranged, the court is formally opened and business is commenced.

<small>Preliminaries.</small>

SEC. 192. The prisoner and witnesses are then called or brought into court. If a rescue or escape is apprehended, to prevent which the guard is insufficient, fetters may be employed, but not otherwise. The prisoner should be treated with decent respect and kindness, and be allowed a seat. The name of each member of the court is next called by the Judge Advocate, according to seniority; after which, the order assembling the court is read aloud.

<small>Prisoner in court.</small>

SEC. 193. The Judge Advocate now asks the prisoner if he has objections to any member of the court present—naming them in order—or any cause of challenge.

<small>Has opportunity to challenge.</small>

Peremptory challenges are not admitted of any sort; but cause must always be alleged, and this before the oath is administered.* The reasons assigned for the challenge, and the reply of the Judge Advocate, ought to be entered on the record. The court is then cleared for deliberation, and the challenged member withdraws until the decision is announced. If it is sustained, the member retires altogether and the supernumerary, should there be one, supplies his place; but if the challenge is not sustained, the member resumes his seat. A Judge Advocate is never the subject of challenge, as he has no judicative voice.

<small>Peremptory not allowed.</small>

<small>Judge Advocate not challenged.</small>

The technical rules and distinctions, and the great

---

* Wharton's Crim. Law, 971.

strictness usually observed by courts of law respecting challenges, do not obtain before military tribunals, and accordingly it is said there should be the most liberal indulgence conceded to the wishes and even prejudices of the prisoner, where this can be done consistently with the public interests.

SEC. 194. It has been heretofore shown that although courts martial are required by law to take a prescribed oath before they can legally exercise any judicial authority, they yet possess before being sworn, wherever the requisite number are present, certain deliberative powers necessary for their organization and the preservation of order. Hence they are competent to decide upon the exception or challenge raised against any member, and such minor questions as do not involve the exercise of judicial powers. *Court may decide on challenge before oath.*

A court martial cannot examine witnesses on oath, prior to its being regularly organized and sworn as required by law. It can therefore only decide the challenge upon a consideration of the statements made informally by the parties concerned—that is, the objector (through the Judge Advocate) and the challenged officer—and also of witnesses not under oath.

The right of challenge is reciprocal, and the Judge Advocate ought to exercise it on a proper occasion.

SEC. 195. It has just been remarked above that peremptory challenges are not allowed. What, then, are the proper grounds of challenge before a court martial? *What are special grounds of challenge.*

It will be unnecessary to enter into the numerous distinctions and niceties of the law on this subject, or to note the various kinds of challenge which it recognizes. All that need be said here may be embraced under two heads:

1. Challenges on grounds which disqualify a member *for reasons beyond his control, such as relationship, or previous connection with the subject matter, or interest.* These *Principal,*

may be called *principal challenges*, as they present *prima facie* causes for objection.

2. Challenges *on grounds relating to the previous conduct of a member*, such as *partiality, prejudice*, or *malice*, etc., which may be designated as *challenges to the favor*. <small>To the favor.</small> Under one or the other of these divisions it is believed all exceptions which are allowed by courts martial may be classified.

SEC. 196. Under the first head may be named objections which arise from the fact that, by conviction, the prisoner would forfeit his commission, which would result in the promotion of the party challenged. This, it is conceived, is a clear case of *interest* in the conviction of the accused. So that the member is a relative, or of the blood or kindred of the prosecutor or prisoner, is also said to be good cause of challenge.

Previous connection with the subject matter is good ground of objection to a member. Thus it is said an officer who has sat on a court of inquiry to investigate the subject of the charge is ineligible as a member of the court martial. So, also, having been a member of an inferior court from which an appeal has been taken.

Whether it is good cause of exception that a member has sat on another court where the same matters have been considered, is yet undecided. It is certainly advisable not to select such a member if another can be detailed, though De Hart expresses the opinion that "unless there be something peculiar in the investigation previously had, and by which a question of the prisoner's guilt may have been agitated, such objection against a member of a court martial would not be sustained."

SEC. 197. Under the *second* head, or *challenges to the favor*, may be named: cases of interest in the result, which do not involve profit or gain to the member — as in a <small>To the favor.</small>

case reported by Captain Simmons, where the "sentence of the court was remitted from the circumstance of an officer being a member whose property the prisoner had attempted to steal."

Malice is cause of objection. But though there is no "prohibition by law or regulation to the appointment of any particular officer as a member of a court martial, and so it may happen that officers bearing an objectionable official relation to the prisoner may be named for such duty," yet, if an opinion has been maliciously declared unfavorable to the prisoner, it is good ground for challenge.*

It is a general rule that the commanding officer of the prisoner ought not to sit on the court which is to try him. Exceptions to this rule ought only to be admitted in cases of urgent necessity. The reason of the rule is stated to be those prejudices which are likely to arise "from previous, or imperfect, or *ex parte* knowledge of the circumstances inducing the trial."

It is also said to be good cause for challenge that the member is a material witness in the case, and has been summoned as such. But if he is to speak of *character only*, the objection would be overruled. In this connection Captain De Hart remarks: "Should a member, not having been challenged, and after being sworn, be unexpectedly called upon as a material witness in the case, he is not thereby disqualified from discharging his duty as a member of the court, though it might prove better that the character of judge and witness were not united. In a case like this, where a member is called on to testify, and the examination is of such a character as to exasperate or irritate the feelings of the witness, it is advisable that the member should not resume his seat; and if the number present be sufficient to continue the proceedings, the court may authorize his withdrawal. In fact, it is a safer rule that

---

* De Hart.

in every case in which a member happens to be examined as a material witness he should be withdrawn from the court; for it is certain that the facts to which he deposes must, to some extent, be an expression of his opinion of the matter in issue."

SEC. 198. It is no ground of objection to a member that he belongs to the same company or regiment as the accused; though, as just stated, the relations existing between the prisoner and his commanding officer often present good ground of exception. Light and unreasonable objections to members, it need hardly be added, are not to be countenanced.

What no ground of.

SEC. 199. The usual time for challenge is before arraignment of the prisoner, whose objections are first heard by the court; then those in reply. And although the general rule is to make the challenge before the court is sworn, yet it will always consider any exception offered upon *good and sufficient grounds, discovered after the swearing of the court.* But if the cause has been previously known to the prisoner, and the opportunity knowingly waived by him, he cannot afterward avail himself of it.

Time of challenge.

SEC. 200. "When practicable, all challenges should be admitted. It is not only right to be as mild as possible toward the prisoner, but it is right to let the public and the prisoner see that such is the case; besides, no officer who has been challenged likes to sit as a member of a court, and it is hard to oblige him so to do unless the good of the service demands it." Commenting on this opinion of an English authority,* De Hart declares the rule to be a good one where it is possible, consistently with the public interests, to observe it. And he adds, "as courts martial are not strictly bound to the observance of proof in the cause of a challenge, such question must be left for determination to the sense of propriety or sound judgment of the court themselves."

Should be allowed, when.

---

* Sir C. J. Napier.

Sec. 201. The great cardinal principle which the court should keep in view in deciding on the sufficiency of any ground of challenge is *absolute indifference and impartiality on the part of its members.* This point should be obtained as far as possible; and taking into view the ordinary principles of human motive and action, the good sense of the court will generally enable it to arrive at a correct conclusion. It is to be observed, however, that while considerations of leniency toward the prisoner in this connection are to be encouraged and commended, they ought to be entertained only in a just and equitable subordination to the public interests.

<small>Cardinal principle to be kept in view.</small>

Sec. 202. Proofs cannot always be obtained to substantiate an alleged ground of challenge; and therefore, acting on certain ideas of military pride and honor, the practice has to some extent obtained of admitting the challenge where the court has confidence in the statements made, or good reasons for believing them.

Sec. 203. *A challenge to the array* is a peremptory objection to the whole court. The phrase is derived from the practice which obtains in certain cases in courts of law of objecting to the whole jury as it stands *arrayed* in the *panel*, or small squares of parchment on which their names are written. Such a challenge is rarely called for in military tribunals, though there may be occasions for it in cases of a want of jurisdiction in the court. The cause of challenge, whatever it may be, as has been heretofore suggested, should be presented through the Judge Advocate, by whom it should, with the decision of the court thereupon, be carefully recorded in the proceedings.

<small>Challenge to the array.</small>

Sec. 204. Of the *oaths* to be administered to the court and Judge Advocate we have spoken elsewhere. It is only necessary here to repeat that if the fact of their being regularly sworn, as required by the Articles of

<small>Oaths to, noticed on record.</small>

war, does not appear on the record, the whole proceedings will be void. It is also indispensable that the record show that the prisoner was asked after reading the order assembling the court whether he had objections to offer to any of its members. Each case should be tried separately where the charges are different.

SEC. 205. After swearing of the court, and before arraignment, is the proper time for any application or motion for the postponement of the trial, though these proceedings are not strictly limited to any particular period. The court is the judge both as to the time and the reasons offered in support of the application.

<small>Motion to postpone.</small>

SEC. 206. If delay is desired in the assembling of the court, authority therefor must be obtained from the same source which convened it. When it is important merely to suspend proceedings for any cause, the reasons assigned ought to be supported by the affidavit of the applicant. If the ground is the absence of a witness, the probable time of his appearance should be given; and in case of sickness of any witness, it is said a surgeon should state the facts by affidavit, or otherwise. The protracted illness of the prisoner is good ground for dissolving the court. It is said that the sickness of the prosecutor, except in very special cases, of which the court must judge, will not justify a suspension of the trial beyond a very limited time, the presence of the Judge Advocate being in general deemed sufficient.

<small>How delay obtained.</small>

SEC. 207. Counsel is allowed the prisoner, if desired, to aid in the defence. He sits by the accused and directs him what questions to ask, which are then put by the Judge Advocate to the witness. Any points to be discussed, or explanations made, are managed in writing in the same manner, for during the proceedings counsel is not permitted to address the court. He may however read to the court a written argument for the defence, and it is customary to allow

<small>Counsel to prisoner.</small>

OF MILITARY TRIALS AND THEIR INCIDENTS. 137

this. If the person selected as counsel is objectionable, the court may refuse to admit him, though this authority is seldom, and ought always to be carefully exercised.

SEC. 208. These preliminaries being arranged, the Judge Advocate reads the charges in full and open court; and the prisoner is now formally *arraigned*, the Judge Advocate addressing him by his proper rank and name, as follows: "You have heard the charges read preferred against you; how say you, are you guilty or not guilty?" Arraigned.

SEC. 209. Here the prisoner may *stand mute*, or refuse to answer; or he may plead to the crime charged. The usual pleas are: To the *jurisdiction* of the court; *abatement;* the general issue of "*not guilty*," or some *special plea in bar* of the trial.

If the prisoner *stands mute*, the case is provided for in the 0th Article of war, which declares that "when a prisoner arraigned before a general court martial shall from obstinacy and deliberate design stand mute, or answer foreign to the purpose, the court may proceed to trial and judgment as if the prisoner had pleaded not guilty."

And so, if the standing mute arise from the inability *only* of being unable to articulate, the court may proceed as though the plea of not guilty had been regularly entered.

SEC. 210. *Plea to the jurisdiction of the court:*

The general grounds of this plea are: that the civil courts only have cognizance of the crime alleged; that a superior court martial only has jurisdiction in the case; that the court assembled has been improperly constituted, either by reason of the member or members, or the authority by which it is ordered to assemble. Plea to jurisdiction.

SEC. 211. *Plea in abatement:* This is a dilatory plea, and must be pleaded with exactness. The true name and facts must also be stated, to enable the Judge Advocate to correct the error. But the court may permit the error Plea in abatement.

to be amended on the declaration of the party, and the formality of a *plea* is therefore rarely resorted to.

SEC. 212. *The plea of guilty:* This admits the crime and facts charged; and sentence follows, unless the court sees fit to receive or the prisoner desires to offer evidence as to the *character* and *degree* of the offence, which may always be done. Where the prisoner is unacquainted with the consequences of such a plea he should be informed; and it is always best to examine as to the nature and extent of the crime, inasmuch as mitigating circumstances may appear proper to be considered.

<small>Plea of guilty.</small>

SEC. 213. *The plea of not guilty* puts in issue the offence charged. Either party may under this plea adduce evidence to prove or disprove the charge, as the case may be; and for this reason it is the plea usually employed where a defence on the merits of the case is designed.

<small>Of not guilty.</small>

SEC. 214. *Special pleas:* Of these there are several—

1. The statute of limitations may be regarded as a special plea, as the party accused *has the right* to plead in his defence that the crime charged has occurred more than two years before the issuing of the order for the trial—all trials for such offences being prohibited by the 88th Article of war. According to the opinion of Mr. Wirt, U. S. Attorney-General, it is not "competent for any individual to waive" this provision or for a court martial to decline, "even on the application of the arrested party, to examine into offences of more than two years standing previous to the order summoning the court," unless the conditions of "absence" or manifest impediment appear, as required in the Article of war.

<small>Special pleas: Statute of limitations.</small>

That the civil courts have charge of the crime or offence, and hence that no court martial could assume jurisdiction of the questions involved during the pendency of the subject before the civil authority, is a lawful impediment to an earlier trial; and therefore such an impediment as is contemplated in the Article just quoted. "Until he is discharged from the prosecution pending before the civil tribunal no court martial can be held upon him."* And the court will assume that some manifest impediment existed to the trial, unless the contrary is shown.†

SEC. 215. 2. *Former acquittal, or conviction:*

As the same remarks apply in each of these cases, with a single distinction, they need not be separated here. An *acquittal*, even without the judgment of the court thereon, is a bar; but this does not necessarily follow on a *conviction on which the court has pronounced no sentence.* Thus, if the court should simply find the prisoner "*not guilty,*" without proceeding further to add the words, "and do therefore acquit him," etc., still it is conceived no further trial could be had, though the former proceedings were thus incomplete; whereas, no *conviction* could be a bar which is not followed up by the sentence of the court. But if the proceedings were full and regular, a second trial after one conviction would be illegal.‡ *Former acquittal.*

SEC. 216. A court martial will not *ex officio* take notice of a former trial. This is the prisoner's privilege, and must be pleaded specially. But such trial must of course have reference to the proceedings of a *court martial*— for, remarks De Hart, "the same acts as may be offered against the rights of private persons may also violate the proprieties of military discipline; and, as such, may be investigated by both civil and military courts." *Former trial, how proved.*

SEC. 217. In order to bring the party within the terms and meaning of the law, however, the former trial must not only have been before a military court, but must have been in all respects a regular and legal proceeding. *Nature of the former trial, when a bar, etc.*

---

* Mr. Wirt's opinion. † De Hart. ‡ Wharton's C. L., 247.

On this point Captain De Hart observes: "If the court had no right to try such persons or such offences as were charged against them, or if it was illegally constituted, or if its proceedings were contrary to law, or the sentence unauthorized, such illegality vitiates the whole proceedings and the prisoner must be discharged. Yet, in such a case, the proceedings had *do not constitute a trial*, as they were not legally conducted; and the prisoner may, upon a new charge, be brought to trial before a new court." So an *arrest* and discharge without trial is not a good plea in bar.* To authorize such a plea, "two things," says Mr. Wharton, "are requisite: first, that the former acquittal should have been regular; second, that the first indictment should have been sufficient." Again, "the court must have been competent, and the proceedings regular. If the court has no jurisdiction, it is no bar to a second proceeding. And if the indictment or charges were sufficient, and the prisoner could have been legally convicted on any evidence which *might have been* properly and legally adduced, his acquittal may be successfully pleaded to a second trial."† And this is in accordance, not only with the Articles of war, but with the provisions of the constitution, which declares that "no person shall be subject for the same offence to be twice put in jeopardy of life or limb." "Twice put in jeopardy," and "twice put on trial," said a learned judge, "convey to the plainest understanding different ideas. Hazard, peril, danger of a verdict, cannot mean a verdict given. There is a wide difference between a verdict given and *jeopardy* of a verdict."‡

"The greatest latitude," again says De Hart, "which it is believed can be claimed in favor of a prisoner on this head is, that where a court of adequate powers has proceeded to judgment, no second trial can take place: for though the de-

---

* De Hart, 142.   Crim. Law, 248.   † Wharton, C. L., 252.
‡ On the construction of this term, see Wharton, 263, *et seq.*

cision may be illegal, and therefore not binding, still it was the act of a legitimate court, exercising a legal authority, but erroneous in result. The prisoner has been by the proceedings, in a legal sense, *jeopardized* in his interests or safety, and he is not responsible for the errors of the court, nor while its powers were exercised was his amenability to punishment destroyed or diminished."

SEC. 218. *A pardon may also be specially pleaded in bar of the trial.* "A pardon is an act of grace proceeding from the power intrusted with the execution of the laws, and exempts the individual on whom it is bestowed from the punishment the law inflicts for a crime he has committed." * * * But, "a pardon is a deed, to the validity of which delivery is essential, and delivery is not complete without acceptance. It may be *rejected* by the person to whom it is tendered. It may be supposed that no being condemned to death could reject a pardon; but the rule must be the same in capital cases and in misdemeanors. A pardon, moreover, may be conditional, and the condition may be more objectionable than the original punishment."*

<small>Pardon.</small>

A pardon must correctly cite the crime or offence pardoned, and a misrecital of it will render it inoperative. If it be *conditional*, the condition must appear to have been duly performed.†

SEC. 219. In addition to the pleas now stated, Captain De Hart informs us that the prisoner may also plead "the want of *definite specification* in the charge, as to matter or *time*, where the latter is an essential part of the offence, or in order to fix the identity. The objection would be that the specifications were couched in terms too vague to admit of a pointed and particular defence; and that should another prosecution be urged against him, he could not consistently plead that he had been previously tried for the same

<small>What of particularity.</small>

---

* 7 Peters, 150. † Wharton.

offence." This objection, he adds, if the prisoner desires, "may be put off until the defence or be made the subject of observation subsequent to pleading," and need not necessarily be presented in the form of a plea.

SEC. 220. "If a special plea in bar be reasonable," observes the same author, "or plausible, though there exist no precedent for the guidance of the court, it is proper to hear evidence on the point raised; and if the plea should be received as valid, the court would adjourn, having committed to record all the facts of their proceedings, and submit the same to the authority by which the court was assembled," for decision.

<small>General rules as to special pleas.</small>

SEC. 221. It is not necessary to *plead a variance* between the charges before the court and those delivered the prisoner. If there proves to be any essential difference, the court will always allow the requisite time to prepare for his defence on the official charges.

<small>Variance.</small>

SEC. 222. We have thus stated and explained the usual *pleas* employed in trials before courts martial.

After the plea has been put in, the next proceedings are to determine the questions which are thus presented and put in issue. These questions are of course to be decided by the court. The manner of doing this will be best explained by considering the course adopted in the most common plea of *not guilty*.

<small>Court to decide issue.</small>

The plea is first to be recorded by the Judge Advocate, who then notifies all witnesses, but the one to be examined, to retire from the court till called—the rule being that the respective witnesses should be examined out of the hearing of each other. It is especially desirable that this should be the case with respect to the witnesses of each party, although the hearing the testimony of one witness would not incapacitate the party listening from testifying.

<small>Usual course of proceeding.</small>

SEC. 223. It is competent for the Judge Advocate to open

the case by such explanations and remarks as he deems necessary; but it is usual to defer any such observations, unless especially called for by circumstances, till the evidence has all been concluded and recorded—when the whole subject may be fully discussed. *Case opened.*

SEC. 224. The witness being sworn by the Judge Advocate in the manner pointed out in a previous chapter, the examination proceeds—being always commenced by the prosecutor. *Swearing witnesses. Separate examination of, a test.*

The separate examination of witnesses is a strong test of their consistency, especially on a cross-examination.* But all examinations must be before every member of the court. The manner and demeanor of witnesses are often not less important than their statements. An over-forward and eager zeal to testify, evasive answers, efforts to gain time in order to consider the *effect* of the reply, are to a greater or less extent marks of insincerity; while, on the other hand, frankness and promptness to state all the circumstances of the transaction are to be taken as indications of sincerity.† The age, inclinations, education, and behavior of witnesses are all to be scanned, in which points, says Blackstone, "all persons appear alike when their depositions are reduced to writing, and read to the Judge in their absence; and yet as much may be frequently collected from the *manner* in which the evidence is delivered as the matter of it." *Other tests.*

A good opportunity to observe the *manner* of a suspected witness may often be obtained by confronting him with an adverse witness, notwithstanding the general rule holds good that they had better be examined separately.

The *form* of examination is immaterial, whether by *narration* or interrogatory. The latter is the more direct and pene-

---

* Starkie on Evidence, vol. I, 134. † Ibid, 458.

trating, and therefore the most certain mode of eliciting the truth.*

SEC. 225. Where a witness whose testimony is important is prevented from attending the trial by sickness, the court may adjourn to his room to receive what he has to testify; but this must be done by all the members, and no one can act for the court.†

Sick witness.

Military persons may be compelled to attend a court martial, as witnesses. No such power exists as to other persons; and where their testimony is required, it may be taken by deposition as provided in the 74th Article of war, before a justice of the peace — the prosecutor and person accused being present at the taking of the same.

Military witnesses.

SEC. 226. De Hart excepts to the prevailing mode of reading the charges to the witness before he is examined. Where the charge would evidently suggest the answer to the witness, by directing his attention to particular phrases, time and place, etc., the objection is perhaps well taken; but in ordinary cases, the reading of the charge is probably the best and readiest way to bring the mind of the witness in an unprejudiced manner to the subject matter of his examination, especially where this is not conducted by means of interrogatories, which, though more direct and searching, are yet a less convenient and more tedious method of proceeding. But, after all, the best rule, as suggested by De Hart, is that the nature of the charges, and the character and standing of the witness, should determine the course to be pursued.

Whether charges should be read to.

SEC. 227. When the course by interrogation is adopted, the questions are written out by the party originating them, and read aloud by the Judge Advocate, who enters them on record. If the question is objected to,

Witnesses, how examined.

---

* Comm. III, 373. † De Hart.

the court is cleared before its propriety is decided; and if it is considered improper to read it in the presence of the witness, this step of clearing the court should first be resorted to. The majority determines whether the question shall be received or not. After an interrogatory is put and entered on the record, it cannot be expunged, except by consent of parties.*

Questions are entered as put by the various parties, as "question by the *court*," by the "*Judge Advocate*," or by "*a member*." If a question originating with a member is approved and received by the court, it thus becomes the question of the court, and cannot be objected to, as all other questions may, although in entering it on the record it should be designated as a "question by a member," in order to distinguish it and present a true record of facts.

<small>Questions, how recorded.</small>

SEC. 228. The examination-in-chief is that to which the witness is first subjected by the party who calls him.

The cross-examination is that conducted by the opposing party, and can never be commenced until the examination-in-chief is complete.

<small>Course of examination.</small>

The re-examination is that made by the first party, when the cross-examination is closed. It is then customary for the court to ask any questions deemed important to elicit a complete narration of the facts and circumstances of the case. This is the usual and better course, as it avoids confusion, and affords a regular and consistent record, notwithstanding the court may examine the witness at any stage of the proceedings, if expedient.

SEC. 229. It is better to read over to each witness his evidence as recorded, to avoid errors; and this ought always to be done if desired by him. Any corrections made by him must of course be recorded. This evidence, however, should never be read to him till his whole examination is complete.

<small>Witness, evidence read to him.</small>

---

* De Hart.

SEC. 230. If a material question has been omitted by either party, it is in the discretion of the court to recall the witness and allow it to be put. This of course confers the right of cross-examination and re-examination to the extent of the first examination, but no further.

Witness may be recalled, when.

When *all the evidence* has been gone through in support of the charges, and the prosecution has been closed, it must be so entered on the record, and no new evidence can afterward be admitted in support of the charges.

SEC. 231. The defence is then commenced; but if necessary the court will grant the prisoner time for better preparation of his case. The same order is pursued in the examination of witnesses for the defence as in that for the prosecution. If either party introduce new facts or witnesses, the opposing party has the right to bring in rebutting proofs. But these subjects will be further treated of in the chapter on evidence. The prisoner having completed his evidence, is then at liberty to address the court in his defence. In doing this, he may present any statements and arguments in his power tending to his exculpation. Much liberty is moreover allowed him in commenting on the evidence of the prosecution, and the consistency and even character of the opposing witnesses, provided, always, this be done in a manner consistent with decency and propriety, and the respect which is due to the court. This address of the prisoner is read by himself, his counsel, or by some friend, or the Judge Advocate, as may be found convenient and desirable to the prisoner.

Defence. Time may be granted prisoner.

SEC. 232. The Judge Advocate, or prosecutor, has always the right to reply when the defence of the prisoner is closed, and here, also, reasonable time for the preparation of this reply is always conceded. When the reply has been read to the court, the *trial* is concluded.

Reply of Judge Advocate.

SEC. 233. As to the course to be pursued by the Judge Advocate in the discharge of his difficult and important duties, the reader is referred to the previous chapter on those subjects.*

SEC. 234. Before the judgment or sentence of the court is announced, there are various defences or pleas which may be offered in *arrest of the judgment of the court;* that is, there may be reasons why, in certain cases, such judgment or sentence should not be pronounced against the prisoner. Although these pleas are seldom employed, as they may be urged in various forms in the *defence*, yet it may be well briefly to refer to the grounds on which they rest. Arrest of judgment.

SEC. 235. *Idiots, insane persons, and lunatics* who, from a want of discretion, are under a natural disability to distinguish between good and evil, are not punishable for their crimes.† But if lucid intervals occur sufficient to enable them to determine on the consequences of their actions, committed therein, they are responsible. What particular degree of lunacy, or insanity, is requisite to excuse the commission of crime, may sometimes be an important question. It would require more time and space, however, than can be here devoted to it, and the reader is, therefore, referred for a full discussion of the subject, to *Wharton's Treatise on Criminal Law, pages* 81 *to* 97, *and the authorities there cited.* Idiots and lunatics.

SEC. 236. 2. *Misadventure, ignorance*, etc., as where a man in the commission of a lawful act commits an unlawful one ignorantly, or without intention. Misadventure.

SEC. 237. 3. *Compulsion*, or the legal restraint of one's will. Upon this subject Captain De Hart makes the following observations: Compulsion, or legal restraint.

"This plea, when founded upon the obligation of subjection to military authority, may present very difficult points to determine; for it is a nice question still, of how far a soldier may plead justification for an act done by the order of

---

* Chapter III.   † De Hart.

a superior officer, which order may prove to be illegal; or be excusable for hesitating to yield obedience to such order, upon the presumption that it is contrary to law. These questions, however, when presented to courts martial, are to be considered in relation to military discipline, and not always referred to as a consideration of personal rights, and therefore courts martial would probably extend the principle of exculpation under the plea. Hesitating in the execution of a military order is clearly, under most circumstances, a serious offence, and would subject one to severe penalties; but actual disobedience is a crime which the law has stigmatized as of the highest degree, and against which it has denounced the extreme punishment of death; and accordingly, an offence of this nature, from the great danger which might result from it, would be very nicely scrutinized by courts martial ere a justification would be admitted upon the ground that there was no lawful authority for the command given."

The 9th Article of war requires, under penalties, obedience to all *lawful commands*. But a difficult and delicate question here arises. Unlawful commands are not obligatory; but what are they, and how are they to be distinguished? They are, says Captain De Hart, "such as are plainly and palpably in violation of the well known customs of the army and laws of the country, and not those in which the question of legality is merely doubtful or undecided. In every case then in which an order is not clearly in derogation of some right or obligation created by law, the command of a superior must meet with unhesitating and instant obedience."

Compulsion may also arise from *duress*, or fear of great bodily harm. This fear must be a well grounded and reasonable one; and when alleged, should of course be proved to the satisfaction of the court.*

---

* 2 Inst., 483. 1 Bl. Comm., 131.

Sec. 238. 4. *Drunkenness.*—This is a species of insanity or madness; yet as it is commonly induced by the voluntary act of the party, it is usually held to aggravate rather than excuse the commission of offences. Mere "drunkenness can never be received as a ground to excuse or palliate crime. This is a sound and long established maxim of judicial policy, from which perhaps a single dissenting voice cannot be found."*

<small>Drunkenness, how far an excuse for crime.</small>

There are cases, however, where this plea ought to be admitted, but only as exceptions to the general rule, which is undoubtedly well founded. Thus, at law, while drunkenness is no defence or palliation, it may be proved, in order to rebut the presumption of malice where that is requisite, as in murder, to make out the crime, or to show the grade of intention.† Much more should this excuse be admitted in the cases of soldiers; especially where it can be presented as a ground of *arrest* of the sentence of the court. To refuse to give proper consideration and weight to such a plea, when we remember "the habits of soldiers and the character of offences most frequently perpetrated by them, would be opposed to the maxims of human reason. Where there is no certain or apparent predisposition to commit the offence, and where its enormity is not such as to shock the sentiment of humanity, courts martial do at times consider this excuse as having some right to consideration, though it must be remembered that it is only received in extenuation, if at all, of smaller and lighter offences."‡

Sec. 239. We conclude this branch of the subject by observing that the matters of defence which have thus been designated as "pleas in arrest of the judgment of the court," are, as already intimated, rarely employed in this form, but are usually presented and relied upon as grounds of defence in the course of the trial. This is

<small>These pleas rarely employed, and why.</small>

---

* Wharton, 92.   † Ibid, 93.   ‡ De Hart, 169.

more especially the case with respect to the excuse of drunkenness, which, if admitted at all, is only to be taken as ground of mitigation or extenuation in the lighter and less aggravated offences. Where, however, the opportunity has been allowed to pass in the *trial*, it might be admissible to urge these grounds of defence in the form of a plea, as now explained.

SEC. 240. III. *Of the Finding of the Court.*—The trial having been concluded by the examination of all the evidence adduced, and the discussion of the case by the parties, the question of the guilt or innocence of the accused is now to be decided by the court.

But the whole, and each part of the charges must first be exhausted, and, notwithstanding the court may be satisfied of the guilt of the prisoner, on any branch of the accusation, so as to render his conviction necessary and certain, they are still bound to continue their examination till the whole subject is disposed of. The whole of the proceedings should then be read to the court by the Judge Advocate, and it is recommended that a fair copy of the same be placed on their table for reference. In important and voluminous cases, this is always requisite. The court should in their investigations exercise all possible forbearance, patience, and prudence, remembering the high responsibility of their office, and the vital interests which are committed to their keeping. Mr. Tytler recommends that "where there are distinct and separate charges, the president and members of the court reason and deliberate separately on each charge, candidly discussing in a free and open conversation the import of the evidence, and allowing its full weight to every argument or presumption in favor of the prisoner."* This practice, says Captain De Hart, is approved by other military writers, and especially by General Kennedy in his work on courts martial.

_{The whole charge to be exhausted.}

---

* Tytler, quoted by De Hart.

OF MILITARY TRIALS AND THEIR INCIDENTS. 151

Sec. 241. When the court are ready to deliver their opinions, they notify the fact to the Judge Advocate, who then proceeds to read the several charges and the specifications thereto in their order, and to take the vote of the members upon each specification or charge, beginning with the youngest member, as required in the Articles of war. The manner in which this is done has already been stated* and need not be repeated. The vote on each specification having been recorded, the opinion on the charge is now given, and also recorded, and so on till the whole are exhausted. Opinions of court, mode of delivery.

Sec. 242. In general a *majority of voices* decides the guilt or innocence of the prisoner; but it is otherwise where the punishment of death is inflicted. The 87th Article of war declares that no person shall suffer death " but by the concurrence of *two-thirds* of the members of a court martial;" nor can any sentence of death be passed by the court, except in the cases mentioned in the Articles of war. In all cases, therefore, where the prisoner is sentenced to death, the record must state that the sentence was concurred in by two-thirds of the court. This statement of the record can, under no circumstances, be dispensed with. If it is omitted, the error would be fatal; unless in cases where the court, not being dissolved, and having a clear knowledge of the fact that the required number actually concurred in the sentence, could, on the return of the record by the authority convening them for revision, so amend their finding as to comply with the terms of the law, without in other respects violating the well known rules which regulate courts martial in all such proceedings. Votes necessary to decide.

Sec. 243. Except in capital cases, the rule is simply to state the fact of acquittal or conviction, without reference to the majority by which the result has been obtained. The reasons on which this rule has been Rule in stating decision of court.

---

* Section 89.

established, as collected by De Hart, are substantially these: It is regarded as important that the opinions of individual members should be concealed, and to reveal them, directly or indirectly, would be in violation of the solemn promise and obligation to secrecy which the law has imposed on each member of the court, as well as the Judge Advocate. To state that the vote was unanimous, would at once reveal what was desired and intended to be concealed; while, on the other hand, to record the particular number of votes given in other cases, might lead to the discovery of individual opinions. The only safe rule, therefore, is the one indicated above.

SEC. 244. It has already been stated that the president of the court votes as other members, and has no casting vote. It follows, therefore, that where an *equality* of votes occurs on the finding of the court (which may happen where the members are reduced by sickness or other accident), the prisoner will be acquitted, upon the principle of law that the benefit of all doubts is to be given in favor of the accused.

President no casting vote.

SEC. 245. *Special verdicts* are sometimes found necessary in military as well as civil courts. Thus, remarks Captain De Hart, "circumstances which are embodied in the charges, and upon which constructive guilt is charged, are necessarily dependent upon motive, by which the degree of criminality is determined." This particular degree it is the duty of the court to ascertain by their findings. The verdict may, therefore, be *special;* i. e., continues the same author, "part of the specification may be found, and other parts declared void of criminality, or the entire circumstances set forth proved, and yet the prisoner declared without guilt. But in all such findings the decision of the court must be clear and specific, so that the amount of punishment be seen to bear a proper relation to the degree of guilt."

Special verdicts.

Sometimes guilt is charged and predicated on a supposed criminal knowledge or intent in the prisoner, which the evidence does not sustain, notwithstanding the facts alleged are proved. When the court is of this opinion, the verdict or finding must so declare. So, also, if the evidence leads to such a conclusion, the court may find the accused guilty as to certain facts in the specification, and may acquit him as to others.

SEC. 246. The distinction, then, between a special and a general verdict in courts martial is simply this, that in the former, the guilt is qualified and confined to particular parts of the charge, while as to other parts of the same charge the accused may be acquitted, either from want of proof as to the fact, or of criminal intent, where the fact is established; but in the latter or general verdict or finding, there is a simple and unqualified declaration of guilt or innocence expressed by the terms, "guilty," or "not guilty." This peculiarity in the manner and form of the special finding in a court martial arises from the fact that the members are judges both of the law and facts in all cases, and are not confined, as would be a jury in civil courts, where a special verdict is rendered, to the bare ascertaining of facts, leaving the court to apply the law. Distinction between general and special verdict.

SEC. 247. It is important that the degree of guilt, or the extent of the charge proved, should be explicitly stated in the finding. In general, it is better that the terms employed be simply of acquittal or conviction. To declare the charges *not proven* is, in the opinion of Captain De Hart, at best an ambiguous expression, and may tend to strengthen the imputations of the charge. So he adds, "acquittals, characterized by the terms *honorable*, *most honorable*, *fully* or *most fully*, should of course be employed only when the nature of the charge makes them necessary." Degree of guilt to be found.

SEC. 248. It is competent for court martials to animadvert on the motives of the prosecutor, when obviously grounded in a spirit of hostility or ill-will to the accused; and, on the other hand, when circumstances Court may censure prosecutor, etc.

require it, "to declare their opinion that he has been actuated by proper motives, and by a sense of duty, and regard for the service."

Thus, also, may the conduct of military witnesses be very properly noticed by the court: "Falsehood and prevarication, when perpetrated by a witness speaking under the solemn obligations of an oath, are certainly most immoral as well as dangerous acts, and therefore all communities which have enjoyed the benefit of a judicial system have punished them as offences; and in noticing misconduct on the part of military witnesses, the court should be specific and not general, so that the offender may be brought to answer by the proper authority."

SEC. 249. Sometimes the degree of guilt proved is not commensurate with the charge. Where this is the case,

Court may find less guilt than charged.

the court may find the accused guilty in a less degree than that alleged against him. But care must be taken that the nature of the offence found is similar to that charged, that is to say, while the degree of guilt, or of the offence may differ from that alleged, its *character* can never be different; thus a party though charged with *desertion*, may only be found guilty of absence without leave. The intention of the party is here received as modifying the degree of guilt imputed to him, and the grade of the offence found is lowered accordingly.

There are degrees of culpability to be considered in every act capable of division into offences of greater or less

Extenuating circumstances.

magnitude. The sentinel overcome by the burdens of the day, or the fatigues of a march, might sleep at his post, but would nevertheless incur the penalty of the law, as being guilty of a grave offence, and yet, though his condition and circumstances could not authorize an acquittal, they might very well be received in extenuation or palliation of his guilt.*

---

* De Hart.

Sec. 250. The minority are bound by the decision of the majority, or such other proportion of the whole court as are authorized by the law to determine the case. *Minority bound by majority.* As has been stated, the exposure of individual opinions is not allowed; and to avoid this the members usually write their decision, guilty, or not guilty, with the desired qualifications, on paper, and the vote is afterward announced by the Judge Advocate in the manner heretofore explained.* The court are not limited to a single vote, but may continue to vote until a decision is obtained, and the result announced, upon each specification and charge.

Sec. 251. IV. *Sentence of the court.*—A court martial, is not, as in the case of a jury in a civil court, obliged to complete the verdict before separating; but may adjourn from day to day to consider their finding and sentence. *Court may adjourn before sentence.* But their acts must be of the entire court, as such, and it would be manifestly improper and illegal to pronounce any decision which had not been considered by the entire court. Every member is moreover bound to vote some punishment upon a conviction by the required number of the court; and therefore, where the accused *Every member must consider the sentence, and vote.* has been found guilty in a legal way, no member can be excused from voting a punishment upon the ground of a want of concurrence in the conviction, or of his having actually voted an acquittal. "The moment the finding is recorded the right of individual judgment ceases;" and the party thus convicted by the court can only be regarded by each member as a legitimate and proper object of punishment. Moreover, "all members must vote some legal sentence; and if that which any member votes for is not carried, some punishment must be voted till a majority agree as to one punishment." Hence, "if a member should vote for death, which is not carried by two-

---

* Page 109.

thirds of the court, he must vote some other punishment."*
And if a diversity of opinion exists as to the nature of the sentence, it will of course be necessary to compromise opinions to an extent, to enable the court to agree upon the punishment to be pronounced, as they are bound to declare some, for the offence of which they have found the prisoner guilty. And not only is it incumbent on each member to vote on the punishment, "but every member is bound to vote on every question which is presented for settlement by the court."†

SEC. 252. Two punishments essentially different cannot, without express authority of law, be inflicted for the same offence; neither can any be awarded which are not recognized by the custom of war, nor prescribed by statute. And where the law prescribes a particular penalty for an offence, no other can be imposed.‡ But on these subjects we have already spoken, and the reader is referred to what has been said.§

Two punishments not to be inflicted for same offence.

In referring to this subject, Captain De Hart has the following observations:

"In passing sentence courts martial should be careful to employ clear and unambiguous language, so that the kind and degree of punishment shall be set forth definitely and precisely; and the mode of inflicting capital punishment should be designated. The military laws do not say how a criminal, offending against such laws, shall be put to death, but leaves it entirely to the custom of war. Shooting, or hanging, is the method determined by such custom. A spy is generally hanged, and mutiny, accompanied with loss of life, is punished by the same means. Desertion, disobedience of orders, or other military crimes, usually by shooting; the mode, however, in all cases (that is, either shooting or hanging), may be declared in the sentence. The

Terms of sentence.

Spies.

---

* Hough, as quoted in De Hart.　　† De Hart.　　‡ De Hart.
§ See sections 154 to 169.

sentence, too, in capital cases, may simply declare the judgment *to be shot to death with musketry, or be hanged by the neck until dead;* or it may add, *at such time and place as the commanding general, or* (as the case may be), *the President may appoint.*

"So, for instance, should the language of the sentence be full and explicit when corporal punishment is to be inflicted, or when the convict is to be marked: as that, he receive —— lashes on his bare back, with a cat-o'-nine-tails, or that he be marked on the ——— hip with the letter D, one inch in length, in indelible ink. Corporal punishment.

"As soldiers are marked for desertion with the letter D, and also, at times, with the same letter for drunkenness, it is recommended that for the first named offence the mark be put on the *left* hip, and for the other on the right hip. This will enable any officer, afterward, should the convict be presented for notice, to determine the offence for which he is marked." Marking with letter.

Sec. 253. Where a statute provides for the punishment of an offence, the words of the law ought, as far as practicable, to be employed in framing the sentence. The judgment of a court martial is only final when approved by the reviewing authority, and, therefore, in sentencing an officer to be *cashiered*, it would be improper to add such words as, "*and he is hereby cashiered accordingly.*"* Words of law to be observed in sentence.

Sec. 254. The term of imprisonment, when not established by the sentence, is regarded as commencing from the day of its promulgation; but if an unusual time elapses between the approval and promulgation of the sentence it is counted as part of the punishment. Where solitary confinement, etc., is directed, the time named must be completed with the requisite conditions. Term of imprisonment.

Sec. 255. Recommendations to the clemency of the execu-

---

* De Hart.

Recommendation to mercy.

tive, or commanding general, are sometimes made by the court, in special cases. When this is done, it may be addressed on a separate sheet of paper, but never embodied in the sentence of the court. The better way is to write it at foot of the sentence, as it is thus in no danger of being lost or overlooked. A recommendation to mercy is not the *act of the court*, and hence may be made by any, even an individual member.

SEC. 256. Previous to the final adjournment of the court, they may modify or change the sentence agreed upon; but their whole proceedings must appear on the record. Hence the previous judgment should not be erased nor interlined, but the sentence should be written out and entered by the Judge Advocate anew, as last agreed upon.

Court may change sentence before adjournment.

CHAPTER VII.

OF THE FINAL PROCEEDINGS.

SEC. 257. We are now to consider the final proceedings upon the trial, and in doing so, will examine—

I. As to the *Revision;* which involves the confirmation or disapproval of the proceedings and sentence.

II. As to the *Execution of the Sentence.*

1. As to the Revision:

In the 65th Article of war it is declared that "no sentence of a general court martial shall be carried into execution until after the whole proceedings shall have been laid before the officer ordering the same, or the officer commanding the troops for the time being; neither shall any sentence of a general court martial, in the time of peace, extending to the loss of life, or the dismission of a commissioned officer, or which shall, either in time of peace or war, respect a general officer, be carried into execution, until after the whole proceedings shall have been transmitted to the Secretary of War, to be laid before the President for his confirmation or disapproval, and orders in the case." Revision.

SEC. 258. The proceedings of the court having been submitted to the reviewing authority, it is incumbent that a strict and careful examination of the whole record should at once be made. If they are found to be regular, he should proceed to approve and confirm, or to disapprove them, as may be determined. On the other hand, Proceedings to be carefully examined.

Proceedings may be returned to court. if mistake or error is discovered in the proceedings, the proper course is to return them to the court for reconsideration and correction. This power of remitting the proceedings of a court for reconsideration is based on the custom of the service, and is analogous to the practice of the civil courts in particular cases. The principal causes for which courts-martial are usually required to revise their proceedings are stated by Captain De Hart to be "where insufficient or undue weight has been given to testimony, which is supposed to arise from inadvertence, or misconception of the law or the custom of war; or where an exorbitant, inadequate, or illegal punishment has been awarded." But whatever be the occasion for which the reconsideration is ordered, the officer directing it should, in reconvening the court, point out the particular cause, or errors, which render it necessary.

SEC. 259. In reconsidering their proceedings, the court must *Duty of court in such cases.* take them as they stand, and cannot have recourse to additional evidence, or new facts of any description, nor recall the former witnesses; their whole duty is *to review the record;* nor can they in any manner obliterate or alter it, as a record. Additions, however, may be made to it, which plainly appear as such, by the court, for this, in part, is the object of its recommittal.

When the case is thus remanded for the reconsideration of the court, it is their duty to examine all the points to which their attention has been directed with the utmost care, patience, and deliberation, which of course would involve a reconsideration of their former opinion, findings, and sentence; these, however, as just observed, must never be erased, but the revised opinion and sentence are sent in as additions to the record.

SEC. 260. In this revision the court may "amend any defects resulting from its own decision not connected *What court may amend.* with questions involving the legality of their proceedings; but it can amend no illegality as to the constitution of the court, or defects in its composition; nor can any illegality in the charge be so remedied;" these latter deficiences must be fatal, and will entirely invalidate all the proceedings.

SEC. 261. If the court are satisfied that the objections taken to their action by the reviewing authority are well founded, they ought, of course, to make such corrections as the law and facts justify; but if of a different opinion, they have only to adhere to their previous decision. In either case, the record must be again returned to the reviewing officer, who is finally to dispose of the case by confirming or disapproving the proceedings, as may be deemed best.

SEC. 262. A distinction has been made between the terms "*approval*" and "confirmation," in this connection. "All such distinctions," observes De Hart, "can only be made by the law itself. Whenever there is a doubt as to the proper terms to be employed to express the decision of the reviewing officer, reference should be made to the statute, and such language or terms selected as are embodied therein; no other rule is safe. According to the language of the 65th Article of war, to *confirm* the proceedings, covers, by this term of approval, all the doings of the court included in the sentence; and to *disapprove* the same, equally rejects all."

_{Approval and confirmation what?}

_{Rule as to.}

"If there be errors in the proceedings which are not so grave as to conflict with the rights of the prisoner, or the demands of justice, such errors would be adverted to and modify the decision of the reviewing officer, but would not necessarily lead to an absolute disapproval of all that the court had done. And so, if the sentence should be too inadequate, or, on the contrary, too severe, the like discretion is left to the reviewing authority to animadvert upon the same, and, according to his opinions as to the wants of the service, either send back for revisal, mitigate, remit, or confirm the sentence.

* * * "Whenever either the first or second part of the

trial is defective, the reviewing authority may in remarking upon the same, either confirm or disapprove, according to the proprieties of the case, the whole proceedings.

SEC. 263. If the court upon revision has adhered to its first decision, the reviewing officer, notwithstanding his opinion that it is erroneous, rather than let the criminal go unpunished altogether, may prefer to confirm the proceedings, should that be legal, and if the sentence is excessive or unusual, may remit such portions of it as he sees best. And in the remission or mitigation of any sentence it is very proper to consider the provocation received by the convicted person.*

<small>Where court adheres to former decision, what done.</small>

SEC. 264. It will be seen that the power to review, for the purpose of confirming or disapproving the proceedings of a court, is, by the 65th Article, already quoted, vested in two distinct parties. 1st, as to certain cases, "in the officer ordering" the court; and 2d, in the President. If the sentence, *in time of peace*, extends to the loss of life, or the dismission of a commissioned officer, or either in time of peace or war respects a general officer, it cannot in any of these cases be executed until the whole proceedings have been transmitted to the Secretary of War, to be laid before the President. In such instances therefore, the officer ordering the court has no authority over the subject. But in those cases to which his authority extends he has power to *pardon* or *mitigate* any punishment; and even the excepted sentences (death and cashiering), which he may *in time of war* carry into effect by virtue of the 65th Article of war, he may suspend by authority of the 89th Article till the pleasure of the President is known—to whom he is required immediately to transmit such suspension, with copies of the proceedings of the court. This power to "pardon and miti-

<small>Power to review.</small>

<small>Duty of reviewing officer.</small>

---

* On the subject of *provocation*, see Wharton's C. L., 436.

gate" is also conferred by the last named Article on any colonel or commanding officer of a regiment or garrison where a regimental or garrison court martial shall be held.

SEC. 265. The duty of the reviewing officer is thus clearly pointed out and limited by law. He has power to *suspend* the execution of the sentence in specified cases; and to *mitigate* it, or pardon, in others. But he cannot, even with the consent of the convicted person, *alter* or *commute* any punishment. To commute a punishment is to exchange it for one of less severity, or to substitute for it one of a different kind. This the law has not authorized. To pardon means to absolve and acquit;* to mitigate is to abate or moderate in degree the same punishment. The language of the law is therefore explicit, and does not permit any change in the species or kind of punishment by the reviewing officer. There seems, therefore, to be no dispute as to the nature and extent of the authority conferred on the reviewing officers, or officer " ordering the court." His power is clearly limited to *pardon and mitigation of the sentence.* Beyond this, says De Hart, he cannot go; and any attempt to change the punishment in kind would be illegal.

SEC. 266. But is the other reviewing authority, the President, thus limited and controlled? Opposite opinions have been expressed and ably maintained on this question; and to give the reader a clearer view of the subject, the arguments on each side will here be substantially set forth. The President as the reviewing power.

In 1820, the United States Attorney-General, Mr. Wirt, gave the opinion that the "power of *pardoning the offence* does not include the power of changing the punishment; but the power to mitigate the punishment decreed by a court martial cannot be fairly understood in any Opinions on this subject —Mr. Wirt.

---

* Webster.

other sense than as meaning a power to substitute a milder punishment in place of that decreed by the court martial; in which sense it would justify the sentence which the President proposes to substitute* in the case under consideration. The only doubt which occurs to me as possible in regard to this construction is, whether the power of mitigating a punishment includes the power of *changing* its species; whether it means any other than *lessening the quantity*, preserving nevertheless the *species of the punishment*. But there is nothing in the force of the terms in which the power is given that ties us down to so narrow a construction. It is proper to state, however, that a different construction is practically given to this power in the War Department, for there the power of mitigation is not understood as giving the power to change the punishment."

Subsequently, Mr. Attorney-General Berrien said: "In those cases which by the Rules and Articles of war are required to be submitted to him [the President] (and the sentences of a general court martial in time of peace, and extending to the dismission of a commissioned officer are among them), the whole proceedings are required to be transmitted to the Secretary of War, to be laid before the President 'for his confirmation or disapproval, and *orders in the case.*' The terms indicate an unlimited discretion; and when it is considered that he is by the constitution the depository of the pardoning power (that this is coextensive with every species of punishment, except only in cases of impeachment, and perhaps, also, for contempts against either house of Congress), it cannot, I think, be doubted that he has authority to mitigate as well as to confirm or reject the sentence of a general court martial, in the exercise of the supervisory power committed to him by the act for establishing rules and articles for the government of the armies of the United States.

<small>Mr. Berrien.</small>

---

* "Service and restraint" for "death."

"It would be singular if in the cases which are entrusted to the supervision of a subordinate officer (see 89th Article of war) a power should be given him over the sentences of a court martial which is denied to the commander-in-chief over those cases which are referred to him."*

The other view of the case is given at some length by Captain De Hart, who, among other things, remarks: Captain De Hart. "There are two distinct species of punishment authorized by military laws which admit of no degrees of severity—1, death; 2, cashiering or dismission. These punishments are evidently different in kind, and are distinctly marked by the manner in which the law declares for what particular offences they shall be inflicted. It is argued therefore that such penalties admit of no mitigation, but must be executed or entirely remitted. * * * Mitigation, in its legal acceptation, means a less degree of the same species of punishment, and were not such the true meaning of the word as there used, it would vest in the hands of the reviewing authority a power to substitute any kind of punishment which, in his discretion, he might deem a mitigated one. If a prisoner were sentenced to death, could it be considered a legal mitigation of the punishment to order the infliction of any number of stripes? In every punishment admitting of degrees of intensity or severity, a mitigated form can be substituted; * * thus, confinement at hard labor for six months may be changed in time to two months, etc. In such cases the species and kind of punishment remain unchanged; and the severity of the sentence is mitigated in accordance with law. But where a sentence is passed which can admit of no alteration without changing its *character*, the only means to shield the criminal is to resort to the power of pardoning. * * * It has been said that the

---

* This seems to be a confusion of the argument. The point is: Does the power of the President authorize him to *change the species of punishment*, which it is conceded an officer cannot do, unless to "*mitigate*" means the same thing as to *commute?*

change of a sentence in the manner referred to is made by the President * * by virtue of his prerogative as chief magistrate of the nation. But this answer yields the entire question. The President is not, like the British sovereign, the fountain of power, and therefore possesses no power of the kind. All his official acts derive their authority from positive laws; and prerogative, or inherent right, or constructive authority, especially in the determination of questions of criminal justice, is not acknowledged, and would be adverse to the principles of our government. * * *

"In the arguments of the several Attorney-Generals the power of the President to mitigate a sentence, by substituting a lighter punishment of a different species, has been claimed as a matter of expediency or convenience, and not as the direct result of any legal or constitutional power. * * * But it must be observed that the defect of the laws does not cure itself; and while we must readily admit that such power, with certain limitations, would be rightly invested in the Executive, and thereby in all cases enable him to execute justice in mercy, still, as the authority has not been given, it cannot be exercised.

"Another objection against the exercise of such authority under existing laws is that it destroys, if conceded, the uniformity of a legal rule, and therefore the law is rendered capricious. It has never yet been maintained that an *officer* having the power to pardon or mitigate the sentence of a court martial could mitigate such sentence by substituting another punishment of a different species, but milder character." * * *

Result.
These views of Captain De Hart are considered sound and well sustained, however they may be opposed to a practice which has in some instances been sanctioned by high authority. Perhaps uniformity of opinion and practice on this subject will hardly be obtained until the question is put to rest by some more definite and positive provision of law than now exists.

SEC. 267. When the proceedings of the court have been disposed of by the proper reviewing authority, the whole matter is closed; and except in the cases of appeal from the decision of an inferior court, as authorized by the 35th Article of war, there is no ultimate or superior source to which application for further redress can be made—the action of the reviewing authority being final and conclusive. *Proceedings closed.*

SEC. 268. The officer who succeeds in command a general commanding an army, or colonel commanding a department, succeeds also to the same powers as his predecessor; his, therefore, is the duty, with its corresponding rights, of reviewing the proceedings of any court martial already ordered, and which may be returned to him. But if his predecessor has exercised the right of reviewal under the law, and has confirmed the sentence of the court, even though his action may have been erroneous, there is no further power of review, and all that the succeeding officer can do is to exercise, in a proper case, the power of pardon or of mitigating the sentence. *Succeeding officer.*

SEC. 269. It may not be amiss here to repeat that the record of every court martial is required by law to be finally deposited in the War Department, there to be carefully preserved.* *Record.*

SEC. 270. II. *Execution of the Sentence.*—The explanations of Captain De Hart on this subject are so clear and explicit, and at the same time so concise, that little change or abbreviation will be attempted. He remarks:

"When the sentence awarded is *corporal punishment*, the troops of the regiment or garrison are drawn up to receive the prisoner, usually in some retired spot, as the ditch of an outwork, to which place he is conducted by a guard or escort. Upon his arrival at the place of punishment, *Corporal punishment.*

---

* See 90th Article of war.

the adjutant or other staff officer reads the sentence of the
court, and its approval; the prisoner during the time occupied
in reading standing uncovered, and advanced a couple of paces
in front of the escort. He is then ordered to strip to the waist,
and is tied to a machine called a triangle, which is formed of
three legs connected by a bolt at the top and separated about
four feet at the bottom. A bar is fastened at a proper height
to two of the legs, against which the prisoner may lean his
breast, who is tied by the ankles to the legs of the machine,
and his hands secured above. Sometimes he is lashed to a gun-
wheel. The strokes with the cat-o'-nine-tails are delivered upon
the bare shoulders, by the drummer or trumpeter. The drum
or trumpet-major counts each lash, giving the executioner
sufficient time to pause between the strokes equal in duration
to three paces in slow time, which is marked by taps of the
drum or by the executioner encircling the cat around his
head. A medical officer is invariably required to attend, to
superintend the punishment. Should any appearances indicate
the propriety of suspending the infliction, the medical officer
reports to the senior officer on parade, who gives orders accordingly. It is well understood that to prolong the punishment
beyond the usual time would be highly improper, and subject
the officer who authorized or caused such to be done to
charges. All means used to cause greater pain to the sufferer
than what must necessarily follow the infliction by the usual
instrument of punishment are strictly forbidden, and therefore the preparation of the cats by steeping them in lime, or
washing them in salt and water during the punishment, would
not be countenanced. It is a well known principle that punishment is shorn of its efficacy by a resort to cruel and inhu-
man means, and the criminal in such cases is no longer viewed
by the bystanders as a malefactor, but is sympathized with as
an oppressed and wronged creature. During the infliction of
the punishment it is necessary that the drum-major should see

that the strands of the cat are not entangled, so as to produce too heavy a blow; they should be kept separated, and if necessary washed in water.

"The cat-o'-nine-tails, the usual instrument of flogging, is composed, as its name imports, of nine lashes of whip-cord, each knotted in three places, one knot being near the end; the lashes are sixteen to eighteen inches long, and fastened to a handle of wood of about a drumstick's length. Common whip-cord is the thickness allowed; a larger description would too much bruise and lacerate the flesh by its weight.

"It is a rule for the regulation of corporal punishment that no greater amount shall be inflicted than what the prisoner is able to undergo at one time. Should, therefore, any number of stripes less than what the sentence prescribes be more than could be given at any time in reference to the physical ability of the prisoner to bear, such number must be considered as remitted, and the punishment complete. * * *

SEC. 271. *Capital punishment.*—"When capital punishment is to be inflicted, great ceremony is made of special observance. When a criminal is put to death by shooting, the troops to witness the execution are formed on three sides of the square. The prisoner, escorted by a detachment, is brought on the ground. The provost marshal leads the procession, followed by the band or field music of the regiment to which the convict belongs, drums muffled, playing the dead march. The party detailed to fire, usually consisting of eight to twelve men, comes next, then four bearers with the coffin, and immediately after, the prisoner, attended by a chaplain; the escort closes the rear. The procession passes in front and along the three sides of the square, facing inward. On arriving at the flank of each regiment, the band of the regiment plays the dead march, and continues until its front is cleared. When the procession has reached the open space the music ceases; the prisoner is placed on the fatal spot where the coffin

[margin: Capital punishment.]

has been put down, and the charge, sentence, and order for the execution read aloud. The chaplain having engaged in prayer with the condemned, retires [as soon as this exercise is over]. The execution party forms at about six paces from the prisoner, and the word is given by the provost marshal. When the firing party forms, the escort moves by the right flank and takes position in rear of that party at ordered arms. Should the fire not prove instantaneously fatal, it is the duty of the provost marshal, or a file which has been reserved for such duty, to complete the sentence. The execution being over, the troops break into column by the right and move past the corpse in slow time.

"When death by hanging is to be inflicted, the troops are formed in square on the gallows as a centre. The prisoner, with the escort, having arrived at their respective places, the charge, sentence, and warrant are read aloud, and the executioner, under the direction of the provost marshal, performs his office. The troops march off the ground at common time; the provost marshal, with the escort, remaining until the body is taken down.

Hanging.

SEC. 272. *Degradation.*—"Soldiers sometimes for disgraceful conduct are discharged the service with ignominy. A sentence of this kind is executed as follows: The troops being assembled, the offender is brought forward in charge of a guard, when the offences of which he has been found guilty, together with the sentence and its approval, are read. The facings, etc., of his dress are stripped off, and he is then trumpeted or drummed out with the 'rogue's march,' through the barracks or quarters of the corps.

Degradation.

SEC. 273. *Imprisonment.*—"When a soldier is sentenced to close confinement in the cells, if sickness should require him to be removed to the hospital, he would upon recovery to health be returned to imprisonment for the remainder of his sentence; but his time in hospital must be

Imprisonment.

computed as part of his imprisonment. When in hospital he is deemed a prisoner.

"A commanding officer could not be justified in releasing prisoners under sentence, allowing them to do duty in presence of the enemy, or at other times, and afterward inflicting the punishment.

SEC. 274. "As there are no particular places provided for the imprisonment of soldiers by sentence of courts martial, it is never stated where the confinement shall be undergone, but is left to the commanding officer of the garrison wherever the prisoner may be (unless specially ordered to be removed to another station) to carry out the sentence by the means within his control. It consequently does not interfere with the right to change the place of imprisonment, should the regiment be removed, or other causes render it necessary. In such cases for ordinary close confinement, the time occupied in effecting the change of place would be counted in the sentence; but when solitary confinement with low diet is the sentence, the prescribed number of days according to the judgment of the court must be fulfilled. *Usual place of imprisonment.*

SEC. 275. "In the rigid execution of sentences awarded by military courts is the most effectual means of preventing offences. * * * In a system which should combine precision and certainty for the jurisprudence of the army, would the country find and secure the high interests of good order and economy; interests which while they would not stand in opposition to any personal rights or humane government, would be doubly appreciated by being associated and connected with all the lofty and enduring benefits which other nations have gained, or hope to acquire by a well regulated army." *Sentence ought to be rigidly enforced.*

Chapter VIII.

OF THE REDRESS OF WRONGS.

Sec. 276. We are now to examine the means provided for the redress of wrongs against officers and soldiers; and it will be convenient to do so, in regard—

I. To new or second trials; and

II. To the particular mode of redress furnished in the Articles of war.

New trial. There are certain cases in which it would be proper to order a new trial; and this is obviously one means of *redressing wrongs* in military as well as civil courts. Under what circumstances then may a new trial be had before a court martial?

Sec. 277. It is to be observed, in the first place, that a new **Not after acquittal.** trial can never be had where the prisoner has once been duly acquitted; for, says Blackstone, "there hath been yet no instance of granting a new trial, where the prisoner was acquitted upon the first."

"After an *acquittal* of the defendant," says Mr. Wharton,* "in an indictment for either a felony or misdemeanor, there can in general be no new trial, though the result be produced by error of law or misconception of fact." The few exceptions which have occurred to this rule are all, it is believed, confined to cases where *fraud* was practised in procuring the acquittal.

To justify a *new trial*, therefore, there must first have been a *conviction*† of the party by a court martial, where *any* judgment has been pronounced.

---

* Crim. Law, 982.   † See sec. 280.

Sec. 278. If the findings of the court were based upon irrelevant matter, or the testimony of incompetent witnesses, the reviewing authority may either confirm the proceedings, and exercise the power of pardon in a proper case, or he may award a new trial, as may be deemed best. Mr. Wirt claimed for the President of the United States the power to order a new trial under the 65th Article of war, requiring the proceedings to be submitted to him for his confirmation or disapproval, *and orders in the case;* "the last words (says Mr. Wirt) having no other just interpretation than the acknowledgment of such authority. In revising a sentence and ordering a new trial, the President is, however, to be governed by the same considerations which would determine a superior court of law in an appeal from the inferior civil courts."

When new trial may be granted.

Sec. 279. So, also, where the constitution of the court has been defective, or the court has assumed jurisdiction improperly, as their proceedings could not legally affect the accused, a new or second trial might very properly be ordered. "A judicial body, which is forbidden by law to entertain jurisdiction of certain offences, and of particular persons, cannot most assuredly by neglect and non-observance of the injunction restrain another tribunal in the exercise of its legal powers. Such a principle, if admitted, would lead to the grossest abuses, and weaken the securities against crime, and the foundations of criminal justice. The language of the fundamental law, both for this country and for England, is that 'no person shall be subject for the same offence to be twice put in jeopardy of life or limb.' And how can a person be put in jeopardy ('legal jeopardy') by the action of a court which has no power to enforce its mandate? An acquittal or conviction in law signifies a *legal* acquittal or conviction, and the judgment of a court having no power to try cannot declare such acquittal or conviction." * * * "It is not sufficient that

For defect in court.

the court which notices the charge or criminal beyond the pale of its jurisdiction should in itself be a legal court to place the prisoner beyond the possibility of another trial," for a court of inferior and inadequate jurisdiction may yet be a legal court; "but it must have full authority for its proceeding to insure such a consequence."*

SEC. 280. It was said above that to justify a new trial there must have been a *conviction* of the party accused; but this of course only refers to cases in which the court proceeds to judgment and sentence; for if in the instances adverted to, such as a want of jurisdiction, illegality in the constitution or composition of the court, or in the charges, the court should adjourn or be dissolved for any such defects, without findings and sentence, it is conceived the party would still be subject to a new or second trial. He could not, surely, interpose the Articles of war, and plead a former *trial,* for in a legal sense he had not been tried; nor could he allege that he had once been in *jeopardy,* for this could not arise till the trial was finished; nor, indeed, does this term mean anything more than acquittal or conviction, *and the judgment of the court thereon.*†

May be after conviction and judgment.

SEC. 281. The application for a new trial is not, as in cases at law, presented to the court, but must be made to the authority which convened the court, or to a superior source, for, says De Hart, "where a prisoner has been found guilty contrary to evidence, or upon irrelevant or improper testimony, a new trial may be granted as an act of mercy," and, it may be added, as an act of justice also.

How application for new trial is made.

SEC. 282. II. Of the particular mode of redress for wrongs provided in the Articles of war:

1. As to the wrongs of officers.
2. As to the wrongs of soldiers.

---

* De Hart, 208. † Judge Washington, 4 Wash. C. C. R., 402.

The 34th Article of war provides that "if any officer shall think himself wronged by his colonel, or the commanding officer of the regiment, and shall, upon due application being made to him, be refused redress, he may complain to the general commanding in the state or territory where such regiment shall be stationed, in order to obtain justice; who is hereby required to examine into said complaint, and take proper measures for redressing the wrong complained of, and transmit, as soon as possible, to the Department of War a true state of such complaint, with the proceedings had thereon."

34th Article of war.

As to officers.

The remedy here pointed out is exceedingly simple and easy. It will be observed that it applies to inferior officers, who, upon feeling themselves aggrieved, may complain first to the colonel or commanding officer of the regiment. This complaint should be in writing, and couched in brief, pertinent, and respectful terms, setting forth the particulars of the grievance, and asking for its redress. If this application be either refused or improperly neglected, the party will then be justified in appealing in the same manner to the commanding general referred to in the Article. This appeal must, however, be made through the regular channel, that is, the commanding officer of the regiment, who is thus furnished the opportunity for a review of his former course or decision, or of making any necessary explanation on the subject in forwarding the complaint to the general. It should be recollected, too, that the second complaint must be the same, or substantially the same, as the first.

Sec. 283. Although, as has been elsewhere remarked, the general commanding is required by the Article to take proper measures for redressing the wrong, and to transmit the complaint, with the procedings thereon, to the War Department, so that he cannot arbitrarily dismiss it without consideration, still, as De Hart observes, "if the charge laid should be incapable of proof, or the grievances

Duty of general commanding.

stated not amount to a crime or offence, at least of military cognizance, it cannot be supposed it was intended to trouble the department with the report," and "this conclusion," he adds, "is the more truthful, inasmuch as the complainant is not thereby debarred of either the right or means of preferring his complaint again to the highest authority."

SEC. 284. The 35th Article further declares that "if any

35th Article of war. inferior officer or soldier shall think himself wronged by his captain or other officer, he is to complain thereof to the commanding officer of the regiment, who is

Wrongs of inferior officers and soldiers. hereby required to summon a regimental court martial for the doing justice to the complainant; from which regimental court martial either party may, if he think himself still aggrieved, appeal to a general court mar-

Court summoned. tial. But if, upon a second hearing, the appeal shall appear *vexatious and groundless*, the person so appealing shall be punished at the discretion of said court martial."

Commenting upon this Article, Captain De Hart remarks that it was originally adopted from the British Articles of war in 1776, and subsequently, in 1806, was varied in its terms by the omission of the words, "commanding the troop or company to which he belongs;" but this he regards as not varying the import or intent of the Article in the smallest degree. He

Object of the court. then proceeds, in another place: "The regimental court martial here referred to is solely for the purpose of doing justice to the complainant, and punishment forms no part of its office, inasmuch as a court of this description is not of adequate powers or jurisdiction to sit in judgment upon, or try a commissioned officer, being limited in this respect by the 67th Article of war. Nor is it," he continues, "a court of inquiry, with powers such as are contemplated by the 90th Article of war; and this because courts of inquiry can only be ordered by the President, or by the commanding officer duly authorized to appoint courts of inquiry when demanded by the accused. But the regimental court martial, now under consideration, is a body organized for special purposes, and therefore much restricted in the range or scope of its powers, and confined in its investigations to a particular species of wrong.

"These wrongs must arise out of the relative connection of the *commanding officer* of a troop or company and a soldier belonging to it. They relate principally, if not entirely, to matters of allowances, and have reference to clothing, pay, messing, repairs, and all things belonging to what is understood as the interior economy of a company; that is, they have reference to matters of account between the captain or commander of the company and the soldier. This is the description of the wrongs contemplated by the Article, and therefore accusations by a complainant, impugning the character of an officer, would be foreign to the view of the article, or injuries growing out of the acts of other persons, not so related (that is, commanding officer of a company and soldier belonging to it), could not be considered by this regimental court martial, but would necessarily be prosecuted by the usual means afforded for the administration of justice to the army. * * *

Nature of wrongs to be redressed.

"The words of the Article, *inferior officer or soldier*, include all persons belonging to the troop or company under the rank of commissioned officer, and them only; and the words (after the word captain) 'or other officer,' signify or other officer commanding the troop or company. * * *

"The wrongs to be redressed must be of such a nature as grows out of the relative connection of the officer commanding the company with the soldier belonging to it, and have reference to some right of the latter improperly restrained, or some abuse committed by the captain or other officer, or by him permitted to another; and *military* offences of which the laws and customs of the service take cognizance would not be

12

a legitimate subject for inquiry by such court for 'doing justice to the complainant.' Such matters must be referred to a superior officer, so that the proper court may be convened for the trial and punishment of the accused."

SEC. 285. 2. *The wrongs of soldiers.*—The 35th Article, it will be observed, applies to *soldiers* as well as inferior officers. And the same limitations as to the particular description of wrongs to be redressed are to be regarded in both cases. The court is to inquire into wrongs inflicted by or suffered from the captain or other officer commanding the troop or company to which the soldier belongs, and none others. The complaint should be addressed to the captain or officer commanding the company, and if redress is denied, or unreasonably neglected, it may then be submitted (through the captain, however, for reasons already explained,) to the commanding officer of the regiment, whose duty it is immediately to summon a regimental court to examine the complaint, and do justice to the complainant.

<small>Soldiers.</small>

If the decision of the court is adverse to the officer against whom the complaint is lodged, justice must at once be done the complainant, and it is the duty of the commanding officer of the regiment to enforce the decision of the court.

SEC. 286. *Appeals.*—The Article of war, it will be remembered, provides that if either party is dissatisfied with the decision of the court an appeal may be made to a general court martial; this privilege, therefore, extends to soldiers as well as officers. But should the officer complained of refuse obedience to the inferior court, and yet fail or decline to appeal from its decision, obedience may be enforced by the authority, as just stated, of the commanding officer, or on failure of that, by the ordinary procedure before a higher court, in which charges against the offending party may be regularly preferred.

<small>Appeals.</small>

SEC. 287. *Either party may appeal*, but if, upon a second

hearing, their appeal appears to the court to have been "*vexatious* and *groundless,*" the appellant is to be punished at the discretion of the court. This discretion to punish, however, must be "tenderly" and cautiously employed, and "only where there is no probable cause for the appeal." Either party may appeal.

This is the only case, observes De Hart, in which an appeal from the decision of a military court can be made. The law thus has evinced, he adds, "a particular consideration and jealousy for the rights and satisfaction of inferior officers and soldiers, and has made an exception to the ordinary course of military trials, which distinguishes it in a very marked manner. It not only authorizes, to some extent, a review of the proceedings in the first instance, but secures the advantages of a new trial, independent of any previous examination, and therefore puts the party in a situation to cure all the inconveniences, errors, and deficiencies of testimony which have marked the progress of the first complaint, and rendered, very probably, an appeal necessary."

SEC. 288. The mode of proceeding before the regimental court is described by the same author, substantially as follows:

Mode of proceeding before a regimental court.

The court and parties being duly assembled, the order convening the court is read, and the complainant and defendant are asked if they have any objections to any member of the court. These questions, and the replies, are noted on the record. The court is then sworn. The complainant first states his case, and proceeds with his proofs. The defendant is next heard, and his witnesses. Neither party can be sworn; but no witness is examined except under oath. When the parties and their evidence have been heard the court is closed for deliberation, and its opinion, when given, is duly recorded.

SEC. 289. When an appeal is taken from the decision of

Appeal from the court proceedings on. this court, as permitted by the Article of war, the proceeding is in effect a new trial; and hence nothing that has transpired in the regimental court is to be taken as evidence in the superior court; therefore the former record cannot be read, but the witnesses must be examined anew, and the entire proceedings conducted without regard to anything that has occurred on the former trial. No one appears as prisoner in either court.

De Hart explains the mode of proceeding in cases of appeal in the following terms: "The court having assembled, and the appellant and respondent being present, the order for the court is read. Both parties have the right of challenging, and the Judge Advocate puts the usual question on this point, first to the appellant, and afterward to the respondent, minuting such, and the respective answers on the proceedings. The members and the Judge Advocate are duly sworn. The statement of alleged wrongs by the appellant is read and recorded, and that party first addresses the court, and lays what he considers his wrongs before it, and exhibits whatever proof he may possess in support of his declarations. The appellant must not in any case be sworn. The witnesses who are called by either party give evidence on oath. When the appellant's case is fully before the court, the respondent is allowed to reply to it, by offering such evidence as he thinks necessary, but the respondent himself should not be sworn, unless required to be so by the appellant, or when the court deem it necessary that he may depose the *facts*. The subject having been thus developed, the court deliberates on the evidence, and gives its opinion thereon.

SEC. 290. "This opinion consists in the simple declaration *Opinion of court on appeal.* that the appellant either has substantiated, or failed to substantiate the grievances complained of.

"And should the court be further of opinion that the appeal is vexatious and groundless, such fact would be stated, and the court would then proceed to pass such judgment upon the appellant as the circumstances of the trial would warrant."

Sec. 291. In concluding this subject, we have only to remark that no complaints are contemplated by the Articles of war but such as immediately concern the parties themselves. A complaint by way of information, therefore, cannot be considered and noticed in this manner. All complaints or applications for redress under these Articles must moreover be presented singly, that is, by the individual, and must not be joined together either for effect or convenience, the design of the law being to afford a speedy and convenient remedy for particular wrongs as they severally occur, and in no sense to encourage *combinations* for the injury or annoyance of particular parties.

<small>Redress only at instance of parties wronged.</small>

CHAPTER IX.

OF EVIDENCE.

SEC. 292. The law of evidence, as applied in military trials, will form the next and last subject of our inquiries. It will be impossible to do more than present a summary of the leading rules and principles on this interesting topic, and we must therefore refer the reader, for all that may be required beyond these, to the various works on this branch of the law, which are generally accessible to all.

SEC. 293. It is well to observe in the outset that as courts martial are constituted both judge and jury, they are, of course, to determine questions of law and fact; hence *pleadings*, designed to separate these subjects and disputed from admitted facts in the ordinary tribunals, are not resorted to in military courts, and we shall have no occasion to advert to various qualifications and distinctions of the law in this connection, which might otherwise be deemed important. For example, on an indictment for larceny, *what* particular facts constitute a felonious asportation is a question of law, while the province of the jury only is to determine whether the particular facts charged have been proved. But in a trial before a court martial, for theft or murder, for instance, there is no necessity for a formal sifting and separate decision of the issue. The simple question is one of guilt or innocence, to be decided by the same tribunal, who are judges of the facts to be proved, and also, under the laws, of the legal consequences of such proof.

[margin note: Court to judge law and fact.]

It will be convenient to examine the subject now before us, under three divisions, as follows:
I. Evidence in general.
II. Direct and positive evidence.
III. Circumstantial evidence.

SEC. 294. I. *Of evidence in general.*—Evidence is defined by Mr. Starkie to be that which is legally submitted to a jury, to enable them to decide upon the questions in dispute or issue, as distinguished from all comment or argument. Evidence defined.

SEC. 295. There are degrees of evidence, from that which merely produces doubt, to that which satisfies the mind of the existence or truth of a fact in dispute. But even the most direct and positive evidence can produce nothing more than a high degree of probability, such as may amount to moral certainty. From the highest degree, it may decline to a mere preponderance of assent to a particular fact. This distinction between full proof and mere proponderance of evidence is important. It is essential to all convictions that guilt should be fully established, and no weight of preponderant evidence is sufficient, unless it generate full belief, to the exclusion of reasonable doubt.* Degrees of.

SEC. 296. There is, therefore, a manifest distinction between *evidence* and *proof;* the former being the particular means or mode by which the latter is secured. A fact is said to be *proved* by *evidence* which induces no doubt of the existence of such fact. Hence, no proof of any fact can be made or attempted except by means of the established rules of evidence. Distinction between evidence and proof.

SEC. 297. The most general division of evidence is into *parol and written.* *Parol evidence* includes all which is unwritten or oral; and thus the testimony of witnesses is embraced in this term. General division into parol and written.

---

* Starkie on Evidence, vol. I, 449.

Written evidence includes, as the phrase imports, all records, letters, orders, documents, and printed matter.

In one or the other of these forms must all evidence be submitted to a court martial. And since personal knowledge can rarely be referred to, as warranting a conclusion upon any past transaction, even in the breast of a single judge, the decision of the court must be based upon information as to facts and circumstances communicated by others, or derived from written documents. By facts and circumstances are meant all things and relations, whether natural or artificial, which really exist, whether their existence be perceptible by the senses or otherwise.*

SEC. 298. Upon this subject Mr. Starkie remarks: The great and general rule seems to be this, that all facts and circumstances upon which any reasonable presumption or inference can be founded as to the truth or falsity of the disputed fact or issue are admissible in evidence; it being assumed that they can be substantiated by legal and competent means. But this rule, he adds, is subject to some exceptions founded on considerations of policy. The rule itself depends chiefly on two considerations:

<small>General rule as to what is admissible.</small>

1st. That where direct evidence can be obtained, it is essential to the purposes of justice that such evidence should be open to contradiction and confirmation from collateral circumstances; and

2d. The frequent necessity of depending wholly upon presumptions, and proofs from collateral circumstances.†

The facts and circumstances then, bearing upon any transaction having reference to the issue to be tried, are to be communicated to the mind of the court—and this is to be done, if practicable, by means of direct and positive testimony, which leads us to the second branch of our inquiries on this subject.

---

*1 Starkie, 15. †1 Starkie, 17.

Sec. 299. II. *Direct and positive evidence.*—Evidence is said to be direct and positive, when the facts in dispute are communicated by those who, by means of their senses, have actual knowledge of what they testify. *(Direct and positive evidence.)* It is thus distinguished from that which is *presumptive*, or which is presumed or inferred from certain facts and circumstances already known and admitted. "In strictness," says Mr. Starkie,* "all evidence is presumptive, as a jury seldom have actual knowledge of a fact by means of their own senses, but infer its existence from their reliance on the information and veracity of others, and must therefore always act upon presumptions more or less forcible; but in common acceptation, direct and positive evidence is communicated by one who has had actual knowledge of the fact; and presumptive evidence is any which is not direct and positive."

Sec. 300. But direct evidence may be either written or oral. Let us then inquire how it may be obtained, and the means by which it is communicated. *(May be written or oral.)*

1. The first, and most obvious way of communicating evidence, is by oral testimony, or the mouth of witnesses. And here a rule of great importance must be noticed, viz: that which excludes all *hearsay* testimony. *Hearsay is not evidence*, as a general rule. By the term hearsay, is *(Hearsay not evidence.)* to be understood evidence which does not derive its value solely from the credit of the witness himself, but rests in part on the credit and veracity of a third party. Such evidence is inadmissible to establish any fact susceptible of proof by witnesses speaking of their own knowledge. Its incompetency to satisfy the mind, as well as the frauds which may be practised under its cover, combine to support the rule which excludes it from judicial tribunals.† Hearsay evidence is moreover delivered, without the required sanction of an oath in the pres-

---

* Vol. I, 19.   † Ch. J. Marshall, 7 Cranch, 290, et. seq.

ence of the accused, and passing as it usually does through several channels of communication, is liable to much abuse and misunderstanding.

SEC. 301. The rule which excludes it, however, has some qualifications. Thus, declarations *in extremis*, or of a *dying* person, may be received as evidence in cases of homicide. But they must have been made under a sense of impending dissolution, which must appear to the satisfaction of the court.* And it is the privilege of the party against whom such declarations are adduced to enter into the circumstances of the deceased in his last moments, and thus to show that they were not of such a character as to lead to the conclusion that he was properly impressed with a religious sense of his approaching dissolution. Much more would this be the case if the declarations were accompanied with expressions of malice or ill-will to the accused, as the very basis on which their admission depends is the regard for truth, and the absence of all feelings of malevolence or uncharitableness, which the law infers on such occasions, not, however, to the exclusion of evidence to the contrary.

<small>Exceptions to rule as to hearsay.</small>

<small>Dying declarations.</small>

SEC. 302. The party whose declarations *in extremis* would be received by a court, must, it should be observed, be one whose evidence, were he alive, would be admitted. Hence, the dying declarations of a *convict* would not, while those of a mere accomplice would be, admissible in evidence.

Nothing, however, can be evidence in a declaration *in articulo mortis* that would not be so if the party were sworn.† The whole statement must be taken, or none, and the mere opinion of the party should be rejected.‡ If possible, the precise words should be recited.

SEC. 303. Where a witness has been examined on a former

---

* Wharton's C. L., 308.   † Wharton's C. L., 311.   ‡ Ibid, 312.

trial, and has since died, what he said at the first trial <small>Deceased witness.</small> may be proved at the second. And so, if the witness is alive, and has been kept away by the fraud or contrivance of the accused, his former evidence may be used on the trial.

Sec. 304. Where a party is tried for *mutiny, riots*, etc., what was said by any of the rioters or mutineers may be proved as going to show the design and intention of <small>Declarations of rioters, etc.</small> the party.

Sec. 305. We return now to the subject of oral testimony, or that derived from witnesses:

We have in a former place spoken of the manner in which the attendance of witnesses, military persons, is procured at a court martial. There is no way of compelling the attendance of one not belonging to the service, though we have <small>Witnesses' expenses.</small> shown how his deposition may be taken. The army regulations also provide for the payment of the expenses of any witness not belonging to the army, by a *per diem* allowance, as is done in the civil courts.

Sec. 306. The testimony of witnesses is delivered *viva voce* before the court under certain rules and restrictions, the principal of which it will here be necessary to <small>Viva voce.</small> notice. All testimony is received under the sanction of an oath, and hence all witnesses must be sworn in the manner required by the Articles of war, as already pointed out.

Sec. 307. In general any one may be examined as a witness who has understanding and memory, and who is capable of being bound by an oath. But there are <small>Who may be witness.</small> circumstances which disqualify a person as a witness altogether, and these are: 1st. *The want of religious belief,* <small>Disqualifications.</small> as in the case of young children, lunatics, idiots and atheists,* and some others.

Sec. 308. A lunatic may be admitted to testify in his lucid

---

* 2 Starkie, 392.

Lunatics and others. intervals; but as an idiot is always *non compos*, his evidence, of course, cannot be received. Intoxication is obviously, for the time being, a ground of disqualification. The ground on which children, as such, are rejected, is their general inability to appreciate the obligations of an oath. There can, therefore, be no settled age at which they can testify; but their competency must depend upon the degree of knowledge and understanding which, upon examination by the court, they are proved to possess.*

Even a person born deaf and dumb, *if he has understanding*, may be examined by a sworn interpreter, who is able to convey his replies by means of signs and motions. The obligation and nature of the oath should be explained to the witness by the interpreter, so as to ascertain if he understands and accepts it.† Or should the witness be able to read and write, as in some instances, the whole process may be conducted by the Judge Advocate by such means.

SEC. 309. Incompetency may also arise in the witness from *Want of religious belief.* *want of religious belief, where there is no defect of understanding.* Persons, therefore, who avow a disbelief in God, and a future state of rewards and punishments, cannot be competent witnesses, inasmuch as they repudiate the only obligation which the law can impose on the conscience of men.

SEC. 310. The proper time for showing the religious opinions of a witness is before he is sworn. The ordinary *How and when to show this.* mode of proving his religious views is to produce evidence of his declarations to others. *The weight of opinion now is that the witness himself cannot be questioned or examined on this subject.*‡ Sometimes the witness has been questioned on the *voir dire* as to his religious belief; but, said W. Serjeant Talfourd,§ "it may be doubted whether a witness

---

* 2 Starkie, 392.   ‡ Wharton's C. L., 369.
† Wharton C. L., 352.   § As quoted in Wharton, 370.

would not be justified in insisting, when so questioned, on the simple answer that he considers the oath administered in the usual form binding on his own conscience, and in declining to answer further, for a confession, thus forced from him, of a disbelief in a state of retribution, would certainly be esteemed as disgraceful in a court of justice, and there seems no reason why a person should thus be taxed, perhaps to his own infinite prejudice, merely because he appears to perform a public duty in obedience to a subpœna. At all events, it is quite clear that a witness may properly refuse to answer any questions which go beyond an inquiry into his belief in a superior Being to whom man is answerable, and that it is the duty of counsel to refuse, however urged, to put such questions, which are altogether impertinent and vexatious."

SEC. 311. The second cause of disqualification in a witness which may be named is *infamy of character.* Persons convicted of crime are called infamous. The crime or offence must be one which is inconsistent with the principles of common honesty.* The usual enumeration of these disqualifying crimes is, treason, felony, and all offences of fraud embraced in the general idea of the *crimen falsi,* such as perjury, piracy, forgery, swindling, etc.† Says Mr. Wharton :‡ " The extent and meaning of the term *' crimen falsi,'* is nowhere laid down with precision; but from an examination of the different decisions it may be deduced that the *crimen falsi* of the common law not only involves the charge of falsehood, but also is one which may injuriously affect the administration of justice by the introduction of falsehood and fraud."

Infamy of character.

SEC. 312. A conviction without judgment does not produce disability. And the judgment must be in a court of competent jurisdiction. Whether a foreign judgment has the effect of disqualifying a witness is yet doubt-

Conviction and judgment.

---

* 2 Starkie, 714. † Ibid, 715. ‡ Crim. Law, 354.

ful. The affirmative of the proposition has been maintained by Judge Story* and Mr. Greenleaf.† This, indeed, would seem to be the better opinion, though the contrary has been held by very able jurists. It may be observed, however, in support of the affirmative position, that formerly the *punishment* pronounced for the crime was the test of disqualification, and this would, of course, vary in different countries. But in modern times the offence or crime itself is alone regarded. *Moral turpitude*, therefore, is now the essence of the objection, and it is difficult to see, on this ground, any just reason for the distinction between foreign and other judgments which has been attempted.

"*Desertion*, though a high crime, is not deemed such an offence as renders the one who has committed it incompetent. It may, however, be considered as affecting the credibility of the witness upon proof of conviction."‡

A witness incompetent for infamy, it is said may have his affidavit read, to defend himself against such complaint, but for no other purpose.§

SEC. 313. But incompetency from infamy may be removed, and competency restored in three ways: 1st, by pardon; 2d, by proof that the party has undergone the penalty of the law, and suffered the punishment denounced against his crime; 3d, by proof of the reversal of the judgment.‖

Incompetency, how removed.

1. A pardon granted after the sentence of the court has been complied with, e. g., the fine paid, or imprisonment expired, purges the disability, and restores competency. It must, however, correctly recite the offence, and a misrecital will render it inoperative. But where disability is attached to the conviction of a crime by express pro-

Pardon.

---

* Story's Con. of Laws, 91, 93, etc.
† 1 Greenleaf Ev., Sect. 376, and see 2 Starkie, 716, note 3.
‡ De Hart, 393.   § 2 Starkie, 722.   ‖ Ibid, 716.

visions of the law, the pardon, it is thought, cannot restore the competency of the offender, the words of the act, in such cases, being held to control the prerogative of the government.*

If conditions are annexed to the pardon, they must of course be complied with, or it will be inoperative. A promise in the pardon excepting legal disabilities is repugnant, and therefore void.

2. When the party has *suffered the punishment* awarded, he is in general restored to competency by this fact. But perjury is said to be an exception to this rule. Penalty suffered.

3. *Reversal of the judgment.*—This will restore the competency of the witness by removing the cause of disability. Such reversal must be proved by the production of the record.† Reversal of judgment.

SEC. 314. The third ground of incompetency to be noticed is that arising from *interest*.

Private interests can rarely interfere to the exclusion of witnesses in ordinary criminal prosecutions, much less are they likely to do so in military trials. But even here there are cases where parties are properly excluded on the ground of interest. Interest.

Mere *bias* is not sufficient to disqualify; neither is interest in a *similar* suit or question. The general rule is that the interest to disqualify must be some legal, certain, and immediate interest, however minute, in the *result* of the cause, or in the record as an instrument of evidence, acquired without fraud.‡

Expectation of benefit does not of itself disqualify. Thus, an informer is a competent witness, though he received part of the penalty; and even where one is entitled to a reward, on the conviction of the defendant, he is yet competent to testify. These may be regarded as exceptions to the rule, but they are

---

* Wharton's C. L., 357. † 2 Starkie Ev., 722. ‡ 2 Starkie, 744.

established on grounds of necessity and policy.* So, on the same grounds, the prosecutor, and a party whose signature has been forged may both be examined, unless in cases where they are so directly and positively interested in the event as to over-balance the policy of the rule admitting them, of which the court are to judge.

SEC. 315. An accomplice is a competent witness, though his expectation of pardon depend on the conviction of the accused. If separately indicted, he may be examined in favor of the defendant.† Where several are joined in one indictment, the court may order the acquittal of one or more against whom no evidence, or insufficient evidence has been adduced, and they may be examined as witnesses against the remainder. But before any such examination could be had in a court martial, the proceedings in the cases of such as are acquitted would require approval, and hence an adjournment of the court would be requisite, until such time as would be necessary for the confirmation. If the testimony of one involved in the same charge is requisite for the defence of the prisoner, he ought as soon as practicable to apply for a separate trial, to the authority ordering the court martial; and if not attended to, his application may be renewed to the court.‡

Accomplice.

SEC. 316. Although a conviction on the testimony of an accomplice or *particeps criminis* is legal, yet it is usual, and perhaps better, generally, to acquit the accused in cases where such testimony is uncorroborated. This is, however, a question to be determined by circumstances. The witness being competent, the court are to decide as to his credibility. But his testimony is to be regarded with much caution, and juries in criminal prosecutions have been advised by the judge that it was "dangerous" to convict on the unsupported evidence of an accomplice in guilt.§ Con-

Weight of evidence of an accomplice.

---

* Wharton's C. L., 364.   ‡ De Hart, 395.
† Ibid 367, 368.   § Wharton, C. L., 367.

firmation, however, is not required, and cannot be expected in every particular of the testimony.

SEC. 317. A party who is *bail* for the accused, is incapacitated; but his capacity may be restored by substituting new bail. So, also, a pecuniary interest may be removed by a release to the witness. Bail.
Release.

SEC. 318. Although a *particeps criminis*, who has testified fully and impartially, cannot demand his own pardon, yet the practice is to grant it. It has, indeed, been decided that if an accomplice be admitted to testify, and has done so in good faith, the government is bound in honor to discharge him.* Accomplice testifying to be discharged.

SEC. 319. *Husband and Wife.*—The relation of husband and wife is another cause of incompetency. The disability in these parties to testify either for or against each other results from the joint consideration of their identity of interests, and the policy of the law in its desire to prevent domestic dissension, and to preserve inviolate the confidence of so sacred a relation. Where husband and wife are admissible against, they are also admissible for each other. But the general rule is that they cannot appear as witnesses either for or against each other. And this rule is so rigid that it is incompetent to examine a party divorced *a vinculo* as to anything that transpired *during the coverture.* There are, however, some few exceptions to the rule, grounded in necessity: thus, the dying declarations of a wife murdered by the husband would be admissible, and so may a wife be examined on an indictment of her husband, for actual violence to her person, or in cases affecting her personal liberty and security. Ground of exclusion.

Exceptions.

SEC. 320. The law includes in this disability only such as are legally bound as husband and wife; therefore, a marriage by force, or a second marriage during the Who included as.

---

* Wharton, C. L., 368.

life of either party to the first, would not disqualify. To give it such an effect the marriage must have been legal.

But it is unnecessary to enlarge on this subject, as questions of this character are not likely to arise before military tribunals.

SEC. 321. *Counsel and Client.*—This is another relation from which incapacity to testify, or rather exemption from any obligation to do so results. Hence, cases of this sort are styled cases of *privilege.* An attorney being bound to keep the secrets of his client, cannot be examined against him. This privilege, however, does not extend to matters within his own knowledge before he has been addressed in his professional character. But when an attorney is consulted on business professionally, the communications between himself and his client are wholly confidential, and he should not be required to divulge them. The rule relates only to professional intercourse, and therefore does not embrace information derived from other sources. But it covers all information obtained from the client, whether verbal, or from books and papers exhibited by him.*

Counsel and client.

This immunity does not extend to any agent, steward, or servant. Neither are communications made to clergymen or medical men considered privileged.† But officers of the Executive Departments cannot be compelled to disclose information which, in their judgment, would be prejudicial, if divulged, to the public interests. Nor will the court compel the disclosure of facts, from any source, when such disclosures would be detrimental to the public interests.‡

SEC. 322. *Credibility of witnesses.*—A witness may be competent to testify, and yet there may be circumstances affecting his credit before the court, so as not to entitle his statement to belief. When such is the case, his credit may

Credibility of witness.

---

* Wharton's C. L., 361. † Ibid, 362.
‡ Wharton's C. L., 363. See, also, 1 Greenleaf Ev., sec. 250.

be attacked or impeached by adducing evidence affecting his character for veracity; but this examination must be confined to his general reputation for truth and veracity. Particular parts of a man's character or conduct cannot be inquired into.*

How attacked.

The questions generally allowed to be put on such occasions are: "Do you know the general character of the witness? and if you do, what is it for truth and veracity?" "Would you believe him on his oath?" But it is inadmissible to attempt to show the estimation in which the witness is held in his particular neighborhood, or to prove that he is a person of infamous character.

On the cross-examination of the attacking witness the inquiry must be confined to his opportunity for knowing the character of the witness impeached, the sources of such knowledge, and the length of time, and how generally such unfavorable reports against him have prevailed.†

Cross-examination.

SEC. 323. But the credit of a witness may be impeached, in the second place, by contradicting him, that is, by showing that out of court he has made statements contrary to his testimony at the trial. This contradiction of a witness, however, must be limited to such matters as are relevant to the issue; but if he *voluntarily*, that is, without being questioned, swears falsely to irrelevant subjects, it is held he may be impeached as to these also. The witness can in no case be admitted, when impeached, to corroborate his statements made at the trial with proofs of declarations made by him elsewhere.‡

Witness may be contradicted.

SEC. 324. Before concluding our remarks on the subject of oral testimony, it will be proper briefly to refer to some of the rules which regulate the examination of witnesses.

---

* Wharton's C. L., 377.   † Ibid, 377.   ‡ Ibid, 378, 379.

Examination of witnesses.—In general, an objection to the competency of witnesses ought to be taken before the examination-in-chief, otherwise an unfair advantage would be obtained by the objecting party, if he were permitted to hear the testimony of a witness, and then avoid it by raising objections where it proved to be adverse. But where the incompetency arises from *interest*, the objection may be taken after the examination-in-chief, if it appear, in the course of the trial, that the witness is interested ;* but not if the objection was known before.

<small>Objections to competency, when to make.</small>

SEC. 325. *Leading questions*, by which are to be understood questions which suggest to the witness the answers to be made, are not in general to be asked. But where the matter about which the witness is examined is merely introductory of that which is material, it is often desirable to lead his mind directly to the subject ; and where the witness is examined as to material facts, it is in general necessary to some extent, to lead his mind to the subject of inquiry. Questions to which the answer *yes* or *no* would be conclusive are inadmissible; and so, also, are questions that suggest the desired answer.†

The court must decide as to the propriety of questions which may be objected to; and will allow leading questions on the examination-in-chief, either where from the nature of the case the witness cannot be directed to the subject of inquiry except by a particular specification of it, or where any attempt is manifest in the witness to conceal the truth.‡ So, if the witness shows that he is decidedly adverse in his feelings to the party calling him, the court may allow leading questions to be put to him. But in general the rule which excludes the use of such questions should be adhered to.

The witness should state only what he knows of his own

---

* 2 Starkie, 121.   † 1 Starkie, 124.   ‡ Ibid, 126.

personal knowledge of the facts he relates; his persuasion or belief are not proper subjects of inquiry, unless such belief is based on facts within his actual knowledge, or relates, as in examinations of professional men, to matters of skill and judgment, where from the nature of things the evidence cannot extend beyond opinion and belief.* *Personal knowledge of facts.*

Sec. 326. *Cross-examination.*— Upon a cross-examination leading questions may be put, but they must not *assume* facts which have not been proved, or anything else contrary to the facts which are proved. *Cross-examination.*

The object of the cross-examination is to elicit the truth as to the evidence of the witness; hence irrelevant questions are not allowed; nor can a cross-examination be made as to any distinct collateral fact, for the purpose of impeaching the witness by contradicting him.† Though the witness has not been examined in chief, yet if he has been sworn, he is subject to be cross-examined by the opposite party.‡

Sec. 327. The mode of examination is generally regulated by the court, according to the capacity and disposition of the witness, and an adverse witness is sometimes allowed to be cross-examined by the party who calls him, where circumstances render it necessary and proper. *Court to regulate examination.*

Sec. 328. After the cross-examination, a *re-examination* is allowed, to explain any facts or circumstances developed on the cross-examination. The re-examination must therefore be confined to the subject matter of the cross-examination;§ and being wholly an explanatory process, no new matter can properly be introduced thereby. *Re-examination.*

Sec. 329. A witness cannot refuse to answer questions which subject him merely to civil liabilities or charges; but it is clear that he is not bound to answer any question if his answer will expose him to any penal *What questions witness may refuse to answer.*

---

* 1 Starkie, 127.   † Ibid, 134.   ‡ Ibid, 131.   § De Hart, 409.

liability or criminal punishment, for no man is required to criminate himself;* neither is he bound to answer any question which would render him infamous or disgrace him,† or which would impeach his conduct as a public officer.‡ The witness is himself to be the judge whether he can safely reply to questions propounded to him, but must always state under oath that his answer would criminate or accuse him, before he can be exempted by the court.§ But if a witness replies to a question the answer to which would criminate him, on the examination-in-chief, it seems he cannot be protected on the cross-examination, but is bound to answer everything relating to the transaction.‖

SEC. 330. Whether a witness is bound to reply to questions merely *tending* to criminate or disgrace him is not so clear. Mr. Greenleaf draws a distinction between questions which are material to the issue, and such as are only collateral to it; in the former case he considers it absurd to exclude the testimony of the witness merely because of its *tendency* to disgrace him. And Mr. Wharton¶ concludes that the weight of authority tends to the opinion that where the transaction to which the witness is interrogated forms part of the issue to be tried he will be obliged to give evidence, however strongly it may reflect on his character.

Questions tending to criminate.

SEC. 331. Although the privilege of declining to reply to such questions is personal to the witness, and cannot be either raised (except by way of advice from the Judge Advocate, where the witness is ignorant of his rights), or be argued by counsel, the question of exemption is finally to be decided by the court after the declaration of the witness that he cannot safely answer. It is, says Mr. Whar-

Privilege personal to the witness.

---

* 1 Starkie, 134.
† Ibid, 137, *et seq.*
‡ 1 Cranch, 144.
§ See sec. 331.
‖ Wharton's C. L., 375.
¶ Crim. Law, 377.

ton,* the province of the court to determine whether a direct answer to the question may criminate; and the witness is never compelled to answer where there is reasonable ground to sustain his objection.

It is hardly necessary to add that the examination of professional men, as such, should be confined to subjects within the scope of their particular profession. *Professional men.*

Sec. 332. 2. *Depositions.*—We have said that evidence of a direct character was to be communicated in two ways: orally, and in writing. The first of these has now been considered. Of the second, or written, direct evidence, little need be observed, as it is communicated in the depositions or affidavits of witnesses themselves, with regard to which the same rules are to be applied as where the examination is *viva voce* before the court. *Depositions.*

The general rule is to require the production of the party to be examined in open court, his evidence thus delivered being regarded as the *best* evidence; which, as will hereafter be shown, must always be produced when possible. Depositions therefore are obviously in derogation of this rule, and hence can never be admitted, except under the sanction of proper authority. This authority in civil cases is usually a commission from the court. But courts martial are authorized by the 74th Article of war to admit the deposition of witnesses not in the line and staff of the army in cases *not capital*. The deposition is directed to be taken before a justice of the peace; and the prosecutor and accused are required to be present, or to be notified thereof. It thus appears that in *capital* cases no deposition can be read in evidence before a court martial.

Sec. 333. III. *Circumstantial evidence.*—We are next to treat of circumstantial or presumptive evidence.

It will be impossible to do more than to state the leading

---

* Crim. Law, 372.

principles of the law on this interesting topic, and even this must be done in very general terms, as to enter into a close examination of its distinctive features would be foreign to the objects of this undertaking; nor, indeed, is it desirable, in the presence of the many valuable and learned texts books on the subject.

The ground of all presumptions, says Mr. Starkie, is the necessary or usual *connection* between facts and circumstances, the knowledge of which *connection* results from experience and reflection. A presumption is an inference as to the existence of a fact not actually known, arising from its necessary or usual connection with others which are known.*

<small>Ground of presumptive evidence.</small>

Circumstantial evidence is, therefore, any which is not direct and positive. It is allowed to prevail, not, as is often supposed, on grounds of necessity and policy, but because in its very nature it is capable of producing the highest degree of moral certainty. For crime can rarely be committed without affording vestiges by which the offender may be traced and ascertained. Human transactions are all interwoven with each other and the natural world, and no fact or circumstance happens which does not owe its existence to others, and which does not in its turn tend to produce a host of dependent facts and circumstances, resting in perfect harmony with each other.† "Hence, if a number of the circumstances which attended a disputed fact be known, and these so coincide and agree with the hypothesis that the disputed fact is true that no other hypothesis can consist with those circumstances, the truth of that hypothesis is necessarily established."‡

The conclusions to be deduced from circumstantial evidence are not, therefore, of a hazardous and unsatisfactory character, but are to be relied on as generally just and accurate;

---

* 1 Starkie, 23.   † Ibid, 482.   ‡ Ibid, 482.

nevertheless it is, says Mr. Starkie, a species of evidence which requires the utmost degree of caution and vigilance in its application.

SEC. 334. To illustrate the general bearing of this evidence Mr. Wharton introduces the following observations from Mr. Greenleaf's work on Evidence, which are clear and pertinent: "After proving that the deceased was feloniously killed, it is necessary to show that the prisoner was the guilty agent. And here, also, circumstances in the conduct and conversation of the prisoner, tending to fix upon him the guilt of the act—such as the motives which may have urged him to its commission, the means and facilities for it which he possessed, his conduct in previously seeking for an opportunity, or in subsequently using means to avert suspicion from himself, to stifle inquiry, or to remove material evidence—are admissable in evidence. Other circumstances, such as possession of poison, or a weapon wherewith the deed may have been done, marks of blood, the state of the prisoner's dress, indications of violence, and the like, are equally competent evidence. But it is to be recollected that a person of weak mind or nerves, under the terrors of a criminal accusation, or of his situation as calculated to awaken suspicion against him; and ignorant of the nature of the evidence and the cause of criminal procedure, and unconscious of the security which truth and sincerity afford, will often resort to artifice and falsehood, and even to the fabrication of testimony; in order to defend and exonerate himself. [2 Hale P. C., 290; 3 Inst., 202; 2d Starkie Ev., 521.] In order, therefore, to convict the prisoner upon the evidence of circumstances, it is held necessary not only that the circumstances all concur, to show that he committed the crime, but that they all be inconsistent with any other rational conclusion.

"But in order to prove that the prisoner was the guilty agent, it is not necessary to show that the fatal deed was done

Importance of.

immediately by his own hand. We have already seen that if he were actually present, aiding and abetting the deed, or were constructively present, by performing his part in an unlawful and felonious enterprise, expected to result in homicide, such as by keeping watch at a distance to prevent surprise, or the like, and a murder is committed by some other of the party in pursuance of the original design; or if he combined with others to commit an unlawful act, with the resolution to overcome all opposition by force, and it results in murder; or if he employ another person, unconscious of guilt, such as an idiot, lunatic, or child of tender age, as the instrument of his crime, he is guilty as the principal and immediate offender, and the charge against him, as such, will be supported by evidence of these facts." *See* 3 *Greenleaf Ev.*, sec. 137, 138.

SEC. 335. When the fact of guilt is not proved by *positive* and satisfactory testimony, the following cautions are suggested by Mr. Wharton:

1. *The onus of everything essential to establish the charge lies on the prosecutor.* In other words, the defendant's guilt must be made out by evidence sufficient to exclude any reasonable supposition of his innocence.

<small>Cautions as to.</small>

2. *There must be clear and unequivocal proof of the corpus delicti.* The fact of the commission of the offence is necessarily the foundation of every criminal prosecution; and until this fact is *proved*, it is always dangerous to convict.

SEC. 336. The observations which have now been made will be sufficient to exhibit the nature and use of circumstantial evidence, and to show that there is no ground for the popular impression that it is necessarily inconclusive or imperfect in its character. Errors and mistakes may sometimes occur in the application of its principles; but, as a learned judge once remarked, the same objection applies where the proofs have been positive and direct from witnesses who have deliberately forsworn themselves. We cannot for such

<small>Not objectionable.</small>

reasons abandon our faith in human testimony, without subverting the whole foundation of administrative justice.*

SEC. 337. We will now pass to a brief review of the most prominent and practical rules which govern courts martial in the admission of evidence, both direct and circumstantial. General rules to be observed.

1. *All irrelevant evidence is to be excluded.* In other words, the evidence is to be confined to the issue. Nothing, then, can properly be received as evidence which does not tend directly to prove or disprove the matter in issue Thus, in an action of trespass for battery, it could not be proved under the general issue that the plaintiff committed the first assault, for that is not the issue. But sometimes facts and circumstances connected with a former offence out of which a later offence has grown, may be given in evidence to show the *quo animo* or motive of the prisoner respecting the subsequent transaction.† There must, however, have been some connection between the two, for it would not be allowed to introduce evidence of a distinct offence, having no reference to or bearing upon that for which the party is on trial. This principle may be illustrated by reference to the crime of *desertion*. Here any fact connected with the absence of the prisoner, going to show an intention on his part *not to return*, may be inquired into. But such evidence is not to operate in any way to determine the nature or degree of punishment for the act of desertion, as it is admitted solely to show the existence of a specific offence.‡ The proper test would seem to be that nothing should be received as evidence from which a natural and reasonable inference may not be drawn as to the truth or falsity of the disputed fact; and the court must exercise a sound discretion in discriminating between facts connected with the issue and such as are merely collateral.§

Evidence to be confined to issue.

* Judge Story.
† Wharton's C. L., 299.
‡ De Hart, 342.
§ 2 Starkie, 380.

SEC. 338. De Hart observes, in this connection, that the prisoner may, under the plea of *not guilty*, which puts in issue the material parts of the charge, give in evidence matters of justification, excuse, or extenuation, and if other acts besides those which are the subject of the charge have been proved against him to show his design, he will be permitted to explain those parts of his conduct; and for this purpose he may give in evidence other *contemporaneous* acts (but such only), to show a different design from that imputed to him.*

<small>Matters in excuse and extenuation.</small>

SEC. 339. *Character.*—The moral character of the accused may sometimes be offered in evidence in his behalf, as in some instances it may afford a presumption of his innocence of a particular act. It can be offered in this general way, however, only in *doubtful* cases, as affording ground for the belief that a person of known probity or humanity would not be likely to commit a disgraceful or outrageous act;† and such evidence, when the testimony against the accused is doubtful, may often be sufficient to warrant his acquittal. But *generally*, character intended to influence the finding of the court must be relevant to the particular charge—for it would be absurd, when considering a charge of theft, to admit evidence of character for courage; or character for honesty, where the charge was cowardice.‡

<small>Character of accused.</small>

<small>Evidence as to.</small>

SEC. 340. The prosecution cannot impeach the character of the accused till the latter has adduced evidence in support of it; and cannot even then go into particular facts,§ but is confined to the general character of the defendant.‖ Nor can the prosecution be admitted to show the *tendency* of the defendant to commit a particular crime, though it be the crime charged, or that the *deceased was of bad character, quarrelsome, and riotous.*¶

<small>Not to be impeached till.</small>

---

* De Hart, 344.   ‡ De Hart, 346.   ‖ 2 Starkie, 365.
† 2 Starkie, 364.   § Wharton, 294.   ¶ Wharton, 295.

Sec. 341. Trials for *mutiny and sedition* frequently occur in courts martial, and it is important to consider the rule of relevancy in the testimony, with regard to them. [Mutiny.]

Evidence such as would be competent to prove a conspiracy would be admissible, according to De Hart's opinion, to prove sedition and mutiny before a court martial. What, then, is a "*conspiracy*"?

"The offence of conspiracy consists not in the accomplishment of an unlawful purpose, nor in any one act moving toward that purpose, but in actual concert or agreement of two or more persons to effect something which, being so concerted or agreed, the law regards as the object of an indictable conspiracy." * * There are two classes of cases where the criminality of a conspiracy is obvious: 1. Where the act to be done is unlawful; 2. Where the means proposed to accomplish a lawful act are themselves unlawful.* A single person cannot be said to be guilty of a conspiracy; it must be by two, at least.† [Conspiracy.]

But it is different in this respect, at least in a military view, as to the offences of mutiny and sedition; for although, says De Hart, two or more persons are frequently parties thereto, it does not require more than one to render such offences complete. They may originate and conclude with a single person, and be as complete with one actor as a thousand. At law, seditious words, though only spoken, no matter by whom or what number, are indictable.

Sec. 342. What evidence, then, may be admitted under the rule of relevancy, in trials before courts martial for these offences? In general, any evidence tending to prove the fact, whether direct or presumptive, is admissible, if referrible to the issue. The acts and declarations of the prisoner bearing on the fact are of course to be admit- [Evidence necessary in mutiny, etc.]

---

* Sergeant Talfourd, in Wharton, 765.   † Ibid, 792.

ted; and as in these cases the act of one is the act of all, those of any parties with whom the prisoner has conspired may be given in evidence against him whenever they are such as could be used against the rest. The same is true of their declarations. Each is deemed to command or assent to what is done by any other in furtherance of the common object. But it is said a foundation must first be laid by evidence sufficient in the view of the court to establish *prima facie* the fact of a conspiracy between the parties before their acts and declarations can be admitted against each other.* Upon the same principle, letters and papers in the custody of the prisoner or of his accomplices, if bearing on the issue, may be used in evidence against him. Such documents, however, must relate to the general design of the parties. If they appear to be mere private opinions, unconnected with that design, they are inadmissible.

SEC. 343. But the whole conduct of the prisoner is to be considered in such cases; and hence it would obviously be improper to read a portion of any paper or letter, or to relate only parts of his conversations, or those of his coadjutors.

Whole evidence to be considered.

It is of course competent for the accused to rebut the evidence against him by testimony of the same character, provided it is connected in point of time and of subject matter with the acts and declarations proved against him.†

Rebutting evidence.

SEC. 344. 2. *It is sufficient if the substance of the issue be proved.*

It is essential that the allegations against the accused should be supported by corresponding proofs. It would be manifestly unjust to convict a man on proof of only part of a separate and independent charge; and even if it could be maintained that part was sufficient to show guilt,

All allegations to be proved.

---

* Wharton's C. L., 324.   † De Hart, 352.

how could it be known by the accused to what particular part of the charge the prosecution would be addressed. To prevent injustice and surprise, it is therefore established as a general rule in the law of evidence, that every material and essential allegation in a charge or indictment must be proved as averred.* Thus, if the charge should be murder, which is killing with malice, both the killing and the malicious intent must be proved. But this rule is qualified by another now to be considered, in connection with which it ought to be taken, for it is also a rule that *it is sufficient if the substance of the issue be proved*, that is, says Mr. Starkie, it is sufficient if part of what is alleged be proved, *provided it be sufficient to support the issue;* but, he adds, no allegation descriptive of that which is essential to maintain the issue can ever be rejected.† The test in such cases is this: if an averment may be omitted or struck out of the charge without affecting it materially, that is, without destroying the cause of complaint, it will be unnecessary to prove such averment.‡ Hence, it is enough to prove so much of the indictment as shows the defendant to have been guilty of the substantive crime charged. Thus, if he is charged with having done, or caused to be done, a particular act, it is sufficient to prove either. So, if two distinct intents are charged, only one need be proved. The offence, however, must be of the same class with that charged; for instance, on an indictment for murder, manslaughter may be found; but a charge of larceny could not be supported by evidence of having merely received the stolen goods.§ A minor offence is included in the greater; therefore it is said a defendant indicted for an assault with a *felonious intent* may be convicted of a simple assault.

And so, a soldier charged with *desertion* may be found guilty

Substance of issue.

---

* 1 Starkie, 387.
† 2 Starkie, 387.
‡ 1 Phil. Ev., 158.
§ Wharton's C. L., 285, 286.

Desertion and absence without leave. of *absence without leave,* for absence is the chief question in issue, while the intent and motive make up the character of the offence. So, also, generally, observes De Hart, "in all accusations where the proof is insufficient to warrant conviction of the specific offence laid in the charge, but a substantial offence has been made out to the prejudice of good order and military discipline, the verdict may be found accordingly. But in every case of this kind, where a minor degree of guilt is found, it must be understood that a breach of a particular Article of war is not expressly and exclusively laid in the charge." *

If in an indictment or charge a person or thing is described with greater particularity than is necessary, it yet may often prove requisite that the particular circumstances set forth should be established for the purpose of identity. Greater strictness is also necessary in requiring proofs in criminal than in civil matters.

Names. The name of the accused ought to be correctly stated; yet wrong spelling is not fatal if it be *idem sonans* with the name which is proved.†

SEC. 345. The jurisdiction of military courts does not depend on the particular place where the crime is committed, but upon the *person* offending, and the description of his offence. "Still, it is necessary in framing a military charge that the *place* where the offence is supposed to have been committed should be laid with certainty, as it may be essential to the defence of the prisoner; but it does not follow that a variance between the proof of the place where the crime was committed and that laid in the charge should acquit the prisoner—it is sufficient to identify him as the perpetrator of the offence."‡ "A soldier, then, accused of deserting from one place on the first day of a

Jurisdiction as to person.

Place.

---

* De Hart, 369.   † Wharton's C. L., 278.   ‡ De Hart, 367.

particular month, but who on the trial was shown to have deserted on the specified day from a different place, would justly be convicted, for the essence of the crime is made out. * * * But if the time and place proved were so variant from those in the charge that there was a possibility of the prisoner having repeated the offence, he would necessarily be acquitted, for the act charged and the act proved may have been different offences."*

SEC. 346. In general the *time* of the commission of an offence is not important, as it does not confine the proofs within the limits of the period stated; and an indictment will be satisfied by proof of the offence at any day anterior to the finding. But this is to be understood only where time is not of the essence of the offence, or is not involved in some material fact; for every *material* fact in issue ought to be laid at a certain time. And if the particular time laid is material to sustain the charge, it must in such cases be proved as laid.†

Time.

SEC. 347. In connection with this subject of time and place may be mentioned the defence which the accused sometimes sets up in the proof of an *alibi*. This defence cannot avail in military trials where the crime alleged is proved to have been committed *by the prisoner at the time stated*, though at a different place: for here the crime and the prisoner are sufficiently connected, and the statement as to the place is mere error. But if the general fact that a crime has been committed at a particular place is proved, and the question is one of the prisoner's identity with the perpetrator, evidence of the prisoner's having been at another place when the criminal act was done establishes the *alibi*, and will be sufficient to acquit him. It is obvious then that both time and place may be material considerations in a charge, and it is important to guard against error in setting them forth. But,

Alibi.

---

* De Hart, 367. † Wharton, 279.

as already noticed, the jurisdiction of courts martial not being limited as to place, mistakes as to place, except where that is material, will not affect the proceedings; and the acts of the accused tending to establish the charge, no matter where committed, are admissible in evidence.*

SEC. 348. In connection with the rule that *"the substance of the issue need only be proved,"* which we have thus briefly examined, Captain De Hart introduces a discussion of the 83d Article of war, and as the subject is one of importance, his remarks are here transferred *in extenso*.

<small>83d Article of war.</small>

The Article is in the following words: "Any commissioned officer convicted before a general court martial of conduct unbecoming an officer and a gentleman, shall be dismissed the service." Upon which Captain De Hart observes:

<small>Conduct unbecoming an officer, etc.</small>

"Such is the language of the law—a law intended to preserve the honor and morals of the army, as a distinctive or professional body.

"In all the legislative enactments or minor regulations for the government of the army, it is to be observed that the object in view is the good order and military discipline of that body; it would therefore appear that no act of a military person which does not offend against such principle could be held as within the cognizance of a court martial. In measuring the turpitude of any conduct by the law just quoted, it is necessary, in the first place, to state with particularity the acts of which the prisoner is accused, in order not only that he may be possessed of all fair means of defence, but that the court may have likewise the power to judge of the reasonableness and justice of the imputations which the charge alleges. The writer is aware of some of the difficulties which have been thrown around this subject by the very indistinct and

<small>Observations.</small>

---

* De Hart, 368.

confused opinions which have been expressed by several British military writers when treating of a similar Article of war, for the government of the English army, and by the difference which exists in the language of the two Articles of war. There are terms employed in the British Article which stand as a guide to the meaning of it, which have been discarded in the American, but when the subject is considered, must necessarily be understood as implied in the latter, in order to give it a proper application.

"The Article of war now under consideration declares that 'any commissioned officer convicted before a general court martial *of conduct unbecoming an officer and a gentleman*, shall be dismissed the service;' whereas the British Article denounces the penalty of cashiering against 'any officer who shall behave in a *scandalous, infamous manner*, unbecoming the character of an officer and a gentleman.' The difference adverted to is very material, and in one affords a rule by which punishment for conduct unbecoming an officer and a gentleman is to be measured, or furnishes the means of ascertaining the description of such conduct so as to bring it by military cognizance within the denunciation of the law.

"Now, it is apprehended that conduct unbecoming an officer and a gentleman before it can be legally made the cause of punishment must be shown to be of that kind as necessarily to reflect disgrace upon the body to which the offender belongs. And this disgrace must not be such as the accidental or capricious judgment of different courts martial might view it; but be referrible to the certain and expressed opinions or feelings of the community at large. *What is conduct unbecoming an officer, etc.*

"By this it is intended to say that the partial judgments of men, based on mere professional conventions or notions of honor (because such may vary with different men, and at various places), are not to be the standard altogether, but that the imputations grounded on the particular acts which make the subject of the charge must be determined or rejected according to the established and acknowledged morals of the Christian world.

"The article in question does not particularize any species of conduct as unbecoming an officer and a gentleman, but leaves that to be determined by the opinions of the world, or by those of the court martial, from the acts alleged, and from which the military community might be prejudiced or receive detriment were it to countenance behavior in any of its members which was of such a nature as to involve scandal and infamy.

The article does not specify conduct.

"There are undoubtedly certain acts, which, however immoral, do not import *infamy*, and are not liable in any of the departments of social life to punishment by declared law. They may in the estimation of many affect the standing of the individual who is guilty of them, and yet be not such as either to debase him in the eyes of the community, or exclude him from society.

"These are cases in which it is believed that a court martial could not apply the stringent powers of this Article of war for correction. The military community cannot expect, nor ought it to be expected of them, to preserve a higher tone of moral conduct than what is sustained by the higher orders of society. The means, therefore, conceded by the Article in question, are not to be considered with reference altogether to such a purpose, for if such were the case, military officers would be subjected to a capricious standard of judgment, or to an ordeal which but very few men could bear.

Standard of military conduct.

"Mr. Samuel in his treatise on 'military law,' when speaking of the similar Article in the English military code, says: 'the words "officer and gentleman," though in general to be understood as one single and indivisible term, appear not to be used so here. The mis-

Mr. Samuel's views of the British Article.

behavior entailing on it the penalty declared by this Article must be such, as I understand it, as to implicate in the first place the *officer;* that is, it must arise in some sort out of his office, and affect *incidentally* only the character of the *gentleman.*'

"But the writer must disagree with such an exposition of the Article, if it is to be received as the interpretation of the American law—nor does the practice accord with such an explanation of it, even in the British service.

83d Article of war.

"In the American army, a charge laid under this particular Article of war *is one single* and *indivisible term,* and cannot be broken by a finding of the court; though, when such conduct as the breach of the particular Article in question is not expressly and exclusively laid in the the charge, the court may, if a substantial military offence be shown by the evidence to have been committed, find a minor degree of guilt, as 'conduct prejudicial to good order and military discipline;' for it would certainly 'be a strange doctrine to maintain that because the court found less proved than charged no punishment should be awarded.'

Court may find a minor degree of guilt.

"The degree to which certain acts may impugn one's character, as conduct unbecoming an officer and a gentleman, is a matter of inference for the judgment of the court, and where such imputation is denied by the evidence, there must be an acquittal; the facts charged may be clearly proved, and yet not involve the guilt alleged by the accuser in the charge. For the court are to try unofficerlike and ungentlemanlike conduct, and to see that it be proved as it is alleged—or to find such minor degree of guilt, under the restrictions before mentioned, as the nature of the evidence will warrant.

"In every prosecution before a court martial for conduct unbecoming an officer and a gentleman, the degree of the offence must be such as to reflect discredit upon the body of the army, or the nature of it such as to militate against the requirements of 'good order and military discipline' before a legal conviction can be declared, or punishment awarded, according to the imperative language of the law for that particular charge, or according to the discretion of the court, if a modified verdict be returned.

"Acts, therefore, which are alleged in a charge of this character, but which by the court are divested of the imputation, which constitutes the crime, and which are at the same time not of such a kind as would of themselves constitute a breach of good order and military discipline, can of necessity involve no guilt—it can only be by such features that they are made cognizable by military courts. This is a matter for the attention and consideration of courts martial, whenever a charge under the particular Article of war now in review is laid before them.

"It is readily perceived that, when deliberating upon a charge of 'conduct unbecoming an officer and a gentleman,' some officers, members of the court, who might be impressed with any high notions of personal and professional honor, or possessing a very refined and delicate perception of the proprieties which should distinguish a gentleman, would, without strictly regarding the intention or consequences of the law in question, pronounce a verdict of guilty when in reality no legal offence had been committed. To prevent such errors of opinion, which involve the legal rights of others, though proceeding from a noble sentiment, is the purpose of a just explanation of the Article.

"The following case, quoted from McArthur, by Samuel, will sufficiently illustrate the subject: 'At a general court martial held at the *Cape of Good Hope*, May, 1801, an officer was tried charged with *scandalous, infamous conduct*, unbecoming the character of an officer and a gentleman, in having sent a charge of £600 or thereabouts, against *Sir George*

<small>Case cited.</small>

Younge, for a horse, which the said officer had declared to be a present to *Sir George*, when Governor of the Colony of the *Cape of Good Hope*.

"'In respect to which charge the court martial made a distinction; they *acquitted* the officer of *scandalous, infamous* behavior, but considered his conduct nevertheless as unbecoming the character of an officer and a gentleman, for which they adjudged him to be suspended from rank and pay for the space of six calendar months.

"'The proceedings having been laid before his majesty, the Judge Advocate-General signified to *Lieutenant-General Dundas*, the commander-in-chief of his majesty's forces at the *Cape*, that his majesty, laying out of the case any question touching either the right or the delicacy of the officer's claim to a compensation for the horse, concerning which the difference had arisen—points not within the cognizance of a court martial—considered the adjudication as irregular, inasmuch as the court had *acquitted* him of the only imputation which could bring the business as a charge before them, viz: of any *scandalous* or *infamous* behavior in the transaction; his majesty could not, therefore, approve the sentence. At the same time it was signified his majesty was graciously disposed to attribute the error to the nice feelings of the officers who composed the court martial, which had marked their dislike of a conduct which appeared to them not decorous.'

"The above case exemplifies what the writer has endeavored to explain—that it is not all conduct which offends against the delicate proprieties and decorum of an officer and a gentleman which can be held amenable to military law, but such only as, while it impugns the character of an officer and a gentleman, at the same time casts upon the military community a shade of discredit and reproach.

"In speaking of the case above quoted, Captain Simmons very justly remarks: 'An officer sending an improper charge for a horse, taken abstractedly, could in no wise affect military discipline, and excepting as it might implicate the individual character of an officer, in a degree amounting to 'scandalous, infamous conduct,' no offence under the Articles of war could be charged, since there is not any provision in the Article for the cognizance of unofficerlike and ungentlemanly conduct (divested of a tendency to affect good order and military discipline) in any degree less than that involving infamy and scandal.'

"The distinction thus observed by Captain Simmons will undoubtedly be of aid in all questions brought before courts martial for adjudication, and which are laid under the 83d Article of war. . Thus, a charge of unofficerlike and ungentlemanly conduct, when divested of all tendency to effect good order and military discipline, and at the same time involving no moral turpitude of such a kind as would reflect discredit upon the military community, cannot be deemed cognizable by a military court.".

SEC. 349. 3. Another of the cardinal rules of evidence is that *the affirmative of the issue must generally be proved*. A negative does not admit of the simple and direct proof

Negative not generally to be proved. of which an affirmative is capable, hence the party who alleges the affirmative of any proposition is required to prove it.* And it is a general rule that the *onus probandi* rests upon the person who seeks to support his case by a particular fact of which he is supposed to be cognizant. Thus, a party who pleads *infancy* must prove it.†

But where the negative involves a criminal omission by the party, of which the law of course presumes his innocence, the affirmative of the fact is also presumed; and the affirmative being thus assumed, it lies on him who denies the fact to prove the *negative*, as in presumptions of the continuance of life, the legitimacy of children, the satisfaction of debts, etc. These,

---
* 1 Starkie, 376.   † Ibid, 377.

and all legal presumptions, continue till they are negatived by the party denying them.*

SEC. 350. 4. *The best attainable evidence must always be produced.* This rule applies to the *quality* of evidence, and not its measure or quantity; for it is not necessary to give the fullest proof in every case. A fact may be sufficiently proved by *one* witness, though known to several. The meaning of the rule is that no evidence of an *inferior character* can be substituted for that which is superior, if the latter can be procured. Thus, the contents of a writing cannot be proved by a copy or by oral evidence when the original can be produced, for that is the *best* evidence.†

_{How the rule is understood.}

SEC. 351. This rule is adopted for the prevention of fraud, and its proper observance is of great importance, for the inference is natural that when evidence of a higher order is withheld it is unfavorable to the party concealing it. But the rule assumes, in excluding inferior evidence that better can be obtained; for it never excludes evidence which is the best that can be produced. Hence, where a deed is shown to be lost a copy may be given in evidence,‡ when duly authenticated, and the law does not require the strongest possible proof of a fact, but only evidence of the best possible *kind* which can be obtained.

_{Object of the rule.}

"Offences are at times committed with such privacy that it is impossible to prove them otherwise than by the testimony of the party injured; such evidence becomes then the best possible kind of which the case admits, * * * and, where no doubt of the credibility of the witness exists, is considered sufficient to warrant a conviction."§

SEC. 352. The result of this rule of evidence is a distinction between *primary*, or the best, and *secondary*, or inferior evidence. Secondary evidence cannot be ad-

_{Primary and secondary evidence.}

---

* 1 Starkie, 377, 380.   Wharton's C. L., 284, and see sec. 361.
† 1 Starkie, 390, 391.   ‡ Ibid, 392.   § De Hart, 357.

mitted until proof is given that better cannot be obtained. But a distinction also exists between secondary and merely defective evidence. The latter may be admissible as *tending* to prove the issue, though insufficient to do so, notwithstanding it is shown that better cannot be had; while the former evidence, though secondary in character, may yet be adequate, when admitted, to establish the point in dispute.*

SEC. 353. It has just been remarked that secondary evidence cannot be received by the court without proof that better evidence cannot be had. The nature of such proof of course depends on circumstances. Where documents are lost or destroyed, the fact must be shown to the satisfaction of the court; or if in the hands of other or adverse parties, notice to produce them must be given and duly proved before copies can be read.† Due diligence to recover the lost document must also appear; but if it cannot be found in its usual and proper place of custody, or accounted for by the legal custodian, the court will presume that it has been lost, and will receive evidence of its contents.

<small>Secondary not received, except.</small>

SEC. 354. There are some exceptions to the rule requiring the best evidence to be produced, which are the joint result of necessity and convenience. A few will be specified. A person who is generally known and admitted as a *public officer*, may generally officiate without producing his commission, and his acts are *prima facie* received as legal. The contents of any record of a judicial court, and of public books and registers, may be proved by examined copies. So, where the evidence is the *result* of voluminous facts on the examination of many books and papers not to be conveniently produced in open court, the general result it is said may be stated, as the solvency of a party at a particular time, or the military character and history of a soldier as shown by the

<small>Exceptions to rule requiring best evidence.</small>

---

* De Hart, 357. † Wharton, C. L., 303.

records of a department. So, also, inscriptions on walls, gravestones, and monuments.* With respect to persons in the army, it is "sufficient to prove that they acted in the character set forth, without producing their appointments; and therefore, upon a charge of disobedience or neglect of orders against an officer or a soldier, it is sufficient to show that the officer giving the order had previously, in the knowledge of the accused, acted in the capacity alleged. And a prisoner may be proved a soldier by showing that he received pay as such, and acted in the capacity of one, without producing or proving his enlistment."† Commission of officer. Soldiers

SEC. 355. *Handwriting* may be proved by the admission of the party; or by any person who has seen him write, or been in the habit of corresponding with him, without seeing him write, or even, it is said, of acting upon his correspondence.‡ But the means of such knowledge in the witness should be carefully scrutinized. A person whose name has been forged is admissible to prove the forgery.§ Generally, comparison of handwriting by witnesses, for the purpose of proving the writer or his signature, is inadmissible; but the court or jury may compare a document with authentic writing of the party to whom it is ascribed, if such writings are in evidence for other purposes in the same cause. It is also competent to adduce the testimony of *experts*, or persons skilled with respect to money and handwriting, and who have seen what have generally passed as the signatures of the officers of a bank, though they have never seen them write.‖ The *best* evidence of handwriting, however, is the admission of the party, or the testimony of witnesses who *know* the writing in question.

---

* Wharton's C. L., 302, 303.   ‡ Wharton's C. L., 586.
† De Hart, 360.   § Ibid, 586.
‖ Wharton's C. L., 586, 587. See, also, 2 Starkie, 650.

SEC. 356. 5. *Confessions and declarations.* Connected with the rule we have just considered, is the subject of the declarations and confessions of the accused.

Confessions, etc.

A free and voluntary confession by the accused, before or after his arrest, to any person, is evidence against him; and when satisfactorily proved, after proof also of the *corpus delicti*, or act constituting the offence, is generally sufficient to convict.* And yet the numerous instances reported in which convictions on the mere confession of the accused have proved erroneous, render this species of evidence far less satisfactory than, reasoning from the ordinary course of human conduct, it may appear to be; so that, observes the author so often quoted already,† there exists a growing unwillingness to rest convictions on confessions alone. But a confession, before it can be received, must appear to have been *freely and voluntarily made;* therefore, if it has been induced by any hope or promise, or extorted by fear or pain, it is inadmissible in evidence. The influence, however, to render it objectionable must, it is said, be of a temporal character only: for such as refer to a future state are not considered in the light of improper influences, and would not, therefore, of themselves exclude the confession.‡

Must be proof of corpus delicti, before confession is used.

Generally unsatisfactory.

Must be voluntary.

Moreover, in order to shut out evidence of a prisoner's confession, it must appear *affirmatively* that some inducement was presented to him, by or in the presence of some person having authority. The precise words or terms are unimportant; but the court are to determine their probable and reasonable effect on the mind of the accused; and if evidence of any declaration or confession be admitted, and it is afterward discovered that it has been made

To exclude, must appear that it was improperly obtained.

---

* Wharton, 313.

† Ibid, 313, and see the cases cited in proof of the danger of relying on such evidence. ‡ Ibid, 317.

under any undue or improper influence, the court will direct it to be stricken out, or instruct the jury to disregard it.*

SEC. 357. A confession obtained by artifice only, without threat or promise, is admissible in evidence: for in such cases the party, though deceived, has spoken under no improper influence, at least none which may be supposed to excite the feelings or bias the judgment. And so it has been held that discoveries made by means of a confession in itself improperly procured, may be used in evidence if in other respects such discoveries are unobjectionable. *Confession obtained by artifice admissible.* *Discoveries by reason of.*

SEC. 358. Confessions are of course evidence only against the party who makes them, except in cases of conspiracy, mutiny, etc., where the declaration of one party may, after *proof* of the conspiracy, be given in evidence against all.† *Confessions evidence only against the party generally.*

It is to be observed, also, that the whole of a man's confessions are to be taken together. One part cannot be offered in evidence and another rejected. The court, however, is not bound to *credit* the whole, but may for sufficient reasons reject a part, and accept as true the rest. Truth and falsehood are often mingled together; and when thus presented in evidence, it is the province of the court who are to try and determine the facts as well as the law, to consider what is true and reject what is false. *The whole to be given.*

SEC. 359. It is proper here to add that as no evidence can be received to contradict the record, so none need be offered to prove any point which the record admits.

SEC. 360. *Presumptions of Law.*—We conclude this chapter by a bare reference to certain conclusions, or, as they are termed, *presumptions of the law,* as to which, until contradicted, no proof is required.

1. *The presumption of innocence.*—Every man is presumed to

---

* Wharton, 321, 322.   † Ante, sec. 342.

be innocent till the contrary is *proved;* and if there

Presumptions of innocence.

be reasonable doubt as to his guilt, he must receive the benefit of such doubt. Hence, in criminal trials the testimony ought to be such as to satisfy the jury beyond a rational doubt of the guilt of the prisoner, or it is their duty to acquit him.

2. *Presumption of intent.*—The law presumes the natural and probable consequences of every act deliberately done

Of intent.

to have been intended by the author. Thus, *malice* is presumed in every act of the deliberate killing of another.

3. *Presumption that official acts are legally and properly performed.*—Where acts are of an official character, or

As to legal acts.

require the concurrence of official persons, a presumption arises in favor of their due execution, for everything is presumed to be duly and rightfully performed until the contrary is proved.

4. There are also presumptions of a less conclusive character, and from which the inference of guilt must be more or less strong, according to circumstances. These are, 1st.

As to other acts of accused.

Presumptions arising from attempts to escape or evade justice. 2d. Such as arise from attempts to forge evidence. 3d. From threats or declarations of the intention of the parties. 4th. Presumptions which arise from possession of the fruits of an offence. Parties who have become obnoxious to any of these, or kindred presumptions, would be under circumstances of very strong suspicion, and it is obvious that a smaller amount of proof would be held to justify their conviction than would otherwise be required.

Mr. Wharton, whose excellent treatise on criminal law has so frequently been quoted and relied upon in these pages, and from which the foregoing summary respecting presumptions has been made, lays down with great precision and accuracy the law on this subject, and to that the reader is now referred.*

---

* Crim. Law, 327-342.

Sec. 361. Thus has been concluded a brief review of such of the established principles and rules of evidence as seemed important to be considered in connection with the subject of military trials, and with it terminates the present undertaking. Nothing new has been attempted, unless in the mode of treating some of the topics discussed, and the general arrangement and style of the work. What has now been accomplished, chiefly, as the learned reader will perceive, by the collection and readjustment of the labors of others, is submitted, with its many acknowledged imperfections, to the indulgent consideration of the military profession.

Conclusion.

APPENDIX.

ARTICLES OF WAR.

AN ACT FOR ESTABLISHING RULES AND ARTICLES FOR THE GOVERNMENT OF THE ARMIES OF THE CONFEDERATE STATES.

SECTION 1. *The Congress of the Confederate States of America do enact,* That, from and after the passage of this act, the following shall be the rules and articles by which the armies of the Confederate States shall be governed:

ART. 1. Every officer now in the army of the Confederate States shall, in six months from the passing of this act, and every officer who shall hereafter be appointed, shall, before he enters on the duties of his office, subscribe these rules and regulations.

ART. 2. It is earnestly recommended to all officers and soldiers diligently to attend divine service; and all officers who shall behave indecently or irreverently at any place of divine worship shall, if commissioned officers, be brought before a general court martial, there to be publicly and severely reprimanded by the President; if non-commissioned officers or soldiers, every person so offending shall, for his first offence, forfeit one-sixth of a dollar, to be deducted out of his next pay; for the second offence he shall not only forfeit a like sum, but be confined twenty-four hours; and for every like offence, shall suffer and pay in like manner; which money, so forfeited, shall be applied, by the captain or senior officer of the troop or company, to the use of the sick soldiers of the company or troop to which the offender belongs.

ART. 3. Any non-commissioned officer or soldier who shall use any profane oath or execration shall incur the penalties expressed in the foregoing article; and a commissioned officer shall forfeit and pay, for each and every such offence, one dollar, to be applied as in the preceding article.

ART. 4. Every chaplain, commissioned in the army or armies of the Confederate States, who shall absent himself from the duties assigned him (excepting in cases of sickness or leave of absence), shall, on conviction thereof before a court martial, be fined not exceeding one month's pay, besides the loss of his pay during his absence, or be discharged, as the said court martial shall judge proper.

ART. 5. Any officer or soldier who shall use contemptuous or disrespectful words against the President of the Confederate States, against the Vice-President thereof, against the Congress of the Confederate States, or against the Chief Magistrate or Legislature of any of the Confederate States in which he may be quartered, if a commissioned officer, shall be cashiered, or otherwise punished, as a court martial shall direct; if a non-commissioned officer or soldier, he shall suffer such punishment as shall be inflicted on him by the sentence of a court martial.

ART. 6. Any officer or soldier who shall behave himself with contempt or disrespect toward his commanding officer, shall be punished, according to the nature of his offence, by the judgment of a court martial.

ART. 7. Any officer or soldier who shall begin, excite, cause, or join in any mutiny or sedition, in any troop or company in the service of the Confederate States, or in any party, post, detachment, or guard, shall suffer death, or such other punishment as by a court martial shall be inflicted.

ART. 8. Any officer, non-commissioned officer, or soldier, who, being present at any mutiny or sedition, does not use his utmost endeavor to suppress the same, or, coming to the knowledge of any intended mutiny, does not, without delay, give information thereof to his commanding officer, shall be punished by the sentence of a court martial with death, or otherwise, according to the nature of his offence.

ART. 9. Any officer or soldier who shall strike his superior officer, or draw or lift up any weapon, or offer any violence against him, being in the execution of his office, on any pretence whatsoever, or shall disobey any lawful command of his superior officer, shall suffer death, or such other punishment as shall, according to the nature of his offence, be inflicted upon him by the sentence of a court martial.

ART. 10. Every non-commissioned officer or soldier who shall enlist himself in the service of the Confederate States shall, at the time of his so enlisting, or within six days afterward, have the Articles for the government of the armies of the Confederate States read to him, and shall, by the officer who enlisted him, or by the commanding officer of the troop or company into which he was enlisted, be taken before the next justice of the peace, or chief magistrate of any city or town corporate, not being an officer of the army, or where recourse cannot be had to the civil magistrate, before the Judge Advocate, and in his presence shall take the following oath or affirmation: "I, A B, do solemnly swear, or affirm (as the case may be), that I will bear true allegiance to the Confederate States of America, and that I will serve them honestly and faithfully against all their enemies or opposers whatsoever; and observe and obey the orders of the President of the Confederate States, and the orders of the officers appointed over me, according to the Rules and Articles for the government of the armies of the Confederate States." Which justice, magistrate, or Judge Advocate is to give to the officer a certificate, signifying that the man enlisted did take the said oath or affirmation.

ART. 11. After a non-commissioned officer or soldier shall have been duly enlisted and sworn, he shall not be dismissed the service without a discharge in writing; and no discharge granted to him shall be sufficient which is not signed by a field officer of the regiment to which he belongs, or commanding officer, where no field officer of the regiment is present; and no discharge shall be given to a non-commissioned officer or soldier before his term of service has expired but by order of the President, the Secretary of War, the commanding officer of a department, or the sentence of a general court martial; nor shall a commissioned officer be discharged the service but by order of the President of the Confederate States, or by sentence of a general court martial.

ART. 12. Every colonel, or other officer commanding a regiment, troop, or company, and actually quartered with it, may give furloughs to non-commissioned officers or soldiers, in such numbers, and for so long a time, as he shall judge to be most consistent with the good of the service; and a captain, or other inferior officer, commanding a troop or company, or in any garrison, fort, or barrack of the Confederate States (his field officer being absent), may give furloughs to non-commissioned officers and soldiers, for a time not exceeding twenty days in six months, but not to more than two persons to be absent at the same time, excepting some extraordinary occasion should require it.

ART. 13. At every muster, the commanding officer of each regiment, troop, or company there present, shall give to the commissary of musters, or other officer who musters the said regiment, troop, or company, certificates signed by himself, signifying how long such officers as shall not appear at the said muster, have been absent, and the reason of their absence. In like manner, the commanding officer of every troop or company shall give certificates, signifying the reasons of the absence of the non-commissioned officers and private soldiers; which reasons and time of absence shall be inserted in the muster-rolls, opposite the names of the respective absent officers and soldiers. The certificates shall, together with the muster-rolls, be remitted by the commissary of musters, or other officer mustering, to the Department of War, as speedily as the distance of the place will admit.

ART. 14. Every officer who shall be convicted before a general court martial of having signed a false certificate relating to the absence of either officer or private soldier, or relative to his or their pay, shall be cashiered.

ART. 15. Every officer who shall knowingly make a false muster of man or horse, and every officer or commissary of musters who shall willingly sign, direct, or allow the signing of muster-rolls wherein such false muster is contained, shall, upon proof made thereof, by two witnesses, before a general court martial, be cashiered, and shall be thereby utterly disabled to have or hold any office or employment in the service of the Confederate States.

ART. 16. Any commissary of musters, or other officer, who shall be convicted of having taken money, or other thing, by way of gratification, on mustering any regiment, troop, or company, or on signing muster-rolls, shall be displaced from his office, and shall be thereby utterly disabled to have or hold any office or employment in the service of the Confederate States.

ART. 17. Any officer who shall presume to muster a person as a soldier who is not a soldier, shall be deemed guilty of having made a false muster, and shall suffer accordingly.

ART. 18. Every officer who shall knowingly make a false return to the Department of War, or to any of his superior officers, authorized to call for such returns, of the state of the regiment, troop, or company, or garrison, under his command; or of the arms, ammunition, clothing, or other stores thereunto belonging, shall on conviction thereof before a court martial, be cashiered.

ART. 19. The commanding officer of every regiment, troop, or independent company, or garrison of the Confederate States, shall in the beginning of every month remit, through the proper channels, to the Department of War, an exact return of the regiment, troop, independent company, or garrison under his command, specifying the names of the officers then absent from their posts, with the reasons for and the time of their absence. And any officer who shall be convicted of having, through neglect or design, omitted sending such returns, shall be punished, according to the nature of his crime, by the judgment of a general court martial.

ART. 20. All officers and soldiers who have received pay, or have been duly enlisted in the service of the Confederate States, and shall be convicted of having deserted the same, shall suffer death, or such other punishment as by sentence of a court martial shall be inflicted.

ART. 21. Any non-commissioned officer or soldier who shall, without leave from his commanding officer, absent himself from his troop, company, or detachment, shall, upon being convicted thereof, be punished according to the nature of his offence, at the discretion of a court martial.

ART. 22. No non-commissioned officer or soldier shall enlist himself in any other regiment, troop, or company, without a regular discharge from the regiment, troop, or company in which he last served, on the penalty of being reputed a deserter, and suffering accordingly. And in case any officer shall knowingly receive and entertain such non-commissioned officer or soldier, or shall not, after his being discovered to be a deserter, immediately confine him, and give notice thereof to the corps in which he last served, the said officer shall, by a court martial, be cashiered.

ART. 23. Any officer or soldier who shall be convicted of having advised or persuaded any other officer or soldier to desert the service of the

Confederate States, shall suffer death, or such other punishment as shall be inflicted upon him by the sentence of a court martial.

ART. 24. No officer or soldier shall use any reproachful or provoking speeches or gestures to another, upon pain, if an officer, of being put in arrest; if a soldier, confined, and of asking pardon of the party offended, in the presence of his commanding officer.

ART. 25. No officer or soldier shall send a challenge to another officer or soldier, to fight a duel, or accept a challenge if sent, upon pain, if a commissioned officer, of being cashiered; if a non-commissioned officer or soldier, of suffering corporal punishment, at the discretion of a court martial.

ART. 26. If any commissioned or non-commissioned officer commanding a guard shall knowingly or willingly suffer any person whatsoever to go forth to fight a duel, he shall be punished as a challenger; and all seconds, promoters, and carriers of challenges, in order to duels, shall be deemed principals, and be punished accordingly. And it shall be the duty of every officer commanding an army, regiment, company, post, or detachment, who is knowing to a challenge being given or accepted by any officer, non-commissioned officer, or soldier, under his command, or has reason to believe the same to be the case, immediately to arrest and bring to trial such offenders.

ART. 27. All officers, of what condition soever, have power to part and quell all quarrels, frays, and disorders, though the persons concerned should belong to another regiment, troop, or company; and either to order officers into arrest, or non-commissioned officers or soldiers into confinement, until their proper superior officers shall be acquainted therewith; and whosoever shall refuse to obey such officer (though of an inferior rank), or shall draw his sword upon him, shall be punished at the discretion of a general court martial.

ART. 28. Any officer or soldier who shall upbraid another for refusing a challenge, shall himself be punished as a challenger; and all officers and soldiers are hereby discharged from any disgrace or opinion of disadvantage which might arise from their having refused to accept of challenges, as they will only have acted in obedience to the laws, and done their duty as good soldiers who subject themselves to discipline.

ART. 29. No sutler shall be permitted to sell any kind of liquors or victuals, or to keep their houses or shops open for the entertainment of soldiers, after nine at night, or before the beating of the reveille, or upon Sundays, during divine service or sermon, on the penalty of being dismissed from all future suttling.

ART. 30. All officers commanding in the field, forts, barracks, or garrisons of the Confederate States, are hereby required to see that the persons permitted to suttle shall supply the soldiers with good and wholesome provisions, or other articles, at a reasonable price, as they shall be answerable for their neglect.

ART. 31. No officer commanding in any of the garrisons, forts, or barracks of the Confederate States, shall exact exorbitant prices for houses or stalls, let out to sutlers, or connive at the like exactions in others; nor by his own authority, and for his private advantage, lay any duty or imposition upon, or be interested in the sale of any victuals, liquors, or other necessaries of life brought into the garrison, fort or barracks, for the use of the soldiers, on the penalty of being discharged from the service.

ART. 32. Every officer commanding in quarters, garrisons, or on the march, shall keep good order, and to the utmost of his power redress all abuses or disorders which may be committed by any officer or soldier under his command; if, upon complaint made to him of officers or soldiers beating or otherwise ill-treating any person, or disturbing fairs or markets, or of committing any kind of riots, to the disquieting of the citizens of the Confederate States, he, the said commander, who shall refuse or omit to see justice done to the offender or offenders, and reparation made to the party or parties injured, as far as part of the offender's pay shall enable him or them, shall, upon proof thereof, be cashiered, or otherwise punished, as a general court martial shall direct.

ART. 33. When any commissioned officer or soldier shall be accused of a capital crime, or of having used violence, or committed any offence against the person or property of any citizen of any of the Confederate States, such as is punishable by the known laws of the land, the commanding officer and officers of every regiment, troop, or company to which the person or persons so accused shall belong are hereby required, upon application duly made by, or in behalf of the party or parties injured, to use their utmost endeavors to deliver over such accused person or persons to the civil magistrate, and likewise to be aiding and assisting to the officers of justice in apprehending and securing the person or persons so accused, in order to bring him or them to trial. If any commanding officer or officers shall wilfully neglect, or shall refuse, upon the application aforesaid, to deliver over such accused person or persons to the civil magistrates, or to be aiding and assisting to the officers of justice in apprehending such person or persons, the officer or officers so offending shall be cashiered.

ART. 34. If any officer shall think himself wronged by his colonel, or the commanding officer of the regiment, and shall, upon due application being made to him be refused redress, he may complain to the general commanding in the state or territory where such regiment shall be stationed, in order to obtain justice; who is hereby required to examine into said complaint, and take proper measures for redressing the wrong complained of, and transmit, as soon as possible, to the Department of War, a true state of such complaint, with the proceedings had thereon.

ART. 35. If any inferior officer or soldier shall think himself wronged by his captain or other officer, he is to complain thereof to the commanding officer of the regiment, who is hereby required to summon a regimental court martial, for the doing justice to the complainant; from which regimental court martial either party may, if he think himself still aggrieved, appeal to a general court martial. But if, upon a second hearing, the appeal shall appear vexatious and groundless, the person so appealing shall be punished at the discretion of said court martial.

ART. 36. Any commissioned officer, store-keeper, or commissary, who shall be convicted at a general court martial of having sold, without a proper order for that purpose, embezzled, misapplied, or wilfully, or through neglect, suffered any of the provisions, forage, arms, clothing, ammunition, or other military stores belonging to the Confederate States to be spoiled or damaged, shall, at his own expense, make good the loss or damage, and shall, moreover, forfeit all his pay, and be dismissed from the service.

ART. 37. Any non-commissioned officer or soldier who shall be convicted at a regimental court martial of having sold, or designedly or through neglect wasted the ammunition delivered out to him, to be employed in the service of the Confederate States, shall be punished at the discretion of such court.

ART. 38. Every non-commissioned officer or soldier who shall be convicted before a court martial of having sold, lost, or spoiled, through neglect, his horse, arms, clothes, or accoutrements, shall undergo such weekly stoppages (not exceeding the half of his pay) as such court martial shall judge sufficient for repairing the loss or damage; and shall suffer confinement, or such other corporal punishment as his crime shall deserve.

ART. 39. Every officer who shall be convicted before a court martial of having embezzled or misapplied any money with which he may have been intrusted, for the payment of the men under his command, or for enlisting men into the service, or for other purposes, if a commissioned officer, shall be cashiered, and compelled to refund the money; if a non-commissioned officer, shall be reduced to the ranks, be put under stoppages until the money be made good, and suffer such corporal punishment as such court martial shall direct.

ART. 40. Every captain of a troop or company is charged with the arms, accoutrements, ammunition, clothing, or other warlike stores belonging to the troop or company under his command, which he is to be accountable for to his colonel in case of their being lost, spoiled, or damaged, not by unavoidable accidents, or on actual service.

ART. 41. All non-commissioned officers and soldiers who shall be found one mile from the camp without leave, in writing, from their commanding officer, shall suffer such punishment as shall be inflicted upon them by the sentence of a court martial.

ART. 42. No officer or soldier shall lie out of his quarters, garrison, or camp without leave from his superior officer, upon penalty of being punished according to the nature of his offence, by the sentence of a court martial.

ART. 43. Every non-commissioned officer and soldier shall retire to his quarters or tent at the beating of the retreat; in default of which he shall be punished according to the nature of his offence.

ART. 44. No officer, non-commissioned officer, or soldier shall fail in repairing, at the time fixed, to the place of parade, of exercise, or other rendezvous appointed by his commanding officer, if not prevented by sickness or some other evident necessity, or shall go from the said place of rendezvous without leave from his commanding officer, before he shall be regularly dismissed or relieved, on the penalty of being punished, according to the nature of his offence, by the sentence of a court martial.

ART. 45. Any commissioned officer who shall be found drunk on his guard, party, or other duty, shall be cashiered. Any non-commissioned officer or soldier so offending shall suffer such corporal punishment as shall be inflicted by the sentence of a court martial.

ART. 46. Any sentinel who shall be found sleeping upon his post, or shall leave it before he shall be regularly relieved, shall suffer death, or such other punishment as shall be inflicted by the sentence of a court martial.

ART. 47. No soldier belonging to any regiment, troop, or company, shall hire another to do his duty for him, or be excused from duty but in cases of sickness, disability, or leave of absence; and every such soldier found guilty of hiring his duty, as also the party so hired to do another's duty, shall be punished at the discretion of a regimental court martial.

ART. 48. And every non-commissioned officer conniving at such hiring of duty aforesaid shall be reduced; and every commissioned officer knowing and allowing such ill practices in the service, shall be punished by the judgment of a general court martial.

ART. 49. Any officer belonging to the service of the Confederate States, who, by discharging of fire-arms, drawing of swords, beating of drums, or by any other means whatsoever, shall occasion false alarms in camp, garrison, or quarters, shall suffer death, or such other punishment as shall be ordered by the sentence of a general court martial.

ART 50. Any officer or soldier who shall, without urgent necessity, or without the leave of his superior officer, quit his guard, platoon, or division, shall be punished, according to the nature of his offence, by the sentence of a court martial.

ART. 51. No officer or soldier shall do violence to any person who brings provisions or other necessaries to the camp, garrison, or quarters of the forces of the Confederate States, employed in any parts out of the said states, upon pain of death, or such other punishment as a court martial shall direct.

ART. 52. Any officer or soldier who shall misbehave himself before the enemy, run away, or shamefully abandon any fort, post, or guard which he or they may be commanded to defend, or speak words inducing others to do the like, or shall cast away his arms and ammunition, or who shall quit his post or colors to plunder and pillage, every such offender, being duly convicted thereof, shall suffer death, or such other punishment as shall be ordered by the sentence of a general court martial.

ART. 53. Any person belonging to the armies of the Confederate States who shall make known the watchword to any person who is not entitled to receive it according to the rules and discipline of war, or shall presume to give a parole or watchword different from what he received, shall suffer death, or such other punishment as shall be ordered by the sentence of a general court martial.

ART. 54. All officers and soldiers are to behave themselves orderly in quarters and on their march; and whoever shall commit any waste or spoil, either in walks or trees, parks, warrens, fish-ponds, houses, or gardens, cornfields, enclosures of meadows, or shall maliciously destroy any property whatsoever belonging to the inhabitants of the Confederate States, unless by order of the then commander-in-chief of the armies of the said states, shall (besides such penalties as they are liable to by law), be punished according to the nature and degree of the offence, by the judgment of a regimental or general court martial.

ART. 55. Whosoever, belonging to the armies of the Confederate States in foreign parts, shall force a safeguard, shall suffer death.

ART. 56. Whosoever shall relieve the enemy with money, victuals, or ammunition, or shall knowingly harbor or protect an enemy, shall suffer death, or such other punishment as shall be ordered by the sentence of a court martial.

ART. 57. Whosoever shall be convicted of holding correspondence with, or giving intelligence to the enemy, either directly or indirectly, shall suffer death, or such other punishment as shall be ordered by the sentence of a court martial.

ART. 58. All public stores taken in the enemy's camp, towns, forts, or magazines, whether of artillery, ammunition, clothing, forage, or provisions, shall be secured for the service of the Confederate States; for the neglect of which the commanding officer is to be answerable.

ART. 59. If any commander of any garrison, fortress, or post, shall be compelled, by the officers and soldiers under his command, to give up to the enemy, or to abandon it, the commissioned officers, non-commissioned officers, or soldiers who shall be convicted of having so offended, shall suffer death, or such other punishment as shall be inflicted upon them by the sentence of a court martial.

ART. 60. All sutlers and retainers to the camp, and all persons whatsoever, serving with the armies of the Confederate States in the field, though not enlisted soldiers, are to be subject to orders, according to the rules and discipline of war.

ART. 61. Officers having brevets or commissions of a prior date to those of the corps in which they serve, will take place on courts martial or of inquiry, and on boards detailed for military purposes, when composed of different corps, according to the ranks given them in their brevets or former commissions; but in the regiment, corps, or company to which such officers belong, they shall do duty and take rank, both in courts and on boards as aforesaid, which shall be composed of their own corps, according to the commissions by which they are there mustered.

ART. 62. If, upon marches, guards, or in quarters, different corps shall happen to join, or do duty together, the officer highest in rank, according to the commission by which he is mustered, in the army, navy, marine corps, or militia, there on duty by orders from competent authority, shall command the whole, and give orders for what is needful for the service, unless otherwise directed by the President of the Confederate States, in orders of special assignment providing for the case.

ART. 63. The functions of the engineers being generally confined to the most elevated branch of military science, they are not to assume, nor are they subject to be ordered on any duty beyond the line of their immediate profession, except by the special order of the President of the Confederate States; but they are to receive every mark of respect to which their rank in the army may entitle them respectively, and are liable to be transferred, at the discretion of the President, from one corps to another, regard being paid to rank.

ART. 64. General courts martial may consist of any number of commissioned officers from five to thirteen, inclusively; but they shall not consist of less than thirteen, where that number can be convened without manifest injury to the service.

ART. 65. Any general officer commanding an army, or colonel commanding a separate department, may appoint general courts martial whenever necessary. But no sentence of a court martial shall be carried into execution until after the whole proceedings shall have been laid before the officer ordering the same, or the officer commanding the troops for the time being; neither shall any sentence of a general court martial, in the time of peace, extending to the loss of life, or the dismission of a commissioned officer, or which shall, either in time of peace or war, respect a general officer, be carried into execution, until after the whole proceedings shall have been transmitted to the Secretary of War, to be laid before the President of the Confederate States for his confirmation or disapproval and orders in the case. All other sentences may be confirmed and executed by the officer ordering the court to assemble, or the commanding officer for the time being, as the case may be.

ART. 66. Every officer commanding a regiment or corps may appoint, for his own regiment or corps, courts martial, to consist of three commissioned officers, for the trial and punishment of offences not capital, and decide upon their sentences. For the same purpose, all officers commanding any of the garrisons, forts, barracks, or other places where the troops consist of different corps, may assemble courts martial, to consist of three commissioned officers, and decide upon their sentences.

ART. 67. No garrison or regimental court martial shall have the power to try capital cases or commissioned officers; neither shall they inflict a fine exceeding one month's pay, nor imprison, nor put to hard labor any non-commissioned officer or soldier for a longer time than one month.

ART. 68. Whenever it may be found convenient and necessary to the public service, the officers of the marines shall be associated with the officers of the land forces for the purpose of holding courts martial and trying offenders belonging to either; and in such cases the orders of the senior officer of either corps who may be present and duly authorized, shall be received and obeyed.

ART. 69. The Judge Advocate, or some person deputed by him, or by the general, or officer commanding the army, detachment, or garrison, shall prosecute in the name of the Confederate States, but shall so far consider himself as counsel for the prisoner, after the said prisoner shall have made his plea, as to object to any leading question to any of the witnesses, or any question to the prisoner, the answer to which might tend to criminate himself, and administer to each member of the court, before they proceed upon any trial, the following oath, which shall also be taken by all members of the regimental and garrison courts martial.

"You, A B, do swear that you will well and truly try and determine, according to evidence, the matter now before you, between the Confederate States of America and the prisoner to be tried, and that you will duly administer justice, according to the provisions of 'An act establishing Rules and Articles for the government of the armies of the Confederate States,' without partiality, favor, or affection; and if any doubt should arise, not explained by said Articles, according to your conscience, the best of your understanding, and the custom of war in like cases; and you do further swear that you will not divulge the sentence of the court until it shall be published by the proper authority; neither will you disclose or discover the vote or opinion of any particular member of the court martial, unless required to give evidence thereof, as a witness, by a court of justice, in a due course of law. So help you God."

And so soon as the said oath shall have been administered to the respective members, the president of the court shall administer to the Judge Advocate, or person officiating as such, an oath in the following words:

"You, A B, do swear that you will not disclose or discover the vote or opinion of any particular member of the court martial, unless required to give evidence thereof, as a witness, by a court of justice, in due course of law; nor divulge the sentence of the court to any but the proper authority, until it shall be duly disclosed by the same. So help you God."

ART. 70. When a prisoner, arraigned before a general court martial, shall from obstinacy and deliberate design stand mute, or answer foreign to the purpose, the court may proceed to trial and judgment as if the prisoner had regularly pleaded not guilty.

ART. 71. When a member shall be challenged by a prisoner, he must state his cause of challenge, of which the court shall, after due deliberation, determine the relevancy or validity, and decide accordingly; and no challenge to more than one member at a time shall be received by the court.

ART. 72. All the members of a court martial are to behave with decency and calmness; and in giving their votes are to begin with the youngest in commission.

ART. 73. All persons who give evidence before a court martial are to be examined on oath or affirmation, in the following form:

"You swear, or affirm, (as the case may be), the evidence you shall give in the cause now in hearing shall be the truth, the whole truth, and nothing but the truth. So help you God."

ART. 74. On the trials of cases not capital, before courts martial, the deposition of witnesses, not in the line or staff of the army, may be taken before some justice of the peace, and read in evidence; provided the prosecutor and person accused are present at the taking the same, or are duly notified thereof.

ART. 75. No officer shall be tried but by a general court martial, nor by officers of an inferior rank, if it can be avoided. Nor shall any proceedings of trials be carried on, excepting between the hours of eight in the morning and three in the afternoon; excepting in cases which, in the opinion of the officer appointing the court martial, require immediate example.

ART. 76. No person whatsoever shall use any menacing words, signs, or gestures, in presence of a court martial, or shall cause any disorder or riot, or disturb their proceedings, on the penalty of being punished at the discretion of the said court martial.

ART. 77. Whenever any officer shall be charged with a crime, he shall be arrested and confined in his barracks, quarters, or tent, and deprived of his sword by the commanding officer. And any officer who shall leave his confinement before he shall be set at liberty by the commanding officer, or by a superior officer, shall be cashiered.

ART. 78. Non-commissioned officers and soldiers, charged with crimes, shall be confined until tried by a court martial, or released by proper authority.

ART. 79. No officer or soldier who shall be put in arrest shall continue in confinement more than eight days, or until such time as a court martial can be assembled.

ART. 80. No officer commanding a guard, or provost marshal, shall refuse to receive or keep any prisoner committed to his charge by an officer belonging to the forces of the Confederate States; provided the officer committing shall, at the same time, deliver an account in writing, signed by himself, of the crime of which the said prisoner is charged.

ART 81. No officer commanding a guard, or provost marshal, shall presume to release any person committed to his charge without proper authority for so doing, nor shall he suffer any person to escape, on the penalty of being punished for it by the sentence of a court martial.

ART. 82. Every officer or provost marshal, to whose charge prisoners shall be committed, shall within twenty-four hours after such commitment, or as soon as he shall be relieved from his guard, make report in writing to the commanding officer of their names, their crimes, and the names of the officers who committed them, on the penalty of being punished for disobedience or neglect, at the discretion of a court martial.

ART. 83. Any commissioned officer convicted before a general court martial of conduct unbecoming an officer and a gentleman, shall be dismissed the service.

ART. 84. In cases where a court martial may think it proper to sentence a commissioned officer to be suspended from command, they shall have power also to suspend his pay and emoluments for the same time, according to the nature and heinousness of the offence.

ART. 85. In all cases where a commissioned officer is cashiered for cowardice or fraud, it shall be added in the sentence, that the crime, name, and place of abode, and punishment of the delinquent, be published in the newspapers in and about the camp, and of the particular state from which the offender came, or where he usually resides; after which it shall be deemed scandalous for an officer to associate with him.

ART. 86. The commanding officer of any post or detachment in which there shall not be a number of officers adequate to form a general court martial, shall, in cases which require the cognizance of such a court, report to the commanding officer of the department, who shall order a court to be assembled at the nearest post or department, and the party accused, with necessary witnesses, to be transported to the place where the said court shall be assembled.

ART. 87. No person shall be sentenced to suffer death but by the concurrence of two-thirds of the members of a general court martial, nor except in the cases herein expressly mentioned; and no officer, non-commissioned officer, soldier, or follower of the army, shall be tried a second time for the same offence.

ART. 88. No person shall be liable to be tried and punished by a general court martial for any offence which shall appear to have been committed more than two years before the issuing of the order for such trial, unless the person, by reason of having absented himself, or some other manifest impediment, shall not have been amenable to justice within that period.

ART. 89. Every officer authorized to order a general court martial shall have power to pardon or mitigate any punishment ordered by such court, except the sentence of death, or of cashiering an officer; which, in the cases where he has authority (by Article 65) to carry them into execution, he may suspend, until the pleasure of the President of the Confederate States can be known; which suspension, together with copies of the proceedings of the court martial, the said officer shall immediately transmit to the President for his determination. And the colonel or commanding officer of the regiment or garrison where any regimental or garrison court martial shall be held, may pardon or mitigate any punishment ordered by such court to be inflicted.

ART. 90. Every Judge Advocate, or person officiating as such, at any general court martial, shall transmit, with as much expedition as the opportunity of time and distance of place can admit, the original proceedings and sentence of such court martial to the Secretary of War; which said original proceedings and sentence shall be carefully kept and preserved in the office of said Secretary, to the end that the persons entitled thereto may be enabled, upon application to the said officer, to obtain copies thereof.

The party tried by any general court martial shall, upon demand thereof, made by himself, or by any person or persons in his behalf, be entitled to a copy of the sentence and proceedings of such court martial.

ART. 91. In cases where the general or commanding officer may order a court of inquiry to examine into the nature of any transaction, accusation, or imputation against any officer or soldier, the said court shall consist of one or more officers, not exceeding three, and a Judge Advocate, or other suitable person, as a recorder, to reduce the proceedings and evidence to writing; all of whom shall be sworn to the faithful performance of their duty. This court shall have the same power to summon witnesses as a court martial, and to examine them on oath. But they shall not give their opinion on the merits of the case, excepting they shall be thereto specially required. The parties accused shall also be permitted to cross-examine and interrogate the witnesses, so as to investigate fully the circumstances in the question.

ART. 92. The proceedings of a court of inquiry must be authenticated by the signature of the recorder and the president, and delivered to the commanding officer, and the said proceedings may be admitted as evidence by a court martial, in cases not capital, or extending to the dismission of an officer, provided that the circumstances are such that oral testimony cannot be obtained. But as courts of inquiry may be perverted to dishonorable purposes, and may be considered as engines of destruction to military merit, in the hands of weak and envious commandants, they are hereby prohibited, unless directed by the President of the Confederate States, or demanded by the accused.

ART. 93. The Judge Advocate or recorder shall administer to the members the following oath:

"You shall well and truly examine and inquire, according to your evidence, into the matter now before you, without partiality, favor, affection, prejudice, or hope of reward. So help you God."

After which the president shall administer to the Judge Advocate or recorder the following oath:

"You, A B, do swear that you will, according to your best abilities, accurately and impartially record the proceedings of the court, and the evidence to be given in the case in hearing. So help you God."

The witnesses shall take the same oath as witnesses sworn before a court martial.

ART. 94. When any commissioned officer shall die or be killed in the service of the Confederate States, the major of the regiment, or the officer doing the major's duty in his absence, or in any post or garrison the second officer in command, or the assistant military agent, shall immediately secure all his effects or equipage then in camp or quarters, and shall make an inventory thereof, and forthwith transmit the same to the office of the Department of War, to the end that his executors or administrators may receive the same.

ART. 95. When any non-commissioned officer or soldier shall die or be killed in the service of the Confederate States, the then commanding officer of the troop or company shall, in the presence of two other commissioned officers, take an account of what effects he died possessed of, above his arms and accoutrements, and transmit the same to the office of the Department of War, which said effects are to be accounted for and paid to the representatives of such deceased non-commissioned officer or soldier. And in case any of the officers so authorized to take care of the effects of such deceased non-commissioned officers and soldiers should, before they have accounted to their representatives for the same, have occasion to leave the regiment or post, by preferment or otherwise, they shall, before they be permitted to quit the same, deposit in the hands of the commanding officer, or of the assistant military agent, all the effects of such deceased non-commissioned officers and soldier, in order that the same may be secured for, and paid to their respective representatives.

ART. 96. All officers, conductors, gunners, matrosses, drivers, or other persons whatsoever, receiving pay or hire in the service of the artillery, or corps of engineers of the Confederate States, shall be governed by the aforesaid Rules and Articles, and shall be subject to be tried by courts martial, in like manner with the officers and soldiers of the other troops in the service of the Confederate States.

ART. 97. The officers and soldiers of any troops, whether militia or others, being mustered and in pay of the Confederate States, shall, at all times and in all places, when joined, or acting in conjunction with the regular forces of the Confederate States, be governed by these Rules and Articles of War, and shall be subject to be tried by courts martial, in like manner with the officers and soldiers in the regular forces; save only that such courts martial shall be composed entirely of militia officers.

ART. 98. All officers serving by commission from the authority of any particular state, shall, on all detachments, courts martial, or other duty, wherein they may be employed in conjunction with the regular forces of the Confederate States, take rank next after all officers of the like grade in said regular forces, notwithstanding the commissions of such militia or state officers may be older than the commissions of the officers of the regular forces of the Confederate States.

ART. 99. All crimes not capital, and all disorders and neglects which officers and soldiers may be guilty of, to the prejudice of good order and military discipline, though not mentioned in the foregoing Articles of War, are to be taken cognizance of by a general or regimental court martial, according to the nature and degree of the offence, and be punished at their discretion.

ART. 100. The President of the Confederate States shall have power to prescribe the uniform of the army.

ART. 101. The foregoing Articles are to be read and published once in every six months to every garrison, regiment, troop, or company mustered, or to be mustered in the service of the Confederate States, and are to be duly observed and obeyed by all officers and soldiers who are, or shall be in said service.

SEC. 2. *And be it further enacted*, That in time of war, all persons not citizens of, or owing allegiance to the Confederate States of America, who shall be found lurking as spies in and about the fortifications or encampments of the armies of the Confederate States, or any of them, shall suffer death, according to the law and usage of nations, by sentence of a general court martial.

INDEX TO ARTICLES OF WAR.

A.
                     No. of article

Absentees from muster 11
Absence without leave 21, 41, 50
Absence not allowed, except 47, 48
Ammunition, wasted 37, 40
Articles of war, read when 10, 101
Arrests, for what 24, 27
   continuance of 79
Arms, wasted or destroyed 38, 40
Army uniform 100

B.
Brevet rank, on courts, etc 61

C.
Cashiered, who may be 14, 32, 45, 85
   sentence, when 89
Capital cases, who not to try 67
Chaplain, negligent 4
Challenge, to fight 25, 26, 27
   of court 71
Civil offences by officers, etc 33
Civilians, when may be tried 56, 57, 60, 96
Congress, disrespectful words concerning 5
Cowardice, punished 52, 85
Compulsory surrender 59
Commanding officer to make monthly returns 19
Committing officer, duty of 80
Conduct unbecoming, etc 83
Command, suspension of 84
Courts martial—number on 64
   who may appoint 65, 66
   sentence of, confirmed and executed, how 65, 66
   garrison and regimental, not to try capital cases or commissioned officers 67
   what sentence garrison and regimental court may inflict ... 67
   marine officer may sit on 68
   to decide challenge 71
   good behavior enjoined 72
   mode of voting 72
   evidence before, how taken 73
   disturbance punished 76

```
                    record sent to war department........................90
                    place of meeting.....................................86
                    offences cognizable by...............................99
Courts of inquiry...................................................91, 92, 93
Crime—officers charged with...............................................77
       non-commissioned officers charged with.............................78
       not capital, and disorders not named in articles, how punished.....99
```

D.

```
Death—when may be inflicted.....7, 8, 20, 23, 46, 49, 51, 52, 53, 55, 56, 57, 59, 87
       sentence of, to be submitted to President.........................89
Desertion.................................................................20
Divine service............................................................ 2
Discharge, should be had before re-enlistment.............................22
Drunkenness...............................................................45
Duelling prohibited...................................................25, 26
```

E.

```
Effects of deceased officers and soldiers.................................94
Embezzlement..............................................................36
Enemy—misbehaviour before.................................................52
       punishment for relieving...........................................56
       correspondence with................................................57
       stores taken from..................................................58
Engineer officers.........................................................63
Escapes...................................................................81
```

F.

```
False returns, etc..............................................14, 15, 16, 17
False alarms in camp, etc.................................................49
Frauds in officers........................................................85
Frays, to be quelled......................................................27
Furloughs.................................................................10
```

H.

```
Hiring another to do duty............................................47, 48
```

I.

```
Inventory of officers and soldiers....................................94, 95
Inquiry—courts of.....................................................91, 93
       oath required in..................................................93
```

J.

```
Judge Advocate—duties.....................................................69
                oath of..........................................69, 92
```

L.

```
Legislature, disrespectful words about..................................... 5
Lying out of quarters.....................................................42
Limitation of trials......................................................88
```

M.

```
Marine corps..............................................................68
Misapplication of property and money.................................36, 39
```

Military boards, rank on..61
Money, etc., misapplied...36, 37

N.

Neglects, punished...36, 37, 38

O.

Oath of allegiance...10
    of officers on courts..69, 93
    of Judge Advocate..69
    of witnesses...73
Officers—to subscribe the Articles of War.. 1
    to attend divine service... 2
    not to swear... 3
    contempt of superiors... 6
    exciting to mutiny...7, 8, 9
    striking superior.. 9
    how non-commissioned officer is discharged..............................11
    taking money...16
    making false returns...15, 17, 18
    not to use reproachful language, etc......................................24
    not to send challenge...25, 26
    to keep order, etc...32
    wrongs, redressed..34
    how and when tried..75
    highest in rank to command...62
    rank by brevet...61
    when charged with crime..77
    committing, duty of..80
    commanding guard to receive prisoner when regularly committed......80
    not to release prisoner without orders....................................81
    when to be dismissed..83
    suspension of...84
    cashiering, what else in certain cases.....................................85
    deceased, effects of..94
    orderly behavior enjoined...54
    orders, who subject to...60

P.

Parade, to be attended..44
President, disrespectful words, about.. 5
        prescribes uniform...100
Prisoners, standing mute..70
Property, to be respected...54
Provost marshal...80, 82

R.

Rank, brevet, on courts...61
    officer highest in, to command..62
Rendezvous, must be attended..44

S.

Safeguards, death to force...56
Sentence of court martial, by whom revised................................89
   mitigated, etc..89
Sentinel sleeping..46
Sleeping on post..46
Soldiers—to attend divine service... 2
   not to swear... 3
   to respect commander... 6
   penalty for mutiny...7, 8, 9
   striking superior.. 9
   how discharged...11
   desertion of...20
   to swear allegiance..10
   to have written discharge..11
   wrongs of, redressed...35
Stores of enemy...58
Sutlers...29, 30, 31, 60
Surrender, compulsory...59
Suspension from pay, etc..84
Spies..101

T.

Trials, capital...67
  not capital..66
  not to occur twice...88
  evidence on..74

U.

Uniform of the army..100

V.

Violence to persons bringing provisions, etc..............................51

W.

Waste, punished..36, 37, 54
Watchwords, rules as to...53
War, who subject to the rules of..60
 Articles of, who to govern......................................96, 97
 Articles of, to be read and published.................................101
 in time of, spies to be punished......................................101

FORMS.

No. 1.

Form of order for convening a general court martial.

GENERAL ORDERS, } ADJUTANT AND INSPECTOR-GENERAL'S OFFICE,
No. — } *January* 5, 186–.

A general court martial will assemble at ———, at 10 o'clock, A. M., the 10th instant, or as soon thereafter as practicable, for the trial of ———, and such prisoners as may be brought before it.

DETAIL FOR THE COURT.

1. Col. A. B., 1*st Regiment of Artillery.*
2. Col. N. M., 2*d Regiment of Cavalry.*
3. Major W. C., 2*d Regiment of Infantry.*
4. Major T. O., 5*th Regiment of Infantry.*
5. Captain S. B., 1*st Regiment of Artillery.*
6. Captain W. L., 2*d Regiment of Artillery.*
7. Captain N. S., 4*th Regiment of Infantry.*
8. Etc., etc., etc.

Captain S. W., of the 2d Regiment of Artillery, is appointed the Judge Advocate for the court.

Should any of the officers named in the foregoing detail be prevented from attending at the time and place specified, the court will nevertheless proceed to, and continue the business before it, provided the number of members present be not less than the *minimum* prescribed by law; the above being the greatest number (when the court is composed of less than thirteen members) that can be convened without manifest injury to the service. (This last sentence to be always inserted in the like case.)

By command of ———.

No. 2.

Form of the proceedings of a general court martial.

Proceedings of a general court martial convened at —— by virtue of the following order, viz:

[*Here insert the order.*]

—— o'clock, A. M., January 10, 186–.

The court met pursuant to the above order. Present:
Col. A. B., *1st Regiment of Artillery.*
Col. N. M., *2d Regiment of Cavalry.*
Major W. C., *2d Regiment of Infantry.*
Major T. O., *5th Regiment of Infantry.*
Captain S. B., *1st Regiment of Artillery.*
Etc., etc.
Captain S. W., 2d Regiment of Artillery, Judge Advocate.
Captain S. M., 1st Regiment of Infantry, the accused, also present.

The Judge Advocate having read the order convening the court, asked the accused, Captain S. M., if he had any objection to any member named therein, to which he replied, ——.

[*If any challenge is made it must be now, and to one member at a time.*]

The court was then duly sworn by the Judge Advocate, and the Judge Advocate was duly sworn by the presiding officer of the court, in the presence of the accused.

[*It is at this stage of the proceedings that the accused makes his request for the privilege of introducing his counsel, and will also, if he desire it, state his reasons for postponement of the trial. These matters being settled, the court proceeds.*]

The charges were read aloud by the Judge Advocate. Judge Advocate (*addressing the accused*), " Captain S. M., you have heard the charge, or charges preferred against you, how say you—guilty or not guilty " ?

To which the accused, Captain S. M., pleaded as follows:

[*Here state the pleas.*]

The Judge Advocate *here gives notice that should there be any persons present in court who have been summoned as witnesses, they must retire, and wait until called for.*

Captain D. N., 2d Regiment of Infantry, a witness on the part of the prosecution, was duly sworn.

By Judge Advocate:
Question. ——— ?
Answer. ———.
Question. ——— ?
Answer. ———.

Cross-examined by the accused:
Question. ———— ?
Answer. ————.
Question. ———— ?
By the court:
Question. ———— ?
Answer. ————.
Question. ———— ?
By the Judge Advocate:
Question. ———— ?
Answer. ————.
Question. ———— ?
Answer. ————.

[*The examination of the witness being completed, his testimony is read over to him, and corrected if necessary—when the next witness is called. The Judge Advocate having presented all the evidence for the prosecution, states such fact, and announces that the prosecution is closed, when the accused enters upon the defence.*]

Lieut. A. B., 1st Regiment of Artillery, a witness for the defence, was duly sworn.
By the accused:
Question. ———— ?
Answer. ————.
Question. ———— ?
Cross-examined by Judge Advocate:
Question. ———— ?
Answer. ————.
Question. ———— ?
Answer. ————.
By the court:
Question. ———— ?
Answer. ————.

[The evidence on both sides having been heard, the accused asks for time to prepare his final defence.]

The court adjourned to meet at 10 o'clock, A. M., on the — inst.

10 o'clock, A. M., ———, 186–.

The court met pursuant to adjournment. Present:
Colonel A. B.
Colonel N. M.
Major W. C.
Major T. O.
Captain S. B.
Captain S. W., *Judge Advocate*, and
Captain S. M., the accused.

The proceedings of yesterday were read over — when the accused, Captain S. M., presented and read (or which was read by his counsel) the written defence (A) appended to these proceedings.

[*Should the Judge Advocate intend to reply, he would notify the court, and ask for the requisite time for preparation.*]

The statement of the parties being thus in possession of the court, the court was cleared for deliberation, and having maturely considered the evidence adduced, find the accused, Captain S. M., of the 1st Regiment of Infantry, as follows:

Of the first Specification of first Charge: "Guilty."
Of the second Specification of first Charge: "Not Guilty."
Of the third Specification of first Charge: "Guilty."
Of the first Charge: "Guilty."
Of the first Specification of second Charge: "Not Guilty."
Of the second Specification of second Charge: "Not Guilty."
Of the second Charge: "Not Guilty."

And the Court do therefore sentence the said Captain S. M., of the 1st Regiment of Infantry, ——— to ———

(Signed)   A. B.,
      Colonel 1st Regiment Artillery, and President of the court martial.
(Signed)   S. W., *Judge Advocate.*

There being no further business before them, the Court adjourned *sine die.*

(Signed)   A. B.,
      Colonel 1st Regiment Artillery, and President of the court martial.
(Signed)   S. W., *Judge Advocate.*

[NOTE.]

MARTIAL LAW.

[See CHAPTER I.]

It is a mistake to suppose that the mere suspension of the writ of habeas corpus of itself imparts additional authority to the military tribunals. The writ is only a help or means to something else. It confers no additional right, and is valuable only in that it assists the complaining party to assert a right already existing—I mean the right of trial according to law. The party tried may be acquitted or convicted as circumstances require, and just as though there never had been a writ of habeas corpus. Hence, where it is designed to confer unusual powers on the military tribunals, something more is necessary than the bare suspension of this writ, otherwise the right to trial by jury is only postponed, not taken away; and a party aggrieved by arrest, or otherwise, might ultimately resort to the civil courts in a suit for damages. It would be no answer to such a claim that the writ had been *suspended* when the arrest was made, for that only afforded the undisturbed opportunity for an exercise of power without warrant or justification, which latter can only be found in positive law. The right to make such a law, if it exists at all, is in Congress only. In other words, martial law cannot legally be declared except by authority of Congress; and when this has been done *in connection with* the suspension of the writ of habeas corpus, then, and then only, is the civil authority so far suspended as to warrant the interference of the military with the personal rights of the citizen. The two measures—suspension of the writ, and the promulgation of martial law should go together. For if the writ be not suspended there would be a dangerous clashing between the civil and military authority on certain occasions; and on the other hand, if martial law do not accompany the suspension of the writ, any exercise of unusual power, no matter how necessary, would be at once shorn both of the sanction and shield of law.

But here arises the question, whence does Congress derive the power to declare martial law? It is not known to the common law, and therefore in England it is based on an exercise of prerogative. No such reason can be offered for it here, and the constitution does not expressly recognize it. A closer inspection of that instrument may throw some light on this perplexing question. Section 7, third clause, provides that the privilege of the writ of habeas corpus shall not be suspended, unless when in cases of rebellion or invasion the public safety may require it. But how does this suspension enure to the public safety? We have just shown that of itself it confers no additional power or right on the public authorities, but only defers, as it were, an existing right of the citizen. The right to suspend, therefore, seems necessarily to imply something else, otherwise it is a barren right. What, then, is thus necessarily implied? If we examine the thirteenth clause of the same section, the seventh, we find that no person is to be deprived of life, liberty, or property, *without due process of law.* What does this mean? The constitution allows the *suspension* of the writ designed to secure the means of trial to all citizens, and yet requires that none shall be tried without due process of law! Surely there must be some mode of trial, some tribunal to decide, else when the writ is suspended, and the citizen arrested by the hand of power, the constitution shuts him up in unlimited confinement. He cannot be tried and released by the civil courts, because this great writ, the only means by which, when under arrest, he can be brought before them, is now unavailable. If it was designed that the military should turn the party over to the civil authority, why suspend the writ; or, indeed, allow the arrest at all? Are we not thus driven to the conclusion that by allowing the suspension of the writ of habeas corpus the civil jurisdiction was designed to be also suspended to a greater or less extent? Where then is the trial by due process of law? All that is left to meet this requirement are the military tribunals and authority provided in the Articles of war, and their action is as much by "process of law," as that of any other court. And this term *"due process of law,"* observes another, is convertible with that of *" by the law of the land."* See 2 Kent, p. 10. What other warrant can be found for the extension of military jurisdiction to civilians?

We conclude, therefore, that the right to declare martial law can only be exercised by authority of Congress, and may be deduced from the provisions of the constitution. How much better to rest it here than upon the dangerous ground of necessity, even when this is to be determined by the best and purest individual.

NOTE.—*See title* " Charge "—*page* 43.

The charge embraces, in general terms, the whole complaint or accusation. The cardinal rule in framing a charge is that it must allege some *single, separate, and specific offence,* provided against in the Articles of war. " Vague charges," says O'Brien, " are always objectionable." Sometimes charges are framed in the words of the Articles of war, which are themselves often couched in general terms, and when this is the case, vagueness in the charge cannot be urged. Thus, the charge of " conduct prejudicial to good order and military discipline," though very general, is yet admissible, as following the words of the law. But it is not, says O'Brien, "requisite that a charge should be in the precise words of any Article of war. It is sufficient if it designates any species of offence for which these Articles provide a punishment. Instead of a charge of 'conduct to the prejudice of good order and military discipline,' it would be as easy, and more equitable, to name the species of offence, as '*drunkenness*,' '*theft*,' or the like; so, instead of 'neglect of duty,' it would be better to state, 'sitting down at a post,' or whatever else way be the offence supposed to have been committed. It is possible there may be some few cases where this distinctness cannot be obtained, and in such cases greater vagueness may be allowed from necessity."

Instead of following the words of the Articles, it is admissible in certain cases, where the article creates an offence, to lay the charge in general terms, as a "violation of the — Article of war." This may be done where the offence clearly constitutes a violation of the Article of war, leaving the particular manner of such violation, and the general facts connected with it, to be set out in the specification.

It is the part of the specification, as distinguished from the charge, to particularize the specific acts which make up the charge. They should be so clearly stated as to leave no doubt of the particular object of the examination. But facts which are unconnected, and have a separate bearing, should not be joined in the same specification. Every allegation, moreover, in the same specification, which when proved would not tend to convict the prisoner of the crime charged, should be regarded as irrelevant. But mere irrelevancy will not vitiate a charge, though evidence upon the irrelevant fact cannot be taken, not even when it constitutes a separate and distinct crime. And if the facts stated in the specification would not, if proved, make up the charge, both charge and specification are to be rejected—"for the court are to pass on the particular crime charged, and no other." The name, surname, rank, company and regiment of the accused ought to be stated. All *inferences* and extraneous matter should be avoided, and nothing alleged which is not culpable in its nature.*

---

*O'Brien's Mil. Law, pages 232, 233, 234.

www.ingramcontent.com/pod-product-compliance
Lightning Source LLC
Chambersburg PA
CBHW031353230426
43670CB00006B/533